The Single Market Review

IMPACT ON SERVICES

AIR TRANSPORT

The Single Market Review series

p II

Table of contents

EUROPEAN COMMISSION

The Single Market Review

IMPACT ON SERVICES
AIR TRANSPORT

The Single Market Review

SUBSERIES II: VOLUME 2

OFFICE FOR OFFICIAL PUBLICATIONS
OF THE EUROPEAN COMMUNITIES

KOGAN PAGE . EARTHSCAN

This report is part of a series of 39 studies commissioned from independent consultants in the context of a major review of the Single Market. The 1996 Single Market Review responds to a 1992 Council of Ministers Resolution calling on the European Commission to present an overall analysis of the effectiveness of measures taken in creating the Single Market. This review, which assesses the progress made in implementing the Single Market Programme, was coordinated by the Directorate-General 'Internal Market and Financial Services' (DG XV) and the Directorate-General 'Economic and Financial Affairs' (DG II) of the European Commission.

This document was prepared for the European Commission

by

Cranfield University

It does not, however, express the Commission's official views. Whilst every reasonable effort has been made to provide accurate information in regard to the subject matter covered, the Consultants are not responsible for any remaining errors. All recommendations are made by the Consultants for the purpose of discussion. Neither the Commission nor the Consultants accept liability for the consequences of actions taken on the basis of the information contained herein.

The European Commission would like to express thanks to the external experts and representatives of firms and industry bodies for their contribution to the 1996 Single Market Review, and to this report in particular.

Office for Official Publications of the European Communities
2 rue Mercier, L-2985 Luxembourg
ISBN 92-827-8778-8   Catalogue number: C1-68-96-002-EN-C

Kogan Page . Earthscan
120 Pentonville Road, London N1 9JN
ISBN 0 7494 2314 5

List of tables

List of figures

List of abbreviations

Aviation Organizations
ACI	Airports Council International (formerly AACC)
AEA	Association of European Airlines
CAA	Civil Aviation Authority, UK
ECAC	European Civil Aviation Conference
ERA	European Regional Airlines Association
FAA	Federal Aviation Administration (US)
IATA	International Air Transport Association
ICAO	International Civil Aviation Organization
OAA	Orient Airlines Association

Units of measurement
ASK	Available seat-kilometre
ATK	Available tonne-kilometre
ATM	Air transport movement
LF	Load factor
MTOW	Maximum take-off weight
NM	Nautical miles
RPK	Revenue passenger-kilometre
RTK	Revenue tonne-kilometre

Other
ASA	Air Services Agreement
ASEAN	Association of South East Asian Nations
CDG	Charles de Gaulle airport
CRS	Computerized reservation system
EEA	European Economic Area
EU	European Union
FFP	Frequent flyer programme
GDP	Gross domestic product
NAFTA	North American Free Trade Area
PPP	Purchasing power parity
VFR	Visting friends and relatives

Countries
AUS	Austria
BEL	Belgium (BE)
DEN/DNK	Denmark (DK)
DEU/GER	Germany (DE) – FR of Germany – Federal Republic of Germany
ESP	Spain (ES)
FRA	France (FR)
GRE	Greece (GR)
IRE	Ireland (IE)
ITA	Italy (IT)
LUX	Luxembourg (LU)
NED	Netherlands (NL)
POR/PRT	Portugal (PT)
SWI	Switzerland
UK	United Kingdom (GB)

Airlines
AF	Air France
AR	Aerolineas Argentinas
AY	Finnair
AZ	Alitalia
BA	British Airways
BM	British Midland
DL	Delta Air Lines
IB	Iberia
KL	KLM
LH	Lufthansa

NW	Northwest Airlines
OS	Austrian Airlines
QF	Qantas
SK	SAS
SN	Sabena
SQ	Singapore Airlines
SR	Swissair
TG	Thai Airways International
TP	TAP Air Portugal
UC	Ladeco Airlines
UK	Air UK
US	US Air
VA	Varig

Acknowledgements

The project was undertaken by a team of air transport industry experts from the Department of Air Transport, College of Aeronautics at Cranfield University, under the direction of Peter Morrell. Members of the team were Dr Fariba Alamdari, Rodney Fewings, Romano Pagliari, Ian Stockman, Dr George Williams, and the independent consultant, Andy Hofton. Support was also provided by Dr Alexandra Fragoudaki and Abhimanyu Bissessur.

1. Summary

1.1.   This study has examined the effectiveness and impact of Community measures taken over the past decade to liberalize air transport in the Community. The study analyses how the airlines concerned have been affected by and responded to the new regulatory and commercial environment. It also provides a detailed assessment of the changes that have taken place in market structure and behaviour. An analysis has been applied to developments since 1985 (and in some cases since 1983), through desk research, the responses to questionnaires from 18 EU airlines and seven civil aviation departments, and interviews with airlines and authorities in France, Germany and the UK. A detailed examination was made of five EU airlines, representing various sizes and types of operation (see case studies, Chapter 6 and Appendix F).

1.2.   From the review of EU measures, it is evident that the three packages of air transport measures have effectively liberalized air transport within the European Union (see Section 3.4). Other sector-specific measures designed to improve the working of the single market have been less effective (see Section 3.5). It should be stressed that the most significant measures only came into force in January 1993, and only a limited number of years' data is available to evaluate any resulting changes. The degree to which the EU measures have had an impact on EU airline strategies, capacity, fares and economics has also been difficult to evaluate against the background of a major economic recession, and global industry changes. The large airlines, such as Air France, British Airways, KLM and Lufthansa, earning under 50% of total revenues from intra-EU and domestic services, are clearly influenced more by world-wide developments than other EU carriers (see Section 2.2).

1.3.   Many of the airlines' strategic changes were more in response to developments in global rather than EU markets: more cross-border alliances and share stakes were made with non-EU carriers than with EU carriers. This was supported by case studies of Air France and British Airways (see Appendices F.1 and F.2). Furthermore, some fairly ambitious alliances (such as Alcazar) were attempted within Europe, but failed through a conflict in desired US partner or the choice of principal European hub (see Section 4.2).

1.4.   In the largest EU countries, such as France, Germany and the UK, there was a trend towards the flag carriers acquiring other domestic airlines that might otherwise have been acquired by hostile interests (see Sections 6.1 and 6.2). Control was also exercised by larger carriers over small regional carriers through code sharing arrangements (e.g. Eurowings with Air France and KLM – see case study in Appendix F.5), or through franchising (see British Airways case study in Appendix F.2). It is difficult to conclude that these last developments should have been prevented by stricter national or EU control on mergers and related arrangements. EU airlines need domestic feed so as to benefit from hubbing at their main base and to compete with other world international carriers. Given the complex web of international alliances, it might be better to pursue a policy of global liberalization, with less control of non-EU investment in EU carriers (negotiated on a reciprocal basis).

1.5.   EU liberalization has not had the same impact on the charter airlines, which were already operating in highly competitive markets prior to the 1990s. Some of them had already attempted to enter scheduled markets, even before the first package, but these were not successful, less because of regulatory restrictions than overexpansion, poor market image and higher than anticipated costs. One exception to this was Maersk Air (see case study in Section 6.4 and Appendix F.4). More recently, a number of charter airlines have started operations in scheduled domestic markets in France, Italy and Spain, but it is too soon to judge how successful they will be (see Section 4.6).

1.6. Total cross-border intra-EU scheduled service seat capacity offered increased by 3% a year between 1989 and 1992, rising to 7% a year between 1992 and 1994, a time of economic recession. This resulted in declining load factors and real yields, particularly in the early 1990s (see Section 5.2.2). Capacity growth for a control group of non-EU countries was significantly lower. This was caused by a substantial growth in regional non-stop services, but redesignation of a number of charter services as scheduled somewhat distorted the picture (see Section 5.1).

1.7. Excluding those airlines based outside the EU, there was a net increase of six in the number of airlines serving intra-EU cross-border scheduled routes between 1992 and 1995, compared to a net loss of four carriers between 1989 and 1992. The majority of these airlines served principally low density regional routes, although a small number of formerly charter airlines (such as EBA in Belgium and Air Liberté in France) started scheduled services in direct competition with EU flag (national) carriers (see Section 5.1). Competition has also increased significantly in French, Italian and Spanish domestic markets as a result of EU liberalization, in some cases accompanied by alleged predatory pricing from the former monopoly flag carrier.

1.8. The first and third packages gave EU airlines more opportunity to carry traffic both between two other EU countries (Fifth Freedom) and within another EU country (consecutive cabotage), both operated as an extension of a cross-border service from their home country. Considerable use was made of these freedoms initially, especially by airlines based in peripheral EU countries (see TAP Air Portugal case study in Section 6.5 and Appendix F.3), but many of these services were subsequently discontinued due to poor economics (see Section 5.1.1). An alternative way of serving routes out of other EU countries is available through the right to establish an airline based in another country. Airlines such as British Airways (TAT in France and Deutsche BA), Lufthansa (Lauda Air in Austria and others) and KLM (Air UK) have done so, but only on a minority basis, the maximum stake being 49.9% (see Section 4.2.1).

1.9. It was estimated that traffic growth during the recent recessionary period (over which the main EU liberalization measures were introduced) was markedly higher than predicted by a model calibrated on past GDP trends over a period of recession and industry regulation. Passenger traffic levels averaged 20% higher than predicted over the period 1992–94. The same model predicted that for every 1% boost to Community GDP that might be caused by single market measures (other studies have attempted to estimate this overall effect on the economies of EU countries), an additional million scheduled passengers would have been generated (see Section 5.2.3).

1.10. Comprehensive data on air cargo carried on intra-EU routes is impossible to obtain. The situation is also complicated by the growing trend in cargo moving by truck between airports and treated in the same way as air cargo. There has been a rapid expansion both in air express and parcel traffic in the EU, and the intra-EU truck network offered by EU airlines.

The removal of EU barriers is thought to have been a major factor in recent express cargo growth (see Section 5.3).

1.11. It is important to note that without the benefits of the liberalization process, EU airlines would not have been able to make use of the dynamic pricing tactics made possible by revenue management techniques. However, airlines have continued to seek revenue increases from the business market segments by increasing these fares, and in this respect it can be concluded that the EU measures have produced an undesired effect. Similar price discriminatory strategies, though, have been pursued by airlines in both the US and Australia, following deregulation (see Section 5.7.1).

There have been exceptions to this experience, for example where entry by carriers such as British Midland in the UK and Air One in Italy has occurred, as both have competed on price for the business market (see Section 5.7). This leads to the conclusion that policies that favour entry by these types of carrier (often one of three or four carriers competing on a dense route) would be desirable with regard to business fares. This last point is supported by the analysis of developments of capacity concentration on cross-border intra-EU routes, which shows, if anything, growing rather than reduced concentration on a city-pair route basis (see Section 5.1.1).

Consumers benefited considerably from deeper discounts from the fully flexible fare for scheduled flights and more widely publicized special offers. The number of passengers taking advantage of such discounts has increased between 1985 and 1994, this trend accelerating in the early 1990s (see Section 5.7.1).

1.12. Cross-border air fares were generally found to be higher than domestic fares for routes of similar distance, especially for fully flexible and business fares. These differentials have been reduced in some countries, for example Germany. They would be expected to decline in the future, but this might take a number of years, given the nature of the causes of the differences (see Section 5.7.3).

1.13. EU carriers have made some progress in reducing costs, although the gap between EU and US carriers is not narrowing. EU airlines have certainly reduced staff numbers (especially in the past few years) and increased labour productivity both in terms of available tonne-kms (ATK) per employee and labour costs per ATK. However, they have not been so successful in reducing the average labour costs per employee. It appears that the airlines are paying their staff on average slightly more in return for proportionately greater productivity increases. These changes were affected partly by EU liberalization measures, partly by international competition from carriers outside Europe and partly by the world and European economic climate. The relative importance of the EU measures would depend on the airline's focus of operations (see Section 5.5).

1.14. It can be concluded that some of the expectations following the introduction of EU liberalization have not been met: there have been few serious challenges to the flag carrier duopolies, and business and fully flexible fares have continued to climb. On the other hand, consumers have benefited from greater competition in promotional fares, and more dynamic pricing tactics overall have led to higher intra-EU traffic growth in the early 1990s than would have been the case without liberalization. There was also a substantial growth in the number of EU cities connected by non-stop services, and some encouraging trends from new entrant airlines in the UK, Belgium, Italy, France and Spain. On balance, it is argued that the net result has been disappointing; but this is hardly surprising given the timing of the final stage of liberalization in the middle of an economic recession, the concern of the larger airlines with more global events, and the time needed to change some of the more deep-seated structural barriers.

1.15. The most important barrier remaining is access to airport slots, which inhibits competition on existing routes and the development of new routes (see Section 3.5.4 and survey results in Appendix B). This is currently being addressed by the Commission, but it is difficult to see a solution that does not involve either confiscation of slots or some form of auction. The latter has the advantage of not requiring procedures for confiscation, and may not be the barrier to new entrants that has often been claimed. Slot pricing may discourage operators of small aircraft, but this already happens under existing landing fee structures.

1.16. The second most important problem is considered to have been state aid (see survey results in Appendix B), and it is argued that many of the conditions imposed in conjunction with the approval of state aid could have been more onerous, and accompanied by such requirements as giving up ground handling monopolies (see Section 3.5.3). Conditions should be strictly monitored and enforced, and, where necessary, modified to take into account changes in the market situation.

1.17. Many of the other benefits that have yet to accrue from the single market are related to horizontal measures. These include the harmonization of indirect taxation and social policies in member countries (see Section 3.7). This would ensure that the key airline input markets such as labour, capital and goods and services were more competitive, a position that some of them do not yet approach.

1.18. As with regulation in other industries, it is necessary to achieve a balance between the strict control of mergers and alliances in order to make Community markets work better, and allowing EU airlines to achieve the necessary economies of scale and scope to be able to compete globally. It is likely that the Commission have tipped the balance slightly in favour of the latter, which means that more intensified efforts should be made to ensure that air transport agreements between the major trading blocs of the EU, NAFTA and ASEAN are liberalized. This would reduce the scope first for EU airlines to cross-subsidize EU operations from lucrative (protected) long-haul markets through increased competition, and second to allow non-EU airlines to take majority stakes in EU airlines and vice versa.

2. Introduction

2.1. Study objectives and approach

In order to examine the impact and effectiveness of Community measures in the field of air transport, it is important to look back at the original aims and objectives of the process. Although the creation of a single market was an objective in itself, it was the benefits which would flow from this which lay behind the liberalization process. Most of the early debate, which led up to the publication of the so-called Memorandum No 1 of 1979[1] was concerned with the perceived need to develop the economic and social cohesion of the Community. This was particularly important for outlying regions.

Given the importance that air transport was likely to play in the economic integration process, the Commission was concerned that the interests of the Community and its outlying regions might not be best served by US-style deregulation (which had taken place in 1978). A central purpose of the Memorandum was therefore to stimulate a policy debate to decide whether the existing system was in the interests of consumers or, in the long term, of the airlines themselves. It was not clear then, just as it is not entirely clear now, that total deregulation and the unconstrained effects of market forces would produce an optimum air transport system for the Community as a whole.

In 1984, after a period of consultation, the Commission produced a second memorandum.[2] This put forward the long-term goal of creating a common air transport market to be achieved by a gradual relaxation of existing controls. It was expected that this would result in lower prices, a stimulus to growth of the industry, lower costs, and profits for efficient airlines. In the longer term, this would create jobs and contribute towards a coherence of the single market which could not be achieved by states acting individually. On the other hand, it was emphasized that national social and economic objectives would be safeguarded, an aim that could work against the benefits of increased coherence and efficiency.

The above background provides a useful starting point for the study in so far that the Memoranda set out objectives (i.e. variety and choice, profits, market stimulation, job creation, cohesion, retain existing benefits and safeguard national objectives). The method by which these were to be achieved in practice were essentially the three packages of air transport measures. An assessment of the progress made so far in achieving these objectives is the primary purpose for this study.

In particular, the study:

(a)   examines any changes in market structure and behaviour which can be traced back to Community initiated or Community inspired changes in the regulatory framework for Community air transport; and

---

[1]   Contribution of the European Communities to the Development of Air Transport Services – Memorandum of the Commission, EC Bulletin Supp. 5/79.

[2]   Memorandum No 2 – Progress towards the Development of a Community Air Transport Policy, COM (84) 72 final.

(b)   assesses the extent to which these have been reflected in the performance and effectiveness of airline operations within the Community.

To meet the study objectives, five discrete but interlinked steps of analysis were undertaken:

(1)   review of Community actions intended to create a single aviation market;
(2)   scheduled and charter carrier strategic responses to liberalization;[3]
(3)   operational changes and marketing innovations;[3]
(4)   financial and economic developments;[3]
(5)   identification of barriers to the full exploitation of the potential of the single market.

The logic of the approach and sequencing proposed for the study are based on the following analysis.

Both the actual and the proposed changes to the regulatory environment in the period from 1985 to 1995 (**Step 1**) forced airlines, both incumbents and new entrants, to change their strategies (**Step 2**) and to introduce new operating patterns and new marketing tools. The operational and marketing changes reflected both the more liberal market environment and the strategic options being taken. These changes also represent the responses (**Step 3**) to actions intended to create a Single Aviation Market and to the more general liberalization trends (see Figure 2.1).

The strategic options adopted led to significant structural changes within the European airline industry through mergers, share purchases and various types of marketing alliances. This supply side restructuring has been aimed at achieving both marketing benefits and cost efficiencies. The various operational and marketing innovations and developments had similar objectives. The success of both strategic (Step 2) and operating/marketing decisions (Step 3) can be gauged by the medium-term changes (**Step 4**). These tend to be structural, organizational, economic or financial in character.

A quantitative and qualitative analysis of the effects of liberalization (Steps 3 and 4) together with an assessment of airlines' strategic responses since 1985 (Step 2) enabled the consultants to identify both the progress towards the creation of a Single Aviation Market with pan-European distribution networks and any barriers which still exist to the full exploitation of the opportunities created by a single market (**Step 5**).

The above steps in the analysis required quantitative as well as qualitative measures, especially Steps 2 to 4. Such quantification tended to be either Community-wide or related to specific markets or groups of routes. It was supported by six detailed case studies of the behaviour and performance of individual Community airlines conducted in parallel with the preceding five steps in the analysis.

---

[3]   Case studies of five Community airlines were undertaken to support these areas of work.

Figure 2.1.   Study structure

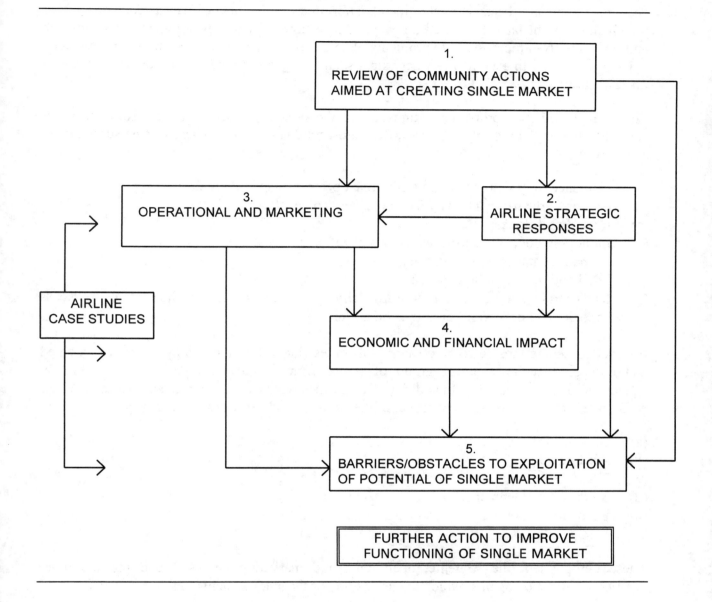

2.2.   Distinguishing the impact of Community measures

The gradual liberalization of intra-Community air services began when Europe's airlines were going through a profitable period (1983–89), but the more fundamental changes arising from the second (effective November 1990) and third (effective January 1993) liberalization packages occurred at a time when economic recession and a downturn in demand growth pushed many airlines into deficit and several into a loss-making spiral. Against that background airlines would in any case have taken a variety of actions to improve their worsening economic fortunes. How can one, in the present study, distinguish responses and actions which would have occurred anyway from those that arose directly as a result of the liberalization process and of the Community liberalization in particular? This poses a crucial methodological problem.

In some areas the distinction is relatively straightforward. For instance, many effects such as new Fifth Freedom services or entry of new airlines on major intra-Community routes could only have happened because of the liberalization measures. Others, such as code sharing or franchising, might have happened anyway. An examination of developments in yields and unit costs involves more intricate problems of causality. The case studies and interviews with key executives try to establish to what extent such changes were induced by the trend towards liberalization.

There are significant problems with isolating the effects of EU measures from the other variables that explain changes in air traffic, fares, productivity, etc. These can be summarized as follows:

(a)   influence of global factors on EU airline operations (see Figure 2.2);
(b)   economic determinants (GDP, disposable income, etc.);
(c)   oil and fuel prices;
(d)   monopoly controlled airport and air navigation charges;
(e)   exchange rates and interest rates;
(f)   hotel and related holiday costs;
(g)   leads and lags in the aircraft ordering/delivery cycle, which has, in the past, led to excess capacity and downward pressures on air fares.

In order to isolate these effects, a sample of routes (individually or grouped) were evaluated and compared with a control group of routes from countries which were not directly influenced by EU measures. In addition, five airlines were examined in detail as case studies, each one representing a different aspect of the Community's air transport industry:

(a)   British Airways;
(b)   Air France;
(c)   TAP Air Portugal;
(d)   Maersk Air (Denmark);
(e)   Eurowings (Germany).

These complement the strategic, operational and marketing analyses, and provide more detailed information against which to check some of the study conclusions.

Two of the five case studies involve large but contrasting national carriers. British Airways is included both because it was fully privatized in the mid-1980s and because it is a carrier which has apparently responded most rapidly since 1985 to the regulatory changes affecting European and world air transport. Air France, by contrast, is still state owned and has appeared slow to respond to the emergence of the single market. To represent smaller and peripheral national carriers, TAP-Air Portugal, again state owned, has been selected.

Figure 2.2.   The importance of intra-European revenues for major EU airlines in 1992

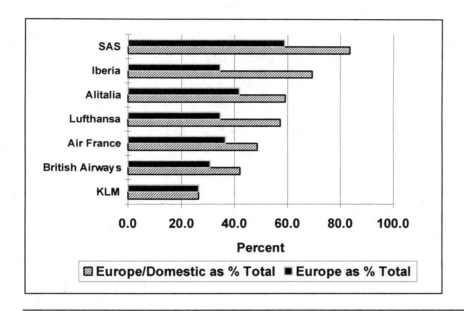

It was important to include a new entrant airline among the case studies. Unfortunately, there are very few truly independent new airlines of significant size which have emerged since 1985 and which are still surviving as truly independent carriers. Most surviving new entrants have become franchisees of larger incumbents or have sold shares to them. To fill this gap the Danish carrier Maersk Air was chosen. This airline operates charters (0.5 million passengers in 1994), but has launched several scheduled routes including some business sectors, and has a wholly owned subsidiary operating regional scheduled services.

The German airline Eurowings was taken as representative of a smaller regional airline. This airline operated regional intra-EU services with turbo-prop aircraft, and has recently agreed to operate larger jet aircraft for charter operator Hapag Lloyd, as well as acquiring some jets for its own services.

2.3. Scope of the study

The analysis of data will covers the period 1985 to 1995 inclusive, but to facilitate understanding, some of the comparative analyses are focused on key years within this time-frame, for example 1986 (before EU liberalization), 1989 (post-first and pre-second EU package), 1992 (post-second and pre-third package), and 1994 and 1995 (the period after the third package came into force). Where necessary, data and developments prior to 1985 have been analysed (for example, 1965–94 for European traffic and yield developments, and post-1980 for employment trends).

The study covers both scheduled and non-scheduled services. The latter are particularly important since around 60% of intra-Community passenger-kms in 1994 were generated on charter flights.

The geographical coverage includes the 15 EU Member States as well as the European Economic Area (EEA) States. Sweden (now part of the EU) and Norway (EEA) adopted the third package measures in August 1993, while Iceland (EEA) adopted them in July 1994.

3. Legal and administrative measures taken to complete the single market

The regulatory developments and changes that have contributed towards the creation of a single aviation market within the European Community are summarized below. This summary takes into account the global nature of air transport, and is introduced by the background to air transport regulation and some of the more important world-wide developments in this area.

3.1. History

As a result of the 1944 Chicago Conference and the 1919 Paris Convention before it, the principle of sovereignty over air space has given countries the right to regulate air services to, from and within their countries. Historically, international air transport regulation developed on the basis of a network of restrictive bilateral agreements between individual states. The regulatory control of the bilateral air services agreements were often supported by inter-airline pooling agreements and the workings of the International Air Transport Association (IATA) tariff co-ordination system, which controlled the fares and rates that could be charged by airlines.

Until the late 1970s most bilateral agreements defined explicitly the routes that could be flown, the number of airlines that could operate, the capacity and frequency that could be offered and the method by which the fares and rates would be agreed. Although similar in format, the precise terms of bilateral agreements varied considerably. Thus the regulatory constraints would vary from market to market, so that international air services between, say, four different countries, could be subject to six different regulatory regimes.

Airlines generally did not compete vigorously against one another, with many being state owned and not subject to commercial realities. Thus the impact of different conditions applying in different markets was limited.

3.2. Barriers to cross-border activity under previous regulatory systems

Up to January 1993, scheduled air services between all EU countries were governed by air services agreements (ASAs), or 'bilaterals'. Such agreements still apply to services between EU and third countries. Bilaterals are in essence international trade agreements, which vary in their detailed clauses, but now tend to follow the basic format that was set out in the standard bilateral agreement proposed by the Chicago Conference. In the course of each agreement, the key issues of economic regulation are dealt with:

(a)   the routes that may be flown;
(b)   the number of airlines permitted to operate (designation);
(c)   the capacity allowed;
(d)   the system for determining the fares to be levied;
(e)   the required ownership of carriers.

3.2.1. Routes

The most fundamental matter that is regulated is whether countries will allow other countries' aircraft into their airspace, whether and where they will allow them to land, and between which points aircraft may carry revenue traffic. The routes that may be flown are listed in a route schedule, which is attached to the bilateral agreement itself. At the most restrictive end of the scale comes an agreement that lists the specific pairs of points that may be operated. At the least restrictive end of the scale comes the provision that airlines may operate to any point in the territory of the state to and from any foreign point.

3.2.2. Designation

Once the routes have been described, there are often restrictions on the number of airlines from each side that may operate the routes. Most agreements up to the 1970s only allowed one airline from each side to operate each route (single designation). Some bilaterals allow routes to be flown by two carriers from each side (double designation), whilst liberal agreements permit operations by an unlimited number of carriers (multiple designation). For example, the US-UK bilateral, known as Bermuda II, originally allowed only one airline from each side on each route, except for two routes that were to be double designation:

'...For the purpose of operating the agreed combination services ... each party shall have the right to designate not more than: (a) two airlines on each of two gateway route segments of its own choosing, (b) one airline on each gateway route segment other than those selected under subparagraph (a)...' (UK-US 1977)

Since 1977, the bilateral has been amended to allow extra designations on further routes.

The ECAC COMPAS report of 1982 indicated that around two-thirds of European bilaterals had no limitations on the number of airlines designated, with one-third restricted to single designation. At that time, however, in practice only 8% of total country-pairs and only 2% of city-pairs operated had more than one designated airline from each state.

3.2.3. Capacity

A key article in many bilaterals concerns capacity. Capacity can be regulated in a variety of ways – by direct limitation of the number of flights that each side's carriers may operate (e.g. Lebanon-UK), possibly in conjunction with a requirement on the aircraft size (e.g. the recent US-Germany interim agreement). Alternatively, the number of seats might be directly regulated. A restrictive form of regulation might require the capacity on offer between two countries to be split precisely 50:50 between the carriers of the two countries. A more flexible regime would allow one side to operate up to 60% of the capacity, a still more liberal agreement might allow one side to have up to 70%. The most liberal capacity regime would involve no controls on capacity whatsoever (e.g. US-Netherlands). Some agreements might apply the capacity splits on a route-by-route basis (e.g. US-UK), although most agreements apply them to the country-pair market. The extent to which carriers may increase capacity is also often regulated.

3.2.4. Tariffs

Another key article relates to tariffs, which concerns the approval procedure for passenger fares and cargo rates. The regulation of fares is particularly difficult for a number of reasons.

If a government decides which fare level it will permit, actually enforcing this fare level is not easy. If the fare is sold in foreign countries, it will be even more difficult for the government to enforce. Furthermore, the fact that various indirect routings are available between any two points makes fare regulation difficult, even when the two governments are co-operating.

Typically, tariff articles in the 1950s included references to the IATA tariff conference procedures, committing carriers to using fares that were agreed at IATA conferences, with government approval largely automatic. This reference to the IATA tariff setting system was gradually removed from bilaterals, and is now no longer a feature, although modern bilaterals continue to commit carriers to establishing fares at a reasonable level, typically including the following clause:

'The tariffs to be charged by the designated airlines of the Contracting Parties for carriage between their territories ... shall be established at reasonable levels, due regard being paid to all relevant factors, including the cost of operating the agreed services, the interests of users, reasonable profit and market considerations.'

The regulation of fares and tariffs generally takes one of the following five forms, shown in order from the most restrictive to the most liberal:

(a) Double Approval   (both governments must approve the fare)
(b) Country of Origin Approval   (government at origin of flight must approve fare)
(c) Home State Approval   (government of airline's home state must approve fare)
(d) Double Disapproval   (fare in effect unless both governments disapprove)
(e) No Government Intervention.

3.2.5. Ownership and control

All bilaterals generally give states the right to refuse to accept the designation of an airline that is not owned and controlled by nationals of the state designating it:

'each Contracting Party shall have the right to withhold, suspend or revoke the operating permission ... in the event that .. that Contracting Party is not satisfied that substantial ownership and effective control of such airline are vested in the nationals of the other Contracting Party.' (US-Italy 1970)

These clauses were introduced into air transport in order to prevent flags of convenience being used as a way of avoiding labour laws and technical regulations – as is apparent in the shipping sector. This will be referred to later in this study.

In addition to the key economic issues, bilateral agreements also cover administrative issues such as the definition of terms used in the agreement, the mutual recognition of aircraft and air crew licences and certificates, the exemption from customs duties of aircraft parts brought into the country for use by foreign aircraft, the commitment to ensure that airport and navigational charges are set at a reasonable level, representation abroad (stationing of personnel), the right to transfer funds from ticket sales abroad, the taxation treatment of revenue (avoiding double taxation), entry into force of the agreement, and the procedure for amending and terminating the agreement.

3.2.6. Charters

Non-scheduled air transport services have historically been subject to far lighter regulation than scheduled services.

The reason for this is that prior to the Second World War, most commercial air transport was scheduled – flights operated to a regular timetable and were openly advertised and available to individual members of the public. The private chartering of aircraft and air taxi operations was very limited and the concept of inclusive tours involving air transport had not yet been created.

At the time of the 1944 Chicago Conference, it was thought that non-scheduled operations would continue to be unimportant and so a more liberal approach was adopted towards them than towards scheduled services [Chataway, 1994]. Whereas Article 6 of the Chicago Convention, which governs scheduled operations, specifically required 'special permission or authorization' from the destination countries for flights to be operated, Article 5 left authorization for non-scheduled services to the discretion of individual states.

This decision placed charter operations outside the scope of bilateral air service agreements and, consequently, in a potentially liberal environment. In practice, most countries have historically required prior authorization of charter flights, but attitudes have varied considerably. Some countries, such as India and until recently Australia, have been very restrictive in their approach, either refusing to allow charter services unless operated by their national carrier or unless it could be shown that it did not divert any traffic from scheduled services. Others allowed charter services, provided their carriers were allowed to tender for the contract. Until recently, Cyprus would permit tour operators to use the flights of charter airlines, provided they also bought a percentage of their total seats from Cyprus Airways. More liberal approaches have been taken by tourist destination countries such as Spain, Morocco and Tunisia, readily authorizing charter services that bring in business for their tourist industries.

As the importance of non-scheduled services increased, charter services began to find their way into bilateral agreements: the UK signed non-scheduled bilaterals with France and Switzerland in 1950 and 1952, but these were superseded by the 1956 Paris Agreement, in which the members of the European Civil Aviation Conference (ECAC) agreed to adopt a more liberal approach to charter services. The states party to the Agreement agreed to freely admit aircraft engaged in non-scheduled commercial flights within Europe, provided the flights did not harm their scheduled services.

In the light of this liberal approach, the member states essentially agreed to waive the right to raise regulations, conditions or limitations on non-scheduled services, the right that was granted in Article 5 of the Chicago Convention. This agreement has greatly facilitated the development of charter services within Europe, most particularly the inclusive tour charters.

An interesting feature of the Paris Convention is that it did not include any mention of ownership and control requirements. This, in contrast to most bilateral agreements, has allowed charter carriers greater flexibility in their ownership structure than scheduled carriers. The UK carrier Monarch is ultimately Swiss owned, while the UK carrier Britannia is owned by the Canadian Thomson corporation.

In the 1960s many governments, under pressure from the International Air Transport Association (IATA) to protect the scheduled carriers, introduced new constraints on the operations of charter airlines. However, through the 1970s these constraints withered away as public demand for cheap air travel increased. Although the charter market continued to be restricted in the extent to which it could compete with scheduled carriers and offer seat-only travel, the core market for inclusive tours was very competitive. By the end of the 1970s, consumers in most countries in northern Europe enjoyed a wide choice of tour operators and charter airlines. This contrasted with European scheduled markets, which, even in countries with clear multiple airline policies like the UK, continued to be dominated by the flag carrier.

3.3. Bilateral liberalization

From the late 1970s through the 1980s the trend towards increasing liberalization of the airline industry spread – unevenly – from the domestic United States industry to international markets. Liberal bilateral agreements were signed in 1978 between the US and various European countries (the Netherlands, Germany, Belgium) and in the following two years between the US and various Asian countries (Thailand, Singapore, Korea). In 1984 the Netherlands and the UK effectively deregulated air transportation services between the two countries with the adoption of an ultra-liberal bilateral, and both countries subsequently endeavoured to sign relatively liberal agreements with other states in Europe.

Such liberal bilaterals pre-dated the Community's first liberalization package of 1988 and, by going much further than this first package, had a more direct impact on air services between the countries concerned. Examples of these were:

UK - Netherlands (June 1984)	Liberal route access/capacity with consultations Country of Origin fare rules
UK - FR of Germany (December 1984)	Liberal route access/capacity Country of Origin rules only for discount fares Minimum conditions for special fares
UK - Luxembourg (March 1985)	Liberal route access/capacity Double Disapproval on fares
UK - Netherlands (June 1985)	Brought into line with Luxembourg agreement
UK - France (September 1985)	55:45 on capacity (vs. previous 50:50); liberal access No change on fares
UK - Belgium (October 1985)	Same as Luxembourg
UK - Switzerland (December 1985)	Same as Luxembourg for capacity Same as FR of Germany for fares

Over the same period, other bilaterals were revised with very limited moves towards liberalization:

UK - Italy (March 1986)	No change from traditional model, apart from freer access (additional UK carriers could be designated)
France - FR of Germany (1986)	Only greater freedom for route access

The effects of these bilateral changes, as well as the impact of measures introduced by the EU over this period (1984–90) – principally the first package – are examined later in this study. Broadly, the impact of the new bilaterals could be compared with the old style ones as follows:

	Traditional bilateral	**New style bilateral**[4]
Routes flown	Only to specified points	Open route access
Designation	One per route from each state	Multiple designation
Capacity allowed	Shared 50:50 between airlines of each state	
Fares levied	Approval of both governments needed (negotiated through IATA)	Double disapproval (only rejected if both governments disapprove)
Ownership of carriers	Nationals of designating state	No change

The impact of the liberalization of UK/Netherlands air services has been analysed in a number of studies. One study (OECD, 1988) suggested that air traffic on these routes was 3–5% higher as a result of the bilateral liberalization. The same study found that the effect on air fares was to increase the normal economy and business fares and to reduce significantly the lowest discount fare available.

3.4. European Community measures

Against this background the task of creating a liberal Single Aviation Market in Europe can be seen as a continuation of the liberalizing trend that had started with the UK-Netherlands agreement of 1984. It can also be seen as a significant challenge and as an essential step in creating fairer competition between existing EU airlines and in reducing the regulatory barriers to entry for new airlines.

The final moves towards the Single European Aviation Market, which came into effect on 1 January 1993 as a result of the third package, had been preceded by a lengthy gestation period. This dated back to the 1974 European Court of Justice ruling (Case 167/73 [1974] ECR 359) which judged that the Treaty of Rome competition rules applied to air transport and the 1975 recommendation by the Commission for the establishment of a European market in aviation. The Commission's Memorandum 1 of 1979 (COM(79) 311) called for a liberalization of the bilateral restrictions and a review of state subsidies. This led to the Inter-regional Directive, which introduced free access on inter-regional routes over 400 kilometres operated by aircraft with less than 70 seats. In 1984 the Commission's Second Memorandum on Air Transport (COM(84) 72) recommended for further liberalization measures.

The *Nouvelles Frontières* ruling of April 1986 (Case 209/84 [1986] ECR 1425), the entering into force of the Single European Act and action by the Competition Directorate of the Commission against airline pooling agreements together provided the catalyst which led to the first package in December 1987. This and the second package of 1990 loosened the constraints of bilaterals between European Community Member States by freeing capacity limitations, allowing additional airlines to be designated and creating additional route rights.

---

[4]   e.g. UK - Netherlands.

These two packages left the fundamentals of the bilateral system in place. However, only those elements of individual bilaterals that were less restrictive than Community legislation were allowed to continue. In contrast, the third package of 1992 for the first time replaced the bilateral system with a multi-lateral system of air transport regulation. The setting of common rules for the award of an air operator's certificate, access to air transport routes within the Community, and the monitoring of air fares therefore replaced the bilateral system and designation of single national carriers.

These rules moved away from the requirement of national ownership and control by creating the concept of a Community air carrier. They also removed the regulatory distinction between scheduled and charter airlines. These liberal rules open up traffic rights on all intra-Community routes for all Community air carriers (with full cabotage from April 1997), with a few exceptions, and remove capacity restrictions.

It is important to note that the three packages only apply to air transport within the Community and subsequently to the EEA countries. Air transport services between Member States and third countries continue to be regulated by traditional air service bilaterals. This, in some ways, places constraints on the effective working of the Single Aviation Market.

3.4.1. The Regional Directive of 1983

The 1983 Council Directive on Inter-regional air services was the first measure introduced by the EU related to air transport. While the Commission had proposed more radical changes, this was as far as the countries opposing air transport liberalization at that time were prepared to go. It categorized all EU airports (with the exception of the Greek Islands) into three groups: category 1 were all capital city airports (except Cologne-Bonn) plus Luton, Düsseldorf, Frankfurt, Munich, Salonika and Milan. The second category included Hamburg, Stuttgart and Cologne-Bonn in Germany; Marseilles, Nice, Lyons and Basle/Mulhouse in France; Naples, Venice and Catania in Italy; Manchester, Birmingham and Glasgow in the UK; and Luxembourg and Shannon. The third category covered all other international airports.

The Directive authorized air services between category 2 and category 3 airports within the EU, subject to:

(a)   aircraft being operated of 70 seats or less;
(b)   over distances exceeding 400 km (or shorter if major time savings were offered);
(c)   states able to object if existing or neighbouring (< 50 km) services were adversely affected.

The Directive had little impact on air transport services in Europe as a whole: it was estimated that only 14 new services were started between regional airports, and many of these would probably have been allowed under existing bilaterals [Wheatcroft & Lipman, 1986]. Amendments were proposed (which were subsequently incorporated into the first package) that would have allowed it to have had a greater impact, namely by the inclusion of services involving category 1 airports, and the removal of the conditions. As it stood, however, it was unlikely to have posed any threat to the major European airlines.

3.4.2. The first package (December 1987)

A major step forward was taken in European air transport liberalization in 1987 with the adoption by the Council of a package of measures to apply from 1 January 1988:

(a)   a Regulation on the Application of the Competition Rules to Air Transport (Council Regulation (EEC) No 3975/87);

(b)   a Regulation on the application of the Treaty to certain categories of agreements and concerted practices (Council Regulation (EEC) No 3976/87);

(c)   a Directive on Air Fares (Council Directive 87/601/EEC);

(d)   a Decision on Capacity Sharing and Market Access (Council Decision 87/602/EEC).

The scope of these measures in terms of market access, capacity, fares and competition is summarized in Table 3.1. Following the Council's adoption of these measures, the Commission terminated proceedings it had begun against 13 European airlines and set out various conditions for allowing some co-operative activities to continue. These subsequently were approved.

The Commission published a report in October 1989 which reviewed the implementation of the above measures (COM(89) 476 final). This was based on a questionnaire which was returned by every member country except Denmark. Broadly, they reported favourable developments in traffic, productivity and efficiency, against a background of stable economic growth, little change in both fuel prices and financial conditions.

The level of the normal economy fare increased more or less in line with inflation, with some increases also in the lowest published fares. The flexibility allowed for fares below the deep discount fare was not requested in five Member States, with only a limited number of airlines using this in the other countries. The number of routes with multiple designation increased from 22 in 1987 to 33 in 1989, although these were concentrated in only five member countries. The capacity shares between bilateral state airlines remained fairly stable over the same period.

A UK study [CAA, 1993] concluded that this first package allowed a number of smaller airlines to enter some of the most important intra-Community routes, offering the mix of capacity and fares that they wished. These included existing airlines such as British Midland and Hamburg Airlines, and new entrants such as Air Europe and Ryanair. However, the initial 55:45 overall country-pair capacity limit was a constraint for UK airlines on French and Portuguese routes (although not Italy or Spain). A number of Fifth Freedom routes were started, notably by Aer Lingus via a Manchester hub [CAA, 1993], but some carriers thought that the 30% upper limit on the capacity offered to such traffic was too restrictive.

Co-operation agreements involving Air France with Iberia, Alitalia, London City Airways, Brymon, and NFD were challenged by the Commission in 1989. While those with the regional carriers were allowed to continue, changes in the agreements were required for those involving major carriers.

3.4.3. The second package (July 1990)

Further progress was made in European liberalization in 1990 with the adoption by the Council of a package of measures to apply from 1 November 1990:

(a) market access (Council Regulation (EEC) No 2343/90);
(b) air fares (Council Regulation (EEC) No 2342/90);
(c) a Regulation on the application of the Treaty to certain categories of agreements and concerted practices (Council Regulation (EEC) No 2344/90).

The main points in these regulations are summarized in Table 3.1. The regulations were based on a Commission proposal of July 1989, although significantly less liberal. In particular, the proposal on consecutive cabotage (limited to 33% of through capacity) was rejected, and the 75:25 capacity safety net proposal was modified to 60:40. Other parts of the package were largely unchanged.

The main changes from the first package were some reduction in the thresholds for multiple designation, and a further loosening of capacity share restrictions. Route access was also significantly improved, and a greater range of fares were to be subject to automatic approval.

3.4.4. The Air Cargo Regulation (February 1991)

Council Regulation (EEC) No 294/91 was introduced in February 1991 which almost completely liberalized flights carrying only freight and mail between EU countries. Complete freedom was given for EU airlines to operate freight aircraft between EU points on a Third/Fourth Freedom basis, and on a Fifth Freedom basis as an extension of these flights (but not cabotage). Prices could be freely established. The definition of EU carrier excluded international integrated carriers such as Fedex or DHL, although these foreign firms tended to contract flying out to EU companies (for example, DHL's air services are operated by their EU-controlled associate company EAL).

3.4.5. The third package (July 1992)

The third package, which largely deregulated intra-EU air services (and domestic services from 1997), consisted of the following three regulations which entered into force on 1 January 1993 for the original 12 Member States, Sweden in August 1993, and Finland and Austria in July 1994 (of the EEA States, Norway adopted the package in August 1993 and Iceland in July 1994):

(a) licensing of air carriers (Council Regulation (EEC) No 2407/92);
(b) market access (Council Regulation (EEC) No 2408/92);
(c) fares and rates (Council Regulation (EEC) No 2409/92).

These are summarized in Table 3.1. Licensing of air carriers was for the time being to be carried out by national governments, but applying uniform procedures laid down in the licensing regulation. Decisions by Member States to grant or revoke operating licences were to be published in the *Official Journal of the European Communities* with, to date, Denmark, Greece, Finland, Spain, France, the United Kingdom, Germany and Sweden in the EU and Norway in the EEA having done so.

Table 3.1.   **Summary of intra-EU air transport packages**

Scope	1st package From 1 January 1988 International scheduled passenger transport	2nd package From 1 November 1990 International scheduled passenger transport	3rd package From 1 January 1993 Intra-Community air transport
Fares	*Fare type* *% of ref. fare* *Fares approved by States* Discount 66-90 Automatically Deep discount 45-65 Automatically All other Dbl approval	*Fare type* *% of ref. fare* *Fares approved by States* Fully flexible 106- Unless double disapproval Normal econ 95-105 Automatically Discount 80-94 Automatically Deep discount 30-79 Automatically All other If dbl approval	*Free pricing* However, provisions made for States and/or the Commission to intervene against - excessive basic fares (in relation to long term fully allocated costs) - sustained downward development of fares
Designation	Multiple designation by a State allowed if: - 250,000 pass (1st year after notification) - 200,000 pass or 1,200 rt flights (2nd year) - 180,000 pass or 1,000 rt flights (3rd year)	Multiple designation by a State allowed if: - 140,000 pass or 800 rt flight (from Jan 91) - 100,000 pass or 600 rt flight (from Jan 92)	No longer applicable
Capacity	Capacity shares between States 45/55% (from Jan 88) 40/60% (from Oct 89)	Capacity shares of a State of up to 60% Capacity can be increased by 7.5% per year	Unrestricted
Route access	• 3rd/4th Freedom region to hub routes permitted • 5th Freedom traffic allowed up to 30% of capacity • Additional 5th Freedom rights for Irish and Portuguese • Combination of points allowed • Some exemptions	• 3rd/4th Freedom between all airports • 5th Freedom traffic allowed up to 50% of capacity • Public service obligations and certain protection for new regional routes • A 3rd/4th Freedom service can be matched by an airline from the other State • Scope for traffic distribution rules and restrictions related to congestion and environmental protection	• Full access to international and domestic routes within the EU including routes between states other than the base of the carrier Exemptions for Greek islands and Azores • Cabotage is allowed for up to 50% of capacity if the domestic sector is combined with a route to the home country Cabotage is unrestricted from April 1997 • More developed public service obligations and certain protection for new thin regional routes • More developed scope for traffic distribution rules and restrictions related to congestion and environmental protection
Competition rules	*Group exemptions regarding* • Some capacity coordinations • Tariff consultations • Slot allocation at airports • Common computer reservation systems • Ground handling of aircraft, freight, passengers and inflight catering • Some sharing of pool revenues	*Group exemptions regarding* • Some capacity coordinations • Tariff consultations • Slot allocation at airports • Common computer reservation systems • Ground handling of aircraft, freight, passengers and inflight catering	*Group exemptions regarding* • Some schedule coordinations • Tariff consultations • Slot allocation at airports • Common computer reservation systems • Joint operation of new thin routes
Licensing of air carriers	Not provided for in the 1st and 2nd packages		*Full freedom to start an airline* Uniform conditions across EU Concept of Community ownership and control replaces national ownership and control Requirements for financial fitness specified Small carriers subject to looser regulatory requirements
Air cargo	Largely deregulated under February 1991 Regulation; free access (except cabotage) and free pricing		Replaces 1991 Regulation

There was to be some protection for single carriers operating small aircraft on thin routes, and states could impose a public service obligation on scheduled air services to an airport serving a peripheral or development region in its territory, or a thin route to a regional airport of vital economic importance to a region.

This study examines the degree to which relevant Council Directives or Regulations have been implemented both in law (*de jure*) and in spirit (*de facto*) in Member States. It would appear that some states were slower than others fully to implement the spirit of the third package by creating administrative or other obstacles. The reluctance of the French government to open up Orly airport to competitive air services in 1994 is an example. Meetings and discussions with aviation authorities and airlines, as well as an examination of publicized cases or referrals to the Commission, are used to ascertain any problems arising with the implementation of the liberalization packages or the competition rules (Appendix B).

3.5. Competition policy

3.5.1. Community action

The three European Community packages dealing with route access, capacity, fares and licences have been supplemented by a range of additional regulatory initiatives designed to foster fair and vigorous competition within the sector. As the basic regulatory constraints have been removed, the importance of protecting the competitive environment has increased. Community action in the field of competition is addressed in this section, while accompanying industry-specific measures on slot allocation and consumer protection are discussed in the next section. A fuller discussion and examination of EU competition policy in relation to the airline industry is to be found in the parallel study for the Commission, *Competition issues*.[5]

Starting in December 1987, a series of regulations were approved governing the procedures for the application of the competition rules to undertakings in the air transport sector. These provided for block exemptions to be made to various airline agreements or concerted practices from the application of the relevant parts of Article 85 of the Treaty. These were granted subject to various conditions and for a limited time period. Currently these cover:

(a)   joint planning and co-ordination of schedules;
(b)   joint operations on new thin routes by small airlines (limited to three years);
(c)   tariff consultations which give rise to interlining;
(d)   slot allocation and airport scheduling arrangements (Council Regulation (EEC) No 95/93);
(e)   CRS operations (Council Regulation (EEC) No 2299/89 as amended).

Thus revenue sharing and pooling, joint services operated by larger carriers, tariff fixing and schedules co-ordination in general are currently illegal with respect to intra-EU operations.

The Commission has taken action to restrict the effects or creation of **barriers to entry** with regulatory initiatives concerning essential inputs, such as slot allocation (Council Regulation (EEC) No 95/93), and essential means of distribution, such as computer reservations systems

---

[5]   European Commission [1997], *Competition issues*, *Single Market Review* Vol. V-3, Office for Official Publications of the EC, Luxembourg, and Kogan Page/Earthscan, London.

(Council Regulation (EEC) No 2299/89 amended by Council Regulation (EEC) No 3089/93). The Commission also studied the competitive consequences of frequent flyer programmes (FFPs) and whether they restricted the freedom of passengers to choose an airline or impede market access of competitive airlines, which arguably function as a barrier to entry.

The Commission's actions to safeguard fair competition include responding to complaints that allege the **abuse of a dominant position** (Article 86). Complaints have arisen in a wide variety of contexts, including refusal to interline (British Midland/Aer Lingus Commission Decision 92/213), overflight charges (SAT/Eurocontrol, Case C-364/92 [1994] ECR I-43), CRS charges (Air UK et al./Galileo, decision outstanding), ground handling monopolies (various complaints, decisions outstanding), and volume discounts for airport charges (Brussels Airport).

3.5.2. Mergers, acquisitions and joint ventures

The Commission's merger policy defined by the Merger Control Regulation (Regulation EEC No 4064/89) has also been an integral part of the establishment of the Single Aviation Market. A number of acquisitions have come before the Commission, the most important of which are outlined below. So far the Commission has not formally opposed any airline merger, and in certain cases (e.g. British Airways/British Caledonian) the Commission has approved a merger of operations which has resulted in high market shares on individual routes, or in individual airport markets. However, in various cases (e.g. Air France - Sabena) conditions, such as guaranteeing the availability of slots to new entrants on particular routes, have been applied to safeguard potential competition. Joint ventures not involving share purchases or exchanges, but with significant implications for competition, also need Commission approval, for example the recent Lufthansa/SAS agreement.

British Airways/BCal: acquisition of 100% of British Caledonian in 1988. The Commission agreed to the take-over in return for various undertakings including a cap on the number of slots used at Gatwick, and an agreement not to appeal against the UK decision to require a number of route licences, including Gatwick to Paris and Brussels, to be returned.

Air France/Air Inter/UTA: acquisition of 100% of UTA and UTA's holding in Air Inter (giving them control of the domestic airline). This was approved by the Commission on condition that Air France divested itself of any shares held in TAT, gave up slots at Paris CDG airport, and allowed at least one other French carrier to serve about half of all internal French routes. The latter did not in fact take place.

British Airways/Dan Air: acquisition of 100% of Dan Air Services. The Commission decided that this did not require examination since Dan Air's turnover was less than ECU 250 million a year. Air France challenged the decision unsuccessfully on the basis that Dan Air's charter revenues should have been taken into account. Its effect on the Brussels/London market were examined at the request of the Belgian government, but it was found not to have a significant effect on competition.

British Airways/TAT: acquisition of 49.9% of TAT's shares by BA, with an option to increase this to 100% by January 1997. Approved on condition that slots are made available to new entrants on London/Paris and London/Lyon if required.

Lufthansa/SAS: this involves co-operation on route networks, schedules, ticketing, frequent flyer programmes, and ground and cargo services. Certain conditions were required to be met before this was approved, including a frequency freeze on a number of routes, slots to be provided for competing carriers at Oslo, Stockholm, Düsseldorf and Frankfurt, the termination of Lufthansa's co-operation with Transwede and Finnair on routes between Scandinavia and Germany, and a guarantee to enter into interline agreements with new entrants if requested.

Sabena/Swissair: agreement signed in May 1995 which resulted in Swissair acquiring 49.5% of Sabena's shares for BFR 6 billion, and Swissair lending a further BFR 4 billion to enable Sabena to reimburse Air France. Approved on condition that slots are transferred in Zurich and Geneva (12) and Brussels (18) to enable (if required) new entrants to obtain sufficient slots to start new services. They must also not increase frequency by more than 25% of the existing level, and must be amenable to signing interline or FFP agreements with new entrants if required. Because Switzerland is not party to the third package, there are also requirements to introduce multiple designation (up to four EEA carriers on routes), country of origin tariffs and to abolish capacity restrictions.

3.5.3. State aid to airlines

The regulation of state aid is also a crucial area of Community regulation in the context of safeguarding competition. In its various decisions approving State aid summarized below, the Commission has imposed conditions to try to ensure that the aid is used to achieve airline restructuring rather than to provide a competitive advantage. Under the Treaty's Article 93 and EEA Agreement Article 62 procedures, the airline requesting Commission approval of state aid was required to submit a recovery plan, which was then examined by Commission consultants. State aid was generally applied in a number of tranches, with Commission approval required for each tranche, subject to adequate progress being made and meeting the conditions. The procedures for the approval of aid are laid down in the December 1994 paper (94/C 350/07), where 'market economy investor' principles are defined. While these include such requirements that equity finance could be provided if the present value of the expected future cash flows from the intended project exceed the new outlay, the paper recognizes the difficulties in applying these principles, given the different accounting practices, cost of capital and other differences between countries. The Commission, in granting approval, has generally imposed the following conditions:

(a)   cost reduction or return to profitability;
(b)   capacity reduction or constraints on expansion;
(c)   no fleet expansion;
(d)   aid not used to acquire other airlines;
(e)   not allowed to act as price leader;
(f)   no government interference in the airline's management;
(g)   no further aid during restructuring plan.

Sabena was the first major airline to get state aid approvals, most recently linked to an investment by Swissair and previously by Air France. Other flag carriers receiving aid have been:

Aer Lingus

The Irish government wished to inject IR £200 million into its national carrier in spring 1994. The Commission approved aid of IR £175 million, while imposing most of the above conditions as well as a requirement that the airline legally separate its transatlantic, European and Express operations. This aid would have amounted to only 5% of their total past three years' revenues.

Olympic Airways

The Greek government originally proposed state aid to their national carrier in 1992, which was subsequently modified to total DR 545 billion (ECU 1.9 billion). This was divided into DR 427 billion for a reduction in the airline's debt, DR 64 billion for converting debt into equity and a capital injection of DR 54 billion. The Commission approved this in October 1994, subject to most of the above conditions, with the following additional requirements:

(a)   removal of Olympic's monopoly on new domestic air services;
(b)   removal of any constraints on charter services, for example seat-only sales;
(c)   removal of Greek island airport exemptions from June 1998.

However, the Olympic case has recently been re-opened, following management changes and problems in connection with the earlier requirements. The total aid of DR 545 billion, paid over three years, would amount to around 86% of the past three years' operating revenues.

Air France

Air France received capital injections of FF 1.25 billion and FF 1.5 billion between 1991 and 1993, the first of which was considered by the Commission to be normal financial transactions and not state aid. The second, however, was required to be repaid. A further FF 5.1 billion was classified as debt. In early 1994, the French government wished to inject a further FF 20 billion of capital into the airline, and this was approved by the Commission in July 1994. This would amount to around 12% of their total revenues over the past three years. The approval was subject to the French government complying with a total of 16 commitments which, in addition to those listed above, included some fairly modest staff productivity targets, that they should sell their shares in the Meridien hotel group, and that the Orly traffic distribution rules be modified. (See case study in Appendix F.)

The Commission reviewed the progress made by Air France under its restructuring programme in November 1995, prior to the payment of the second tranche. They concluded that, although the productivity target for the first year had been exceeded and most of the conditions complied with, the financial results were worse than expected, principally because of a failure to implement the planned savings in labour costs and lower than forecast yields. A further progress report was required before payment of the third tranche in 1996. In the meantime, three airlines have complained to the Commission about Air France's use of subsidies to undercut leisure fares (by up to 40% on the Paris-Stockholm route, according to SAS).

TAP Air Portugal

At the beginning of 1994, the Portuguese government proposed to increase TAP's capital by a total of ESC 180 billion, to be paid in four tranches over 1994 to 1997 (this would amount to around 35% of their total past three years' operating revenues). Following submission of a restructuring plan, the Commission approved the aid, subject to TAP achieving its forecast operating results, the abolition of the airline's tax exemptions, public service obligation open tenders for the routes from the mainland to the Azores and Madeira, and a commitment to liberalize charter services to the Azores (in addition to most of the above conditions). Approval of the third tranche has recently been given. (See case study in Appendix F.)

Iberia

At the end of 1994, the Spanish government submitted its plan to increase Iberia's capital by PTA 130 billion (this would amount to around 17% of their total past three years' operating revenues). The Commission's notice of May 1995 expressed serious doubts that the proposal was compatible with the relevant articles of the Treaty and EEA Agreement, and asked for further information. In January 1996, the Commission decided that the injection of PTA 87 billion of capital did not amount to state aid, particularly in view of the undertakings given by the Spanish government (i.e. reduction of shareholdings in South American airlines).

Other state aid cases examined by the Commission included a capital injection of FF 300 million by Air Outre-Mer of France, and German capital allowances for taxation.

3.6. Other industry-specific measures

3.6.1. Airport slot allocation

Access to congested airports by new entrants is clearly important to enable a competitive single market to emerge. The allocation of slots at congested Community airports is governed by a common framework and rules contained in Council Regulation (EEC) No 95/93, which was approved in January 1993. This regulation designates EU airports as being either 'fully co-ordinated' (53 EU airports had this designation in October 1995), where congestion occurs for significant periods of time, or 'co-ordinated', where a co-ordinator is appointed to facilitate the allocation of slots.

The regulation follows the basic principles of neutrality, transparency and non-discrimination. Airlines have 'grandfather rights' to slots, but slots can be taken away from them under 'use-it-or-lose-it' provisions. After historic precedence, priority in allocation is given to commercial air services (whether scheduled or charter) over other new requests and *ad hoc* or general aviation requirements. New or withdrawn slots are put into a pool, of which 50% are allocated to new entrants. The definition of new entrant, however, is too narrow to help airlines such as British Midland to be treated with priority in the allocation of slots from the pool at airports such as Heathrow.

Coopers and Lybrand [1995] were asked by the Commission to review the regulation and make proposals for improving it. Their report focuses firstly on identifying the effectiveness of the regulation across Member States and secondly on suggesting some improvements to the existing mechanism. Its main conclusions were that there appeared to be a degree of inconsistency across Member States as to the extent to which the EU slot regulation had been fully implemented. They proposed the following main changes in Regulation (EEC) No 95/93: first, that the definition of new entrant should include those operators with up to 10% of the slots on the day in question; second, that new entrants should be given a stronger position concerning the distribution of slots from the slot pool (but that the percentage of slots reserved for them is reduced); and third, the need for a greater degree of transparency both in determining capacity levels at congested airports and in the slot allocation process itself. The report also recommended that the co-ordinators should be fully independent of airport authorities, national governments and airlines. However, in general, the Coopers and Lybrand study falls short of endorsing any radical change in the method of allocating slots.

It has been argued that the present mechanism for allocating slots represents a barrier to entry and as such is at variance with the basic thrust of EU competition policy. Indeed, of those airlines surveyed for this study, 83% identified lack of airport slots as a significant barrier to entry (see Appendix B). Over the last 10 years a number of alternatives have been suggested which could help remove this inconsistency. The UK CAA (Civil Aviation Authority) has carried out a number of in-depth investigations of the allocation of slots at congested airports (CAP 623 and CAP 644); its most recent proposals involve the husbanding of slots as they become available so that sufficient slots can be given to new entrants to enable them to compete on high density short/medium haul routes. One of the documents (CAP 644) suggested that 14 short-haul international duopoly routes from London Heathrow could theoretically accommodate a third carrier on the basis of assumed levels of new entrant service frequency and aircraft size. However, in order to accommodate third carrier competition, a mechanism would need to be introduced which, on the one hand, generated a sufficient number of slots at those times demanded by new entrant carriers and, on the other hand, minimized any potential disruption to incumbent carrier schedules. The CAA proposals are, however, largely ineffective in the sense that they do not advocate the confiscation of incumbent slots which would release the required quantity of slots to accommodate new entrant competition.

Using London Heathrow as an example, Figure 3.1 illustrates the difficulties experienced by new entrant airlines in obtaining slots at congested airports, where only a small proportion of total slot requests were actually granted at their preferred time. These bids were either rejected completely by the scheduling committee or the new entrant was persuaded to shift its preference to less congested periods of the day, resulting in a high percentage of allocations before 06:00 and after 20:00. Amongst those airlines which failed to obtain its requested slots was Air Liberté which wanted to operate four daily services from London Heathrow to Orly. It received no slots at Heathrow and subsequently began services at Gatwick. Contiflug also applied for slots at London Heathrow in order to operate a twice daily service to Berlin. The scheduling committee granted Contiflug evening period slots later than requested and at varying times across the week. Unable to operate such a fragmented schedule, Contiflug's slots were subsequently returned to the co-ordinator.

The problem facing many new entrant carriers is that they must first obtain the number and timing of slots that can match, as far as possible, passenger travel time preferences, and second ensure that the slots obtained are consistent with optimum schedule efficiency. The problems for new entrants could be resolved by a mechanism formulated along the lines proposed by the CAA [1993], where incumbent airlines holding a portfolio of slots above a threshold would be required to surrender a proportion to the scheduling committee. Table 3.2 outlines the number and percentage share of slots held by major carriers at London Heathrow between June 1992 and June 1993.

Table 3.2. Slots held by carriers: London Heathrow 1992/93

	Number	% of total
British Airways	157,929	38.5
British Midland	55,014	13.4
Lufthansa	19,452	4.7
SAS	14,988	3.7
Aer Lingus	14,658	3.6
Air France	14,187	3.5
United Airlines	11,023	2.7
KLM	9,978	2.4
Alitalia	8,892	2.2
Iberia	8,550	2.1
Others	95,534	23.2
Total	**410,205**	**100**

Source: UK Civil Aviation Authority CAP 623, 1993.

Figure 3.1. New entrant slots requested and granted: London Heathrow (summer 1994)

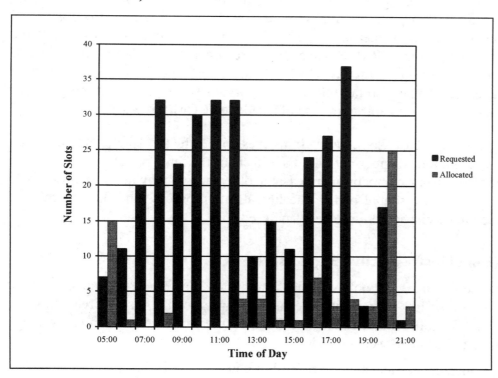

Source: UK Civil Aviation Authority CAP 644, 1995.

The process could involve requiring those airlines holding more than 2% of slots at a fully co-ordinated airport to surrender a fixed percentage in a one-off transfer to the scheduling committee or a phased transfer covering a two or three year period. This could theoretically generate a sufficient number of slots which could be made available to new entrant airlines. Priority rules could also be established where preference would be given to new entrants seeking to operate services on intra-EU monopoly and duopoly routes. However, this could clearly have serious repercussions on the incumbent carriers and their ability to compete world-wide.

Money exchanges through an auctioning process have been suggested as an alternative to the problem of congestion. An example of slot pricing can be found in the United States where the Federal Aviation Administration (FAA) introduced a system of slot trading at four high-density airports in 1986. The conclusion that can be drawn from the US experience is that barriers to entry, especially for small carriers or operators of small aircraft, may be reinforced. The UK CAA did recommend, however, that the current exchanges of slots, sometimes involving secret money payments, should be formally recognized, with the registration of such deals.

The present system of allocating slots represents probably one of the most effective barriers to entry within European air transport. The only way to resolve is to expand capacity.

3.6.2. Consumer protection measures

These measures include establishing common standards of compensation for denied boarding (Regulation (EEC) No 295/91). The regulation of excessive pricing could also potentially serve as a consumer protection measure. The Commission initiatives on regulating computerized reservation system (CRS) displays can be regarded as consumer protection, as can the initiatives on tour operators (Directive 90/314/EEC). Any future initiative on a code of conduct for travel agencies would also fall into this category, as would the recent proposal for a Council regulation on air carrier liability in case of accidents (COM(95) 724).

Thus, in assessing the impact of Community initiatives to create the single market in air transport, it proved essential to consider not only the effects of the three packages, but also the consequences of the European competition rules and other accompanying measures. The competition rules are also an essential part of the liberalization process and their method of application and effectiveness have therefore been analysed.

3.7. Horizontal (non-industry-specific) EU measures

Key non-industry-specific areas of policy which might have affected air transport were identified and the effects of EU policy initiatives and progress, or the lack thereof, in these areas were reviewed. The following areas, where EU measures have been taken (or in many cases are still required to be taken) were considered:

(a)   the removal of physical barriers and the control of goods;
(b)   indirect taxation;
(c)   public procurement;
(d)   free movement of labour and the professions;
(e)   access to capital;
(f)   company law and accounting legislation;

(g)   corporate taxation.

The areas summarized below are likely to be of most significance in their effect on air transport.

3.7.1. Social legislation

Social legislation, with regard to minimum wages, maximum hours and health and safety issues could have a significant effect on airlines' costs, particularly with regard to unskilled labour. The UK's opt-out from the Social Chapter might give UK airlines and service providers a competitive advantage.

3.7.2. Indirect taxation (VAT)

The Commission submitted a proposal for harmonizing indirect taxation (VAT) on passenger air transport sold in the EU. At the moment VAT levels are not harmonized throughout the Community. The application of VAT to domestic air travel is not uniform: Germany (15%), Italy (10%), Sweden (12%), Austria (10%) and Spain (7%) apply a standard rate, and Belgium (6%), France (5.5%), Finland (6%), Luxembourg (6%), the Netherlands (6%), Portugal (5%) and Greece (8%) a reduced rate. The UK is zero rated, while Ireland and Denmark are exempt. The proposal suggests that a reduced rate of no more than 5% may be applied at least until 1997. For cross-border air travel, all countries zero rate tickets, although VAT does apply to surface transport in some EU countries. This zero rate is to be maintained, and air transport to third countries will be exempt from VAT. EU legislation regarding duty free sales and excise duty on fuel will have significant effects on airlines.

3.7.3. Immigration controls

There has been a relaxation of immigration controls for travellers within the EU, with particular regard to the arrangements in place in the Schengen group of countries. The introduction of Schengen has led to a major reorganization of passenger flows at airports, and resulted in the different treatment of transfers between EU and non-EU flights, depending whether or not the airport followed Schengen rules: multi-sector flights from non-EU countries are cleared for immigration at the final destination for non-Schengen countries, and at the intermediate point for Schengen countries. This means that EU countries that do not apply Schengen rules, such as the UK, gain a competitive advantage for the airlines based there. For example, British Airways passengers travelling from New York to Frankfurt via London clear immigration at the final destination of Frankfurt. On the other hand, KLM's New York to Frankfurt passengers have the inconvenience of having to clear immigration in Amsterdam.

3.7.4. Customs controls

The relaxation of customs controls between EU states may have had a beneficial effect on the air cargo industry in particular. However, the abolition of duty-free concessions to intra-EU air travellers in 1999 is likely to have an adverse impact on airport charges.

3.7.5. Consumer relations legislation

Consumer relations legislation, including the Directives on unfair terms in consumer contracts (Directive 93/13/EEC), the code of conduct on electronic payment, and the protection of personal data of individuals, may have implications for the way reservations and ticketing are organized. The proposed distance-selling Directive has caused substantial concern in the travel trade and transport is now scheduled to be exempted. If it is not exempted, there would be very serious cash flow implications, particularly for tour operators and charter airlines.

3.7.6. Public procurement

So far this has not been a significant problem, with cases in three countries of governments dictating travel on the national carrier. These distortions have generally been removed by informal Commission intervention.

3.7.7. State aid

State aid to competing modes of transport, especially the railways, is both a barrier to airline entry and a significant single market distortion.

3.8. Structural implications

There has now been a history of more than a decade of measures at a European Community level which have sought to modify the previously established framework within which air transport operated. However, it is widely recognized that the current structure of the industry is still heavily influenced by the former regulatory regime which had lasted for around four decades and still persists in most areas of international regulation. The effect has been to slow progress towards the Commission's ambition of creating a single market and the realization of the benefits it was anticipated would result. The current and future position is thus bound to be strongly influenced by the past. Any attempt to examine the effects of the various initiatives has to take this starting point into account, in addition to the increasingly global nature of the industry.

While the identification of the remaining barriers to the full exploitation of the single market forms the basis for Chapter 7, it is important to recognize the structural implications which arise from the industry's history. These are:

(a)   Local concentration which results from the privileged position of national airlines and from the predominance of single designation bilaterals.

(b)   Public ownership of airlines and a public service outlook amongst management and staff. Senior appointments made from the political not the business establishment.

(c)   A significant charter sector which has tended to have been regulated more liberally than the scheduled sector.

(d)   A close relationship between the national airline and the local regulatory authority.

(e)   Networks which are dominated by a single hub for each state located at the national capital (for historical reasons Germany is an exception).

(f)   A philosophy of co-operation and co-ordination, not competition and confrontation, amongst airlines, resulting from the history of fares co-ordination and pooling agreements.

(g)   Slot allocation systems which are dominated by incumbents.

(h)   Fares which are directional and not easy for consumers to purchase in the optimum way (i.e. at the cheapest source).

(i)   Terms and conditions for airline customers which are imposed by a strong trade association and which reflect those of public utilities rather than customer oriented enterprises (i.e. compensation for non-delivery).

(j)   Fleets of aircraft which have been acquired for reasons of national aerospace strategy, not simply on the basis of financial or economic justification.

However, it is also necessary to recognize that it would not have been easy, nor is it likely that it would have been effective, for any individual Member State to address these issues individually. Acting together, sometimes with reluctance on the part of some Member States, the series of legal and administrative measures described above has been taken. Subsequent chapters of this report examine their effectiveness.

4. Airline strategic responses

4.1. Introduction

This second step in the study examined the strategies which airlines developed after 1985, both in response to the imminent prospect of liberalization, and following the three EU packages. The speed and extent of any strategic response depended on factors that varied by country: government treatment of airlines in terms of public utility or competitive enterprise; the social, political and cultural environment; and the geographical position of the country. Some scheduled airlines accepted the reality of liberalization and the need to restructure and change, and had the support of government and employees. Others had less support and strong opposition from unions. For airlines that did change, their strategic responses generally involved:

(a)   pre-emptive moves to block market entry by competitors, or to increase barriers to entry;
(b)   an attempt to achieve the marketing benefits of larger scope;
(c)   a more sharply focused competitive stance in European markets.

For charter airlines, liberalization opened up the opportunity to enter hitherto inaccessible scheduled markets. Several adopted a strategy of launching into scheduled services with mixed results.

Establishing the extent to which strategic responses were due to EU liberalization faces two significant problems:

(a)   Many of the large European Community airlines depend on air services between the EU and other parts of the world for more than half their total revenues (see Figure 2.2). These services are still governed by agreements between individual EU countries and third countries. The strategic actions of such airlines are therefore likely to be based more on global air transport developments.
(b)   Given the more competitive nature of air transport markets, airlines are now more reluctant to reveal details of their strategies. Data collection, especially related to revenues and costs for European operations, proved to be difficult.

In order to understand the responses of both scheduled and charter airlines in all the above areas, the evolution of European airlines' strategies since 1985 has been examined. The strategies of the national carriers were assessed as well as those of the larger second and third level carriers and the key charter airlines. The aim is to identify when key strategic decisions were taken and, if possible, the degree to which they could be attributed to the growing liberalization. At a more detailed level this part of the study examines:

(a)   mergers, share purchases and sales (privatization), and alliances;
(b)   new marketing tools and initiatives;
(c)   the nature, timing and scope of cost-cutting measures;
(d)   charter airline strategies.

The aim of this second step of the analysis is primarily to identify the changes being implemented as a result of airlines' strategic decisions. The quantification of such changes will be addressed in the next chapter.

4.2.   A search for size

The airlines' search for size was carried out principally through mergers and share purchases involving both domestic and foreign airlines as well as through marketing alliances and franchises (both involving code sharing). Three linked strategies were followed. The first was to dominate one's home market by buying out or buying into major domestic competitors as Air France did with UTA and Air Inter. The second was to gain a foothold in one or more of the three largest Community markets, those of the UK, Germany or France. An example was the SAS purchase of 24.9% of British Midland in 1988 (subsequently increased to 40%) and the British Airways acquisition in 1992 of 49% of Deutsche BA and 49.9% of TAT in France. The third strategic step was to establish a global presence as Iberia attempted to do by purchasing shares in Aerolineas Argentinas (30%), VIASA (45%) and Ladeco (35%), all South American carriers.

4.2.1. Equity investments in other airlines

Any analysis of equity investments between airlines needs to be preceded by an examination of foreign ownership requirements in general and the requirements for airlines in particular. These need to be viewed both before and after the most significant set of industry-specific measures, namely the third package. Since airline ownership requirements were generally stricter than foreign ownership requirements, only the former are considered here.

Pre-third package

Scheduled intra-EU and other services: governed by national airline licensing regulations and air services agreements (ASAs), with ownership of airline(s) licensed or designated by an EU country to be controlled effectively by nationals of that country. This would have been subject to interpretation by individual countries, but it was generally thought that no more than around 25–30% of the airline's voting capital could be controlled by a foreign airline or other entity for the bilateral treaty to be valid. This would ensure that the supplier benefits from the exchange of air traffic rights would go largely to the countries that negotiated them.

In the UK, the Civil Aviation Authority needed to be satisfied that any applicant for an air transport licence (for whatever type of air service) was a UK national or a corporation controlled by UK nationals. However, there is a procedure whereby the Secretary of State can grant an exemption, and this has been used in the case of two charter licence holders, Britannia (owned by Canadian interests) and Monarch (owned by Swiss interests). In both cases the regulatory authority takes note of the fact that, although owned by non-UK interests, they are both managed on a day-to-day basis by UK nationals.

Privately-owned carriers such as British Airways have a mechanism for limiting the number of voting shares held by non-UK nationals in the event that they are denied operating rights under an Air Service Agreement as a result of becoming effectively controlled by foreign nationals. This is done by disallowing the registration of shares, the purchase of which causes such a situation, or forcing disposal of such purchases. This is only possible because all shares are registered. Airlines such as Lufthansa issue bearer shares, and thus are beginning to encounter problems in this respect, as their government's stake is reduced.

Post-third package

Scheduled intra-EU services: no upper limit on ownership of the airline by nationals of another EU country (alternatively the airline must be effectively controlled by EU nationals), but if that airline also flies non-EU international routes, then the bilateral clause above applies and could be a problem. This is one of the reasons why British Airways has limited its shareholdings in TAT and Deutsche BA to 49.9% and 49.0% respectively.

Other scheduled international air services: governed by licensing and air services agreements as described above.

In most EU states, the competent authority now needs to be satisfied that any applicant for an air transport licence (for whatever type of air service) is an EU national or a corporation controlled by EU nationals. For example, the British Airways powers described above have been modified to include the monitoring of non-EU voting control.

4.2.2. Alliances with other airlines

Partnerships between European airlines and with airlines based in other regions of the world have existed ever since the airline industry began. Apart from the traditional interline agreements, technical co-operation occurred in the exchange, leasing and pooling of aircraft and aircraft parts and the maintenance of aircraft and engines (e.g. the KSSU and ATLAS maintenance groups). However, the main differentiating factor between previous types of agreement from today's airline alliances is that they have become increasingly strategic. In other words, the degree of commitment in and the importance carried by alliances in the corporate portfolio of European airlines has increased dramatically since the beginning of this decade. Attempts to gain benefits of synergy through arrangements such as code sharing, blockspacing, franchising and combined frequent flyer programmes (FFPs) are now widespread in the airline industry.

Airline alliances can be classified as either market-orientated or cost-orientated. Market-orientated alliances involve practices such as joint scheduling, hub co-ordination, code sharing, blockspacing and FFP combination. In the main they are geared towards increasing traffic flows and market share, but can also reduce price competition. Cost-orientated alliances, on the other hand, are designed to reduce costs via joint services, reciprocal sales, creating catering and maintenance joint ventures, and sharing assets. Figure 4.1 distinguishes between the two types of alliance. At first glance, one can conclude that most of the EU majors (with the exception of Air France and Lufthansa) use alliances mainly as marketing tools aimed at increasing the amount of passenger traffic on their networks. The number of marketing alliances is 117, or on average about 10 per airline, which is one and a half times that of cost-oriented alliances (78, or around seven per airline). In particular, Air France is geared to using cost-reducing alliances which is consistent with its current financial situation.

An examination of the development of alliances and code sharing over the past 10 years, and an assessment of the impact of EU measures on such arrangements is to be found in Section 5.4.

Figure 4.1.   Breakdown of EU alliances by type in 1995

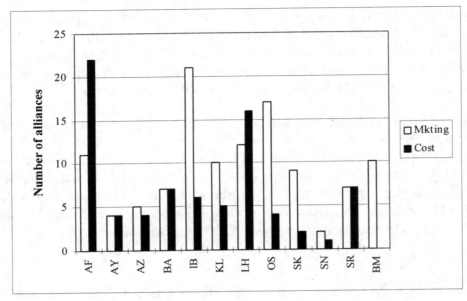

Source: Airline Business, June 1995.

Strategic vs tactical alliances

The alliances of EU airlines can be further classified into two broad categories – strategic and tactical – depending on the degree of co-operation existing between the airlines in the partnership. Strategic alliances are so termed because co-operation exists in a wide range of activities ranging from sales and marketing to purchasing and maintenance, and take a long-term view. Most notable examples of strategic airline alliances which have been widely documented and commented upon are the European Quality Alliance (EQA) with SAS, Swissair and Austrian Airlines (recently dissolved because of the SAS/Lufthansa strategic alliance), the Alcazar project which intended to unite KLM with the European Quality Alliance but which never came to fruition, the Global Excellence consisting of Swissair, Singapore Airlines and Delta Air Lines, the alliances of British Airways, the KLM-Northwest Airlines and Lufthansa-United tie-ups and the Latin-American alliances of Iberia. Tactical alliances, on the other hand, are very narrow and focus on only one field of co-operation, for example, code sharing on one route (for example, between British Midland and Alitalia, or TAP and Delta Air Lines). These alliances are mainly designed to reap benefits in the short term though they could act as stepping stones to wider-ranging arrangements.

The size of the strategic alliances of EU airlines in terms of numbers of passengers carried is given in Figure 4.2. (With the stepped up co-operation between SAS and Lufthansa, the EQA now seems to have been reduced to Swissair and Austrian Airlines, although Sabena might now join their major shareholder, Swissair, in EQA.) One can observe that the Lufthansa strategic alliance is the largest in terms of passengers carried (because of their link with United), followed by those of Swissair and British Airways. Though the KLM grouping is small relative to those three, it has been quite successful mainly because of the anti-trust immunity which the KLM-Northwest alliance enjoys (this allows more open and wide-ranging collaboration on air fares and capacity). The EQA alliance is also relatively small and this could be one of the reasons why SAS has preferred to opt out of it and consolidate its alliance with Lufthansa.

Figure 4.2.   Total passengers carried by EU airline strategic alliances

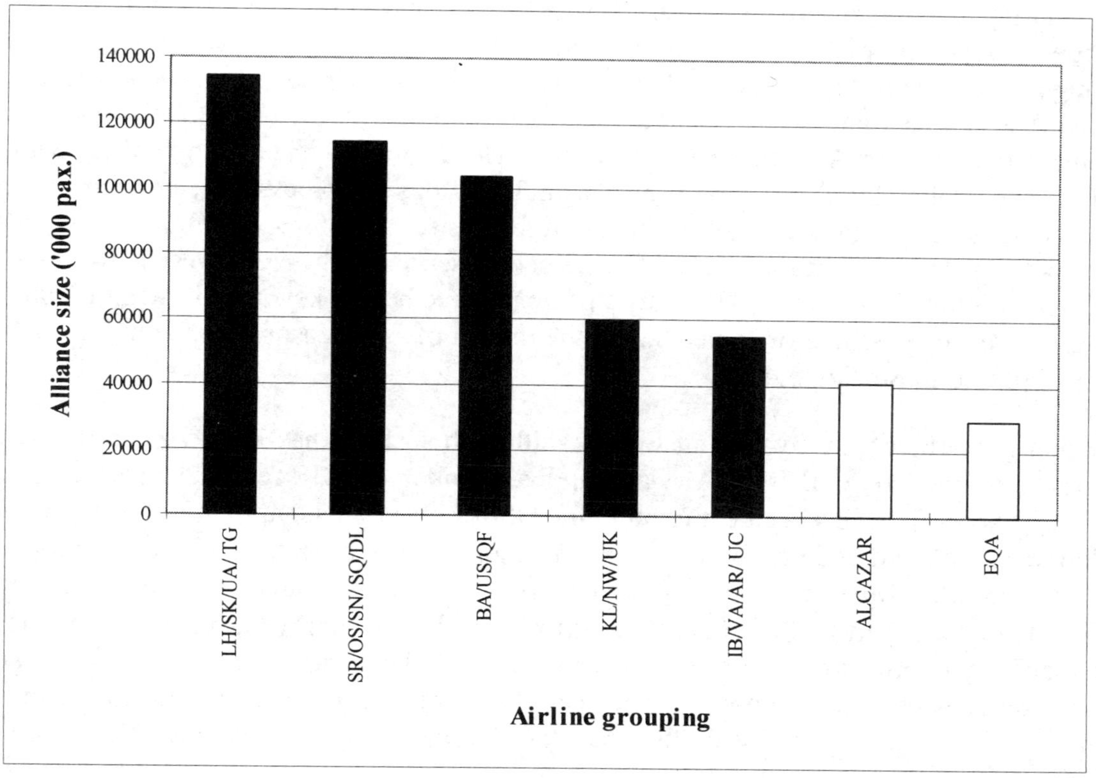

Source: IATA WATS, June 1995.

One particular characteristic of modern strategic alliances, which could arguably be an indication of the commitment of European airlines to their alliances, is that of equity purchases. Proponents of equity purchases, namely British Airways, argue that such financial transactions are essential to cement the relationship. Commitment to the alliance's success is enhanced and, where the equity stake is substantial, a certain degree of control over the partners is possible. On the other hand, opponents to the involvement of equity purchases argue that they are signs of unhealthy agreements and are sometimes a symptom of airlines in distress. Regardless of these diverging opinions, there has been limited evidence to date of cross-border equity stakes between EU airlines, purchases tending to be confined to shoring up national markets. Minority equity stakes by EU airlines in airlines based in other continents have generally not been very successful to date.

4.2.3. Code sharing and franchising

Code sharing originated in the US, and, although first used by USAir and its Allegheny commuter airlines, was more widely introduced after deregulation. In its basic form, code sharing is the practice of one or more airlines putting their code on another airline's flight. That flight is then marketed as if it were operated by the other airline(s). It enables two airlines to offer connecting flights which appear as though the same airline were operating both flight segments as one through flight. It has the effect of upgrading an interline service to on-line status, offering substantial advantages in selling (especially in terms of CRS display).

To be effective it also involves schedule co-ordination and convenient gate positions, agreements on baggage handling, and one-stop check-in.

Code sharing can be offered by itself ('naked code sharing'), together with the features described above, or even as part of a strategic alliance, franchise agreement, or equity exchange. It can be used on services connecting two alliance partners' hubs, where one airline operates the services and the other code shares sometimes involving a block seat purchase agreement (e.g. Virgin Atlantic services between Heathrow and the US, operating with both Virgin's and Delta Air Lines' code, and with Delta buying blocks of seats from Virgin). However, it is more often used on a feeder flight basis, with, for example, the transatlantic airline putting its code onto an intra-EU connecting service (e.g. Northwest putting its code onto a KLM intra-EU service). These arrangements have been a key part of many EU airlines' strategies over the past five or so years, and the impact of EU measures on such developments will be explored in Section 5.4.

Franchising is a recent innovation in Europe, although so far it has largely been restricted to UK based airlines (e.g. British Airways and a number of UK regional airlines, such as CityFlyer Express). It has been common in the US for many years, allowing the major airlines to add their brand and code to small regional airlines, usually operating with turbo-prop rather than jet aircraft. More recently, some of these franchisees have been acquired by the franchisor, to form part of their commuter divisions. It has positive advantages in enlarging the effective network of the major airline which acts as the franchisor. On the other hand, it may neutralize a potential competitor. It also allows the franchisors to offer travel over the sector at lower cost (especially pilots) than they would be able to achieve with their own services.

Franchising will usually involve code sharing, painting the aircraft in the franchisor's colours and having cabin staff wearing franchisor uniforms. It differs from arrangements common in France and Germany, where the small regional airline operates the service for the major airline (e.g. Air France and Lufthansa) on a wet-lease basis, possibly with aircraft and cabin staff wearing the colours of the flag carrier, but with the regional airline having no sales or marketing responsibility.

4.3. New marketing strategies

4.3.1. Route/network development strategies

A key issue was whether and to what extent existing airlines, whether national or second-level carriers, would take advantage of the opportunities to enter new markets and launch new services or routes. An example was Aer Lingus's strategy of developing routes from Dublin via Manchester in the UK to various European destinations, following the first package. Other airlines based in countries on the periphery of Europe, such as TAP Air Portugal and SAS, also emphasized adding Fifth Freedom routes to build up traffic volumes. Also of relevance is the greater use of hubbing, notably by KLM. However, KLM's strategy was aimed more at increasing its market share on longer-haul routes to and from points outside Europe than developing point-to-point EU traffic, and had not previously been constrained by the bilateral system. Other airlines were also concerned about their competitive position on the more lucrative long-haul routes, and pursued similar goals through alliances and code sharing, not related to the EU liberalization process.

British Airways expanded inside Europe through associate airlines, and to a lesser extent through franchisee airlines. Lufthansa is more dependent on domestic feed to its Frankfurt hub than other major EU airlines, because of their more even population and economic distribution. This also makes it more vulnerable to other airlines attracting German originating traffic through foreign hubs. Thus, Lufthansa placed great emphasis on their domestic network in the late 1980s and early 1990s, re-launching the product as Lufthansa Express (later abandoned), and considering secondary hubs at Cologne-Bonn and Munich, of which only Munich is now belatedly being developed. This could be seen as a strategy aimed at pre-empting opportunities for non-German airlines to enter its home market.

4.3.2. Product developments

Few product initiatives were introduced as a direct result of the opportunities opened up by liberalization. The increased competition amongst European carriers has encouraged them to offer a more distinct and market-orientated service. Airlines such as BA have a more clear market segmentation policy in Europe with products such as Club Europe, relaunched in 1994, targeting the growing number of European business passengers. Another example is Lufthansa revamping its domestic services with extra flights, faster check-in and simpler fare structure.

Other product innovations included merging first and business class, improving airport-related product features such as faster and more convenient check-in facilities, and franchising. Others are less directly dependent on liberalization but were reinforced by the more competitive regulatory regime. These include code sharing, branding, frequent flyer programmes and introducing in-flight entertainment technology. New entrants often introduce product innovations, for example EasyJet's no frills, no agents and ticketless approach.

Results from the questionnaire indicate that 50% of airlines claimed that EU measures had a significant effect on product development (see Appendix B).

4.3.3. Pricing strategies

Automatic approval of discount and deep discount fares within pre-defined limits was introduced in the first package in January 1988 (see Table 3.1). There is some evidence that this helped to stimulate the introduction of a wider range of discount fares, particularly to and from Germany and to a lesser degree to and from France. Later packages may have encouraged this trend. However, the expansion in demand during the economic upswing of the late 1980s arguably held back their development, while the recession and excess capacity of the early 1990s encouraged their greater use at deeper levels. This is because airlines generally, and in particular during recession, have difficulties selling all their seats at official or published prices. As a consequence, they routinely remainder some of them through wholesalers. As competition in Europe and elsewhere has intensified, this grey market has increasingly become part of the official market.

The tariff structure for cross-border routes has changed in the period since liberalization began, with first class now almost entirely withdrawn and most airlines offering club class services as their premium product. There have also been some pricing innovations, notably Sabena's Skypass, which offers a monthly season ticket that allows unlimited travel between London and Brussels.

Increased competition on domestic routes, following the third EU liberalization package, has encouraged some carriers such as Lufthansa, which faces competition from Deutsche BA, to adopt simpler and standardized pricing in their domestic markets. Lufthansa has recently reduced its current range of fares to just four booking classes, and divided its network into six fare zones offering low fares. Another example of intense domestic fare competition is Ryanair services on the Stansted-Prestwick route offering fares as low as UK £59 return.

Results from the questionnaire indicate that over 60% of airlines claimed that EU measures had a significant effect on pricing (see Appendix B).

4.3.4. Promotion

It is hard to find evidence of changes to strategic promotional campaigns which can be ascribed to the EU liberalization process. The large European carriers like Lufthansa, British Airways and Air France have attempted to develop global rather than regional brand positions, but cultural differences still appear to be powerful influences – and the retention of the names TAT and Deutsche BA by the British Airways partner airlines, the absence of KLM logos on Air UK aircraft, or SAS logos on BMA, bear witness to the sensitivities surrounding these issues.

The move to a more dynamic pricing environment has, however, introduced a new layer to tactical promotional activity. It has been developments in revenue management and information technology which have made this possible, and market clearing offers are often promoted through electronic media rather than through traditional techniques.

It is important to note that without progressive moves towards tariff freedom through the packages of reforms (i.e. freedom from filing and approval regulation), tactical pricing as now practised through revenue management and CRS displays would not have been (legally) possible.

4.3.5. Distribution

Market forces only indirectly connected with the three packages of liberalization measures have resulted in growing concentration in the travel agency business. This has been partly because agents have moved to increase their bargaining power in relation to the airlines, as the airlines themselves have attempted to gain the benefits of scale. It has also been a result of the airline industry's system of progressive commission payments which give bonuses for volume. However, following agent commission capping in the US, a number of European carriers such as British Airways, Air UK and Lufthansa are looking into ways of reducing agent commissions. In practice, some agents are now forced by corporate clients to book low cost carriers' flights despite the airlines' policy of not paying commission.

The influence of new technology in this regard has been less clear and there is some debate whether it has provided a barrier to the entry and growth of smaller agencies, or whether it has given them cost-effective access to world-class distribution systems.

One of the most significant moves has been the formation of two European CRS, Amadeus and Galileo. The motivation to develop these was global competition, not EU liberalization. It was caused by concern about the advance of the US systems lead by American Airline's Sabre. Most EU airlines were preoccupied with their own national systems developed in the era of home-market focus. EU rules covering bias were developed as a reaction to the growth of global distribution systems and the danger to users and smaller airlines from biased displays and other abuses and not as a pre-emptive single market initiative.

In terms of cross-border moves in the travel trade to exploit the single market the most noticeable has been the acquisition of Thomas Cook by the German bank, West LB, which also owns LTU. So far, this move does not appear to have brought any clear benefits of scale, scope or synergy. The slow pace of such moves is not unusual in other sectors of retailing (i.e. food, clothing).

New entrant airlines have a very real problem in distribution, and this is explored in the two case studies involving such airlines. A new start-up in the UK, EasyJet, is hoping to rely almost entirely on direct telephone bookings by passengers, and is also using the Internet.

The overall effect of the three EU packages on distribution appears marginal, given the results obtained from the airline questionnaire, with only 28% believing that EU measures had a significant impact on distribution policy, whereas 44% believed that these measures had little impact.

4.4. Cost-cutting strategies

While these were partly a response to worsening economic performance, the need to cut costs as a long-term strategy was reinforced by the competitive pressures arising from the liberalized market. The recession and greater competition meant that revenues could not be enhanced through significant price increases; cost-cutting strategies were therefore the preferred or even only method of improving financial results. To achieve long-term cost reductions European airlines undertook one or more of several measures. As the single largest controllable cost, labour was targeted by many airlines in pursuit of cost-cutting strategies. Staff numbers were reduced and existing wage rates and conditions of employment were renegotiated. Some discontinued unprofitable first class services; some set up low-cost or low-wage subsidiaries or contracted out flying to low-cost regionals; in a few cases, carriers began outsourcing key functions such as catering and engineering. More recent cost-cutting activities were aimed at reducing marketing and distribution costs, which represent between 18% and 26% of airlines' total operating expenses. Agent commission capping is now being considered by a number of European carriers.

Whilst prevailing economic conditions would have been expected to have significantly influenced the nature of cost-cutting strategies, EU measures appear to have had some impact. According to the questionnaire results, 67% believed that these measures had at least some impact on their cost-cutting strategy (see Appendix B).

4.5. Corporate developments

There has been a general trend by EU airlines to focus more on core activities, and outsource non-essential or non-specialist tasks such as office and airport cleaning. Flight catering has been contracted out by some airlines such as British Airways, but others such as Lufthansa and SAS see this as part of the core business.

Lufthansa, while retaining catering as a subsidiary, has moved to separate other activities like air cargo, maintenance and information technology into their own legal and operating entity.

The aim is to improve efficiency, with the parent company negotiating with these entities for cargo and maintenance services. Aer Lingus has traditionally cross-subsidized unprofitable airline operations with profits from maintenance, hotels and consulting. However, they have recently sold their hotel group, as a result of the conditions attached to EU approval of state aid. Air France also recently sold their Meridien hotel group, and Alitalia sold its stake in Rome Airport to another subsidiary of the state holding company, IRI.

Some vertical integration has taken place, especially in Germany where Lufthansa has taken stakes in various travel agencies and tour operators. Charter airlines were already largely integrated with tour operators and hotel groups prior to EU liberalization, but some cross-border acquisitions have taken place more recently, for example Airtours' purchase of a Swedish travel group which included the charter carrier Premiair, and the German WestLB/LTU grouping adding Thomas Cook and Owners Abroad in the UK.

Horizontal integration was already discussed in Section 3.6, much of it driven by EU liberalization. Since 1993, EU airlines can take 100% stakes in other EU carriers without any risk of withdrawal of intra-EU route licences. However, if the airline that the EU carrier invested in operated non-EU routes, its designation under the Air Services Agreements of that country might be compromised. So far, airlines with minority stakes in other EU carriers, such as British Airways with its 49% share of TAT, have not increased this to a majority (although in the example given they have an option to do so).

4.6. Charter airline strategies

4.6.1. Introduction

Although the regulatory distinction between charter and scheduled has been removed by the third package, the conceptual distinction, which is one of distribution methods, remains broadly in place. The key point is who takes responsibility for selling seats to the passenger. Where the seat is still sold in combination with hotel accommodation and ground transport, it is likely that seats will be distributed on a wholesale basis to tour operators. They will assume the risk on their block of seats, which may or may not amount to the entire capacity of the aircraft. On flights to leisure destinations in southern Europe, most seats are still sold in this way, but charter airlines are increasingly selling a proportion of seats on a seat-only basis. This is mostly done through the travel trade, but some airlines, such as LTU in Germany, sell direct to the public. In Germany, seat-only sales are estimated to account for about 20% of capacity on such flights, many of them now sold direct to the passenger by the carrier.

The strategic issues faced by charter airlines as a result of EU liberalization were somewhat different from those facing scheduled airlines. The most critical was whether to take advantage of their much lower operating costs to enter the scheduled markets that were being opened up. Several charter airlines, most notably Air Europe and more recently EBA (Belgium), did so. Britannia and some other UK charter airlines changed a number of their Spanish flights from charter to scheduled, principally to avoid possible future bilateral restrictions on charters before these were dismantled by EU legislation (and to a lesser extent to avoid any future restrictions on charters at Gatwick Airport). Seat-only sales were also developed in particular leisure markets (not always in compliance with government regulations), especially from the UK and Germany. Another issue was whether to expand by developing outgoing traffic from charter originating countries other than their own. Finally, the question of increasing size and vertical integration with tour operators also required a strategic response.

The charter airline industry was very liberally regulated before the third package and the regulatory initiatives of the EU did not affect the sector until 1993. Thus, a review of strategic developments over the last ten years, which considered only innovations resulting exclusively from EU-based measures, would have limited relevance. Moreover, many of the developments affecting the charter airlines are driven by strategies adopted within the broader package travel holiday market, a competitive industry which is not directly governed by air transport regulation. For example, in recent years there has been a trend towards longer-haul holidays to destinations outside the EU, such as the US, the Caribbean and Asia. The broad range of strategic developments undertaken by charter airlines is described below.

Some charter airline strategies relate to the liberalization of the scheduled sector which started with the first package, and were:

(a)   launching scheduled services;
(b)   redefined relationships between charter carriers and scheduled flag carriers.

Other developments relate to the most recent EU legislation, which applied directly to the charter sector. After two years of application, the developments have generally been quite limited in scope:

(a)   entry into other countries' charter markets;
(b)   destination-based charter carriers;
(c)   carrying cargo on passenger charter flights.

Other trends are more general strategic moves by companies operating in a competitive industry, such as vertical and horizontal integration, product enhancement and cost reduction.

However, these latter moves can also be related to EU liberalization: the charter carriers were under pressure to defend their market positions from the scheduled carriers and from new charter entrants. The former are becoming more market orientated and profit driven as a result of European liberalization. Thus, the broader competitive developments in the charter sector might also be seen as results of EU measures.

4.6.2. Developments arising from the liberalization of scheduled markets

Going scheduled

One of the most obvious strategies for charter carriers over the last ten years has been to launch scheduled services. In many European countries the charter sector comprised profitable low-cost airlines accustomed to operating in a highly competitive market. By contrast, many scheduled airlines were unprofitable, high-cost, low-productivity airlines operating in relatively uncompetitive markets. There appeared to be an attractive opportunity for charter carriers. As a result, some launched scheduled services in a variety of different forms, which are discussed individually below.

Going scheduled: head to head with the national flag carriers

Some charter carriers have been attracted by the inefficiencies of the incumbent European flag carriers and have entered mainstream business markets in competition with the majors. These instances of significant market entry have often been facilitated by the EU's liberalization measures.

In the UK, Dan Air and Air Europe tried to establish European networks from London Gatwick, encouraged by the moves towards dual designation and the removal of bilateral capacity clauses. Elsewhere in Europe charter entrants have included EuroBelgian Airlines (Brussels to Barcelona, Madrid, Nice, Rome and Vienna), Air Liberté (Paris-London and French domestic), AOM (French domestic and overseas territories), Norway Airlines (Oslo-London), Maersk (Denmark-London), Transwede (Swedish domestic and Stockholm-London), Aero Lloyd (German domestic), Lauda (centred on Vienna and Milan hubs, the latter recently discontinued) and Transavia (Amsterdam-London).

Some carriers have succeeded – many have not. While this section does not seek to describe the general challenges facing new entrant carriers in Europe (such as access to slots), there are some specific issues which the charter carriers face in launching scheduled services.

The charter carriers face particular problems with regard to marketing. Even in their home countries they often have a weak brand position and low levels of recognition among individual consumers. This makes it especially hard for them to attract high yield business passengers, as Dan Air found when it launched scheduled services. In foreign markets they struggle to gain market acceptance, as the retail travel agents and travelling public do not know who they are or where they fly to.

Both these problems mean that charter carriers have to spend very substantial amounts of money on product development which may involve a change of seating configuration, interiors or the acquisition of different aircraft. Charter carriers, used to a very simple form of marketing, may underestimate the expense of promoting and distributing their services at both ends of their routes. This issue becomes particularly acute if the carriers try to launch a full network of routes to several different countries.

Charter carriers may be tempted to utilize the same aircraft for scheduled and charter operations. However, the high density, single-class, configuration of charter aircraft is unattractive for passengers on scheduled services and inappropriate for routes hoping to attract high yield business class traffic. The large size of aircraft typically used for charter operations may also be inappropriate for business markets, which demand high frequency. Moreover, aircraft that operate charter flights have a higher tendency to suffer delays, as they operate, particularly in summer, at very high levels of utilization with limited back-up aircraft. They also suffer from air traffic controller disruption caused by industrial action. If aircraft are cross-utilized on charter and scheduled services, the delays that build up on the aircraft flying charter services can affect scheduled operations.

Going scheduled on leisure routes

Some established charter carriers converted existing charter services to scheduled mode, selling seats directly to passengers, in order to offer the passengers greater flexibility in their travel and accommodation arrangements. Often the airlines reduced the risk of operating these services by continuing to sell a significant proportion of the seats in advance to tour operators. So although the airline faced greater risk than with a regular charter flight, it did not face the full risk of scheduled carriers.

By adopting such a policy, charter carriers added to their costs in paying commission to travel agents, establishing reservations and ticketing departments and in advertising their services, although the difficulties and costs are less significant than those associated with launching business services. The leisure routes are marketed mainly in the home country of the carrier, where the company is already known.

Compared to launching scheduled business routes, there is less need to alter the on-board product and to operate high frequencies, meaning that the existing fleet can be utilized.

Some of the carriers that have most successfully introduced scheduled-style services on leisure routes include the Dutch carrier Transavia on routes like Amsterdam to Faro, Malaga, Palma, and Tenerife; and the German carrier LTU on both long-haul routes to the Caribbean and South-East Asia, as well as to the Mediterranean. The Lufthansa subsidiary Condor also operates a network of leisure routes on a scheduled basis, as does Hapag Lloyd Flug.

Another successful charter carrier flying scheduled leisure routes was Viva, the low-cost charter subsidiary of Iberia and, originally, Lufthansa. Viva developed a network of scheduled leisure routes, which were operating profitably. However, in summer 1995, Iberia, in a move which is markedly out of line with current trends, took these low-yield routes back from its low-cost subsidiary as part of its corporate restructuring. Viva has reverted to being purely a charter carrier.

While Monarch Airlines continues to operate a limited number of scheduled leisure services, other UK charter carriers have seen a different evolutionary process than their German counterparts. Britannia launched a range of scheduled routes to its leisure destinations in the 1980s, but this experiment was at least in part motivated by the possible threat of traffic distribution rules that might exclude charter flights from London Gatwick. Britannia found it impossible to achieve satisfactory load factors and once the threat of traffic distribution rules at Gatwick had subsided, it withdrew its scheduled services to the Mediterranean altogether. The circumvention of regulatory constraints also underlies Air 2000's scheduled services from Gatwick, Manchester and Birmingham to Cyprus. The Cypriot authorities, in an effort to protect Cyprus Airways, restrict the proportion of seat-only passengers on charter flights from the UK to 20%. To get round this constraint, Air 2000 flies as a scheduled carrier on the route, albeit with a high proportion of part charter passengers on board.

Going scheduled: part scheduled by selling some seats on a seat-only basis direct

Some carriers have moved more cautiously to take advantage of the new opportunities by continuing to operate charter-style flights that are sold mainly as seat blocks to tour operators, but retaining some seats to be sold direct to the public. An example of this is the Hanover-based Hapag Lloyd which sells around 15% of its capacity in this way. This is an attempt to gain higher revenues from the seat-only passengers, although the policy also generates costs in controlling reservations, issuing tickets and promoting the seats.

These flights are hybrid charter/scheduled flights, closer to the original charter concept than the scheduled leisure flights described above. Carriers are utilizing the freedom of European liberalization to serve passengers who require more flexibility and independence than the mainstream package holidaymaker, without directly launching scheduled services.

Table 4.1 provides a summary of the types of scheduled service currently being supplied by EU-based charter carriers.

Table 4.1.   Scheduled services operated by EU charter airlines

State	Carrier	Non-leisure routes			Leisure routes	
		Domestic	Intra-EU	Long haul	Intra-EU	Long haul
Austria	Lauda Air		✈	✈		✈
Belgium	Virgin Express[1]		✈			
Denmark	Maersk	✈	✈			
Finland	Karair	✈				
France	Air Liberté	✈	✈			✈
	Air Toulouse	✈	✈			
	AOM	✈				✈
Germany	Aero Lloyd				✈	
	Condor				✈	✈
	Hapag Lloyd				✈	✈
	LTU	✈			✈	✈
Greece	Air Greece	✈				
	Venus	✈				
Italy	Air One	✈				
	Noman	✈				
Netherlands	Martinair			✈		✈
	Transavia		✈		✈	
Spain	Air Europa	✈	✈	✈		
	Centennial				✈	
	Spanair	✈				
Sweden	Nordic East	✈				
	Transwede	✈	✈			
UK	Air 2000				✈ [2]	
	Monarch				✈	

[1]   Formerly known as EBA.
[2]   Scheduled service outside the EU (Cyprus).

4.7.   Summary of airline strategic responses

At the beginning of this chapter three types of strategic response were given, which could be summarized as first, the blocking strategy; second, going for expansion and greater economies of scope; and third, aiming for a more focused competitive stance. Europe's flag carriers that have made a successful transition from state-owned public utility to market-orientated enterprise have proved to be the most adept at adopting measures designed both to protect their existing markets and to develop new ones.

British Airways is an example of an airline that has pursued a combination of all three types of response outlined above: the carrier, through its acquisition and franchising policies, has been able to secure its position in the UK market, as well as achieving greater scope by making better use of its Heathrow hub. Similarly Lufthansa, through its alliance with SAS, has been able to increase its presence in northern Europe, strengthen its links with the Baltic states, and shore up its southern flank through a shareholding in Lauda Air. It has also pursued the second type of response through alliances with United, Thai and South African. An airline making more use of the second and third types of response was KLM, which, as a result of its code sharing alliance with Northwest Airlines, has been able to enhance considerably its long haul route network, gaining economic benefits of scope in the process.

Examples of less successful strategies have been Iberia's South American airline investments, and Air France's Sabena and CSA share purchases which were subsequently unwound. Air France, however, did undertake some fairly vigorous blocking strategies through its acquisition of UTA which gave it control of Air Inter, although this does not, so far, appear to have been very effective.

Charter airlines have been somewhat cautious in entering scheduled markets in head to head competition with flag carriers, possibly because of some of the earlier experiences with this strategy, although recent experience in France, Italy and Spain has gone against this general trend. However, they have converted some of their charter routes to scheduled and put more emphasis on direct sales of seat-only products. There has also been some tendency for these markets to become dominated by vertically integrated travel groups. How far the strategies pursued by scheduled airlines have been influenced by EU measures is summarized in Figure 4.3.

Figure 4.3. **Airline views on the importance of EU measures**

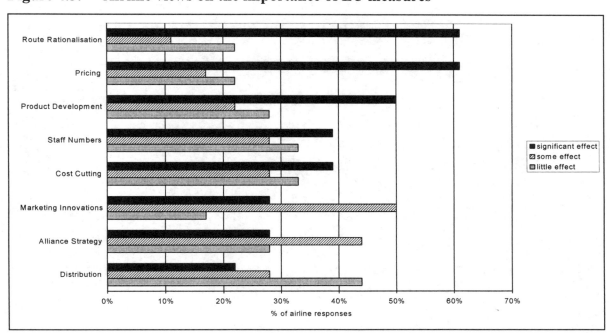

Source: Questionnaire responses: Appendix B.

While these changes have clearly resulted in increases in efficiency for many airlines, continued efforts are necessary if EU carriers are to match and keep abreast with global competitors. In securing and expanding their own markets, the larger scheduled airlines have made it that much more difficult for prospective entrants, whether they be other flag carriers, charter operators or start-up airlines, to achieve their objectives in providing the necessary competition. Ensuring that the entry barriers created by the more successful of Europe's carriers are not so great as to stifle innovative effort must continue to form a key focus of the Commission's work.

5. Impact of EU measures on EU airlines

This step in the analysis is undertaken in parallel with, and feeds off, the analysis of airlines' strategic responses to liberalization discussed in the preceding chapter. The aim is to provide a detailed examination and measurement of changes in EU airline operations and efficiency, and to identify how far such changes have been caused by EU measures. It should be noted that the timing of carriers' responses to liberalization has varied according to the nature of the airline, with some reacting faster than others. Thus, some effects of the third package will not yet be evident (especially in terms of financial results where publication of data is often delayed).

The first part of this chapter is concerned with capacity, and the second with traffic. Subsequent sections deal with marketing innovations, productivity and costs, pricing, profitability and the environment.

5.1. Capacity and air services

This section is concerned with capacity offered by scheduled carriers within the Community across the years 1989, 1992, 1994 and 1995. Extensive use has been made of the computerized database of flights supplied by Reed Travel Group. Data prior to 1989 are not held in a conveniently accessible form.

The report addresses capacity in two ways. Analysis of replies from airlines and directorates of civil aviation to the questionnaire and subsequent face-to-face interviews gave some insight into strategic and tactical responses of carriers to Community initiatives, market growth and competition, while this section analysed published schedules. These capacity studies investigate the number of non-stop services linking city pairs, frequency of service, the number of seats offered on each route, and the number of carriers supplying seats. The reference period for each year is June, and throughout this section frequency, seats and routes should be read as referring to frequency, seats and routes offered per week in June of the relevant study year. As travellers are generally interested in reaching, say, Paris from London rather than flying from Paris Charles de Gaulle to London Stansted, a route refers to a city pair rather than an airport pair. Although it is recognized that passenger selection of specific airports under these circumstances occurs, the existence of high levels of transfer traffic at certain airports serving single catchments would distort the analysis of route traffic and capacity if considered on an airport to airport basis. Such distortion would be particularly evident in airport systems where air traffic distribution rules exist, such as between Milan Malpensa and Milan Linate.

The analysis covers those Member States which have adopted single market legislation throughout the study period (i.e. the 12 states). Analysis has also been carried out of a control group of European states operating throughout the same period outside the Community's regulatory environment, which comprised Austria, Finland, Iceland, Norway, Switzerland, Turkey, Poland and Cyprus (the first four countries applied the regulations only in the last one or two years of the period).

5.1.1. Capacity concentration on cross-border services

Within the Community in June 1995, 21,000 scheduled cross-border flights were made each week, serving 1,450 one-way routes, offering a total of 2.5 million seats and creating over 2.3 billion available seat-kilometres (ASK). Table 5.1 shows the capacity offering by state.

Table 5.1.   Intra-Community cross-border scheduled capacity, June 1995

Member State	Total weekly capacity				Routes producing 50% of seats	
	Routes	Seats (10³)	Flights	ASK (10⁶)	% total routes	Mean carriers/route
Belgium	63	130	1,450	90	13	2.8
Denmark	45	82	755	75	12	3.0
France	183	334	3,099	232	6	4.5
Germany	347	441	3,570	484	10	2.8
Greece	46	59	326	105	11	3.0
Ireland	59	100	980	54	4	3.0
Italy	137	253	1,986	242	9	3.3
Luxembourg	24	15	231	8	14	1.3
Netherlands	66	162	1,759	103	12	4.1
Portugal	57	71	449	109	10	2.8
Spain	233	281	1,881	429	9	3.0
United Kingdom	190	520	4,664	382	6	4.8
Total	**1,450**	**2,448**	**21,150**	**2,313**	**7.8**	**3.2**

The concentration of the market is remarkable. For the Community of 12 as a whole, less than 8% of total cross-border routes are supplied with over 50% of total seats. At the extreme, half of Ireland's available seats to other Community states are concentrated on services joining Dublin with the UK cities of London, Manchester and Birmingham. It also emerged from the analysis that a high number of routes were operated by only one carrier: over 60% of the Community total, with a further 30% served by two carriers (Figure 5.1). The data used in this analysis include Fifth Freedom services by non-EU carriers (under 2% of total seat capacity for the UK routes with the generous assumption that the full capacity of the aircraft is available for intra-EU traffic), and refer only to non-stop services. The single carrier routes are generally low density in terms of the number of seats offered, and the frequency of service: they link regional centres or operate from regional airports to major hubs. That the proportion of these single carrier routes has grown over the 1989–95 study period – a period of increasing expansion in total cross-border routes – is an indication of the fragile nature of the new markets served.

In terms of capacity, measured in seats offered, routes served by two carriers offer around 37% of total capacity. This figure has not changed significantly over the study period 1989–95. Since 1989 a number of non-EU-based Fifth Freedom operators offering insignificant capacity on major trunk routes have left the routes (e.g. Kenya Airways weekly service between London and Athens on a London-Athens-Nairobi service): this has reduced the capacity offered on routes served by six or more carriers quite dramatically, from 25% of all seats to 11% in 1995. A similar picture is recorded when the number of flights is used as a measure of capacity offered on a route, although here it becomes clear that single carrier routes are generally operated by low capacity aircraft (almost 30% of total flights supplying less than 20% of seats).

Figure 5.1. The development of carriers per route by seats, flights and routes: intra-EU services in June 1989, 1992, 1994 and 1995[1]

Percentage of total seats

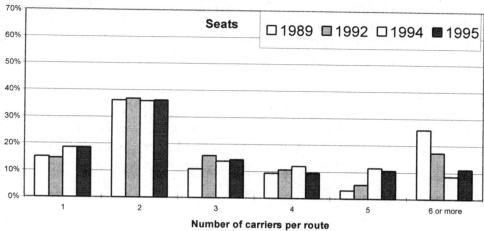

Percentage of total flights

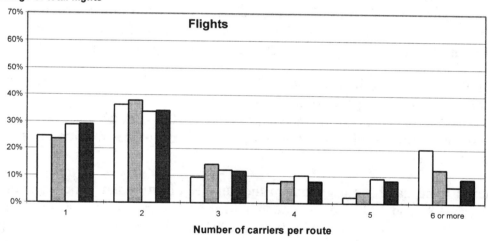

Percentage of total routes

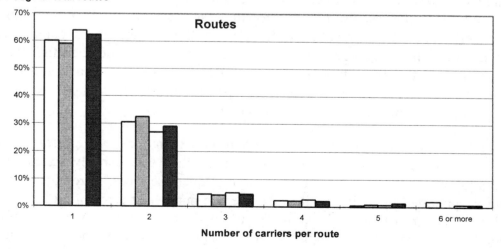

[1]   For absolute figures for the above charts, see Appendix C.0.

A number of EU carriers introduced Fifth Freedom services within the EU, largely as a result of the first package. By December 1992 there were 19 such services operating between 16 EU countries. Only seven of these are still operated, and of the 22 services added in 1993, only 13 remain [CAA, 1995]. Airlines generally find it difficult to market successfully such services, some of which are introduced merely as a way of employing aircraft that would otherwise remain idle (e.g. SAS's Stuttgart-Thessaloniki extension, subsequently discontinued). There were ten consecutive cabotage routes operated in December 1994, three of which were already operated in 1992. A further 12 routes were served since 1992, but later discontinued.

The average frequencies offered on all intra-EU routes increased from 13.9 departures per week in 1989 to 15.5 in 1992, subsequently declining to 15.0 in 1994 and 14.5 in 1995. This indicates some frequency competition in the first period, with the fall since 1992 explained by the addition of new non-stop regional services (and some charters switching to scheduled) with below-average frequencies, rather than by any reduction in frequency on the denser routes.

Between 1989 and 1995, capacity, measured in seats produced per week on each EU route, appears to have become more concentrated on key routes (Figure 5.5). For example, in Spain 12% of EU routes consumed 50% of Spain's EU seat capacity in 1989, falling to 9% of routes for 50% capacity in 1995 (Table 5.1). This general increase in capacity concentration on a smaller proportion of routes appears to be a function of the growth of new EU services rather than a disproportionate increase in capacity on the densest routes (Figure 5.2).

Market concentration appears to limit the scope for meaningful competition between carriers to routes with the potential for high capacities and frequencies. For this reason the 'Top 50' statistic was developed: the routes from each state offering 50% of total seat capacity. The weight of analysis of capacity evolution throughout the study period has fallen on this section of the air transport market.

During this period there has been a growth in the number of city pairs joined by non-stop services. Between 1989 and 1992 the compound annual rate of growth in routes was around 3%, increasing to 7% per annum between 1992 and 1994 (see Figure 5.2). In the final study year, June 1994 to June 1995, there has been a growth rate of 12% in city pair routes. When this is compared with services offered between the control group countries, and between the control group and EU countries, the rate of growth is significantly lower in each of the periods. Since there has been no direct benefit from any of the packages in the control group countries (air services still being governed by bilaterals), it can be concluded that the EU measures had some impact on the number of routes served. However, some caution is needed before drawing any inferences on net consumer air service benefits, since some new routes were merely redesignated scheduled routes (largely Germany/Spain).

As noted previously, new routes are unlikely to support more than one carrier, at least in their initial stages of growth, and low levels of demand mean they are probably suited to low frequency operation of medium-sized aircraft or more frequent services by regional aircraft. This reasoning is supported by a slight fall in the average number of seats offered per flight over the period. The growth in regional routes is no doubt in part due to Community initiatives which have made it more straightforward to begin cross-border operations, but the increasing competition in the supply of aircraft of a size to match the requirements of thin routes should not be underestimated: it has allowed airlines to act on opportunities available to them. Figure 5.3 focuses on the change in aircraft size on intra-Community routes, showing that as new routes have been developed aircraft of appropriate size have been employed. The 1989 peak in aircraft with a capacity of between 40 and 50 seats had by 1995 split into two pronounced peaks at 30 seats, and 50 seats. Lufthansa's downsizing was completed by 1987, driven as much by the need to provide connections to a more decentralized German network (in contrast to British Airways and Air France who are more focused on their principal hubs of Heathrow and Charles de Gaulle respectively). Air France's move to smaller aircraft took place over two periods, 1985-87 and again since 1991.

Figure 5.2.   Route development: EU cross-border services vs control group services, 1990-95

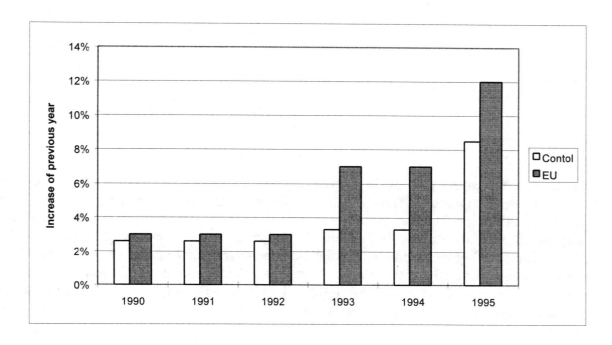

The Top 50 routes are those where evidence of increasing competition in the form of route entry by new carriers might be expected. This is not the case. The average number of carriers on these densest of European routes has fallen within the Community of 12 from 4.5 per route in 1989 to 3.2 in 1995. For individual states the picture is more complicated: Portugal, Greece and Belgium saw increases in the average carriers per route while the remaining states showed a falling average, sometimes dramatic (Figure 5.4). On the densest routes, the presence of Fifth Freedom carriers operating at low frequencies such as Philippine Airlines between Frankfurt and Paris, and the US carrier TWA between Lisbon and Madrid, distorts the picture. In order to get a clearer picture of capacity split between carriers, a more sophisticated index of capacity share was required to weight carriers on a route by the proportion of capacity they offered. This was developed as a capacity index.

Figure 5.3. **Distribution of seats per flight: cross-border intra-EU non-stop services, one week, June 1989 and 1995**

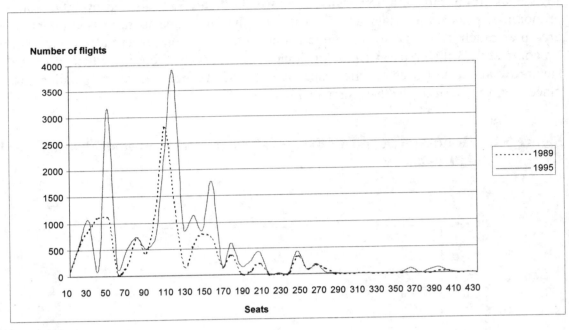

Essentially the capacity index developed sums the square of percentage of total seats offered by each carrier on a route. Thus for a route with two carriers, each offering equal shares of the total seats, the capacity index would be $(0.5)^2+(0.5)^2$, or 50%. Similarly, if one of the carriers dominated the market with a 90% share of seat capacity, the index would be $(0.9)^2+(0.1)^2$, or 82%. Thus, the higher the index, the higher the concentration of capacity. The capacity index was calculated for all Top 50 routes of all states for the four study years. Appendix C.2 shows the Top 50 routes for Spain in 1989, 1992 and 1995, as an example. A summary of the results of the capacity index analysis is presented in Figure 5.5.

Figure 5.4. **Average carriers on EU cross-border routes carrying 50% of total capacity from each state: June 1989, 1992 and 1995**

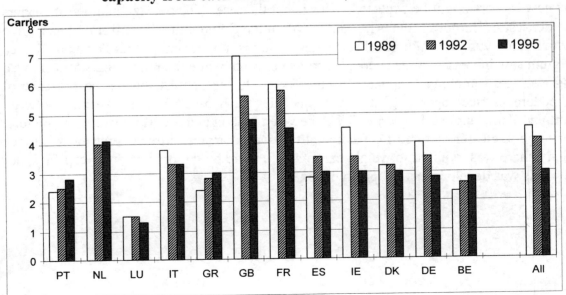

The average index has moved only a few percentage points for most states, although Belgium, Ireland and Portugal record a significant reduction in capacity concentration. In all three cases this is due to the entry of new carriers on established routes; for example, in the case of Portugal, the entry of Air Liberté on routes linking Paris to Lisbon and Porto, and Portugalia serving Brussels and Madrid from Lisbon. Germany, on the other hand, shows an increase in its capacity index from 42% to 50%. In part this is due to the loss of two carriers (Finnair and Hamburg Airlines) on the Hamburg to Amsterdam route, leaving KLM as the only carrier between the two cities. On the Frankfurt to Paris route the number of carriers has fallen as Fifth Freedom carriers Aeromexico, Avianca and Kuwait Airways have withdrawn. Luxembourg has its supply of capacity weighted strongly towards Luxair, sole operator to Frankfurt, and the only airline flying scheduled services between Luxembourg and Palma.

Figure 5.5.   Average capacity share index: services generating 50% of total seats offered: summer 1989, 1992 and 1995

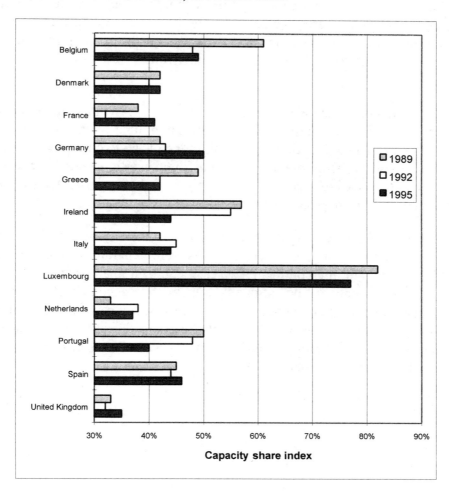

The average capacity indexes for the Top 50 routes of Belgium, Germany, Luxembourg and Spain are higher than those of other Member States, and significantly higher than those of routes to and from the UK. This situation reflects the high index values of a number of routes operated between the states of the former group and the rest of the EU. Apart from this, routes between Germany and the rest of Europe have a much flatter distribution than those of the UK, whereas only a small number of very high density routes (such as London-Paris, London-Dublin) dominate the UK's intra-EU capacity. For Germany, 50% of EU seat capacity is produced on 9% of total EU routes; in the UK 50% capacity is employed on only 6% of routes. The result of this is that only four of Germany's 32 Top 50 routes produce more than 10,000 seats per week, while in the UK all produce more than 10,000 seats: or put in another way, all the Top 50 routes from the UK support three or more carriers, but of the top German routes, almost two-thirds have less than three carriers. Indeed, as noted above, the route between Hamburg and Amsterdam, one of the German Top 50 group, was operated in June 1995 by KLM alone, giving it a capacity index concentration of 100%.

Designation as scheduled services of LTU's high density leisure routes between Germany and Spain further distorts the picture of capacity concentration in those two states. For example, the route between Düsseldorf and Palma de Majorca is ranked third in capacity of German and Spanish cross-border EU routes: over 75% of the capacity on this leisure dominated route is provided by LTU, which moved from charter into the scheduled market in the early 1990s. LTU also operates between Düsseldorf and Ibiza with a similar share of capacity, again distorting the distribution of capacity concentration within the Top 50 routes of Germany and Spain. EU routes from Belgium are dominated by the Brussels-London route, which in June 1995 provided almost 20% of all seats leaving Brussels for destinations in other EU states. The route supported four carriers, but of the seven other routes only three had more than two carriers.

Table 5.2 lists carriers operating cross-border services within the EU in June of one study year, but not in June of the following study year (leavers), or in June of the previous study year (entrants). Thus, an entry and exit taking place within one of the two three-year periods is not recorded. The table does not record entry to and exit from specific routes. Airlines operating international routes under codes of other carriers are not recorded, e.g. Lar Transregional (TAP Air Portugal) and SEEA (Virgin Atlantic).

An explanation for each airline leaving the market is added: the exit of non-EU carriers from Fifth Freedom routes should be noted. These services were generally offered on dense intra-EU routes as add-on sectors to intercontinental service, e.g. Ethiopian Airways flying to Rome then London from Addis Ababa. The rationalization of the schedules of these carriers on intra-EU routes contributed to the reduction in the number of routes with six or more carriers within the EU (Figure 5.1). If the non-EU Fifth Freedom carriers are excluded, the net increase in number of carriers operating intra-EU routes was six between 1992 and 1995, with a net loss of four airlines between 1989 and 1992.

Table 5.2. **Carriers entering and leaving cross-border EU operations, 1989–92 and 1992–95**

1989–92			1992–95		
Leavers		Entrants	Leavers		Entrants
	Reason			Reason	
Air Gambia	1	Aeroflot	Aeromexico	1	Aero Lloyd
Air Zaire	1	Air Belgium	Air Canada	1	Air Liberte
American Airlines	1	Air Corbiere	Air Lanka	1	Air New Zealand
Canadian	1	Air Dolomiti	Air Mauritius	1	Air Normandie
Egyptair	1	Air Exel Netherlands	Avianca	1	Air Nostrum
Gulf Air	1	Air Inter	Emirates	1	Air South West
MEA	1	Air Lanka	Garuda	1	BASE
Qantas	1	Air UK	Iran Air	1	CAE
Somali Airlines	1	Alsair	Japan Airlines	1	Cameroon
Syrian	1	AOM	SAA	1	Centennial
Yemenia	1	ATI	Sudan Airways	1	China Eastern
Zambia Airways	1	Aviaco	TWA	1	Condor
Air Bremen	2	Avianova	United Airlines	1	Eastwest Airlines
Air Europe	2	Corse Méditerranée	Air Corbiere	2	Euro City Line
Air Sardinia	2	Delta	BASE	2	Eurobelgian
Business Flight	2	Emirates	Dan-Air	2	Finnair
Capital	2	Euralair	Flexair	2	Gulf Air
German Wings	2	Europe Aero-Service	GB Airways	3	Icelandair
PanAm	2	Flexair	Loganair	3	Interline
Region Airways	2	Ghana Airways	Maersk UK	3	Interot
Scottish European	2	Gill Aviation	TAT	3	Karlog Air
Templehof Airways	2	LAN Chile	Air Jet	5	Love Air
Finnair	4	Newair	Avianova	5	LTU
Flandre	4	OLT	Hamburg Airlines	5	Macair
North Flying	4	Portugalia	Aigle Azur	6	Muk Air
TACV	4	Proteus	Air Sicilia	6	Royal Nepal
TAROM	4	SAL	AOM	6	Suckling Airways
TAS Airways	4			6	Venus Airlines
Transavia	4				Virgin Atlantic
Virgin Atlantic	4				
Air Exel	5				
Alibu	5				
Brit World	5				
Britannia	5				
KLM City Hopper	5				
Netherlines	5				

Key 1: Fifth Freedom operator abandons intra-EU sectors
2: Company no longer trading
3: Changed to franchise operator for another carrier
4: Network restructuring due to economic recession
5: Airline restructuring or merger
6: Abandoned intra-EU routes

5.1.2. Capacity concentration on domestic services

Appendix D.1 shows the three densest domestic routes for all EU countries with domestic services, as well as the proportion of total EU domestic capacity produced within each country. The sum of seats offered on these routes approaches one-third of the total EU domestic output. The table also shows the number of airlines flying the 30 routes: of these, 15 routes in 1995 had only one operator, and 11 had three or more. All three dense routes in the United Kingdom, France and Spain have three or more operators. Since the beginning of 1996, Italy has also experienced a substantial increase in the level of competition on its most dense domestic routes. Further analysis of domestic capacity and air fares is described in Section 5.7.2.

5.2. Air passenger traffic

5.2.1. Recent air traffic structure

Obtaining a complete picture of origin/destination traffic in the Community is complicated by the difficulty in obtaining comprehensive data on charter flights. The UK Department of Transport attempted to give a complete picture for 1990, after obtaining data from the 12 states that were then Community members (see Table 5.3).

Table 5.3.   **Cross-border EU air passenger movements for 1990 and 1994**

	Total passengers ('000)	Total passengers ('000)	EU as % total international	Scheduled passengers as % total	
	1990	1994	1990	1990[1]	1994
Belgium	6,084	n/a	n/a	66	n/a
Denmark	4,408	n/a	44.3	n/a	n/a
France	18,580	13,707	48.4	78	88
Germany	25,303	31,025	51.4	65	68
Greece	10,224	n/a	n/a	30	n/a
Ireland	5,882	6,929	n/a	67	87
Italy	12,631	n/a	63.3	82	n/a
Luxembourg	730	n/a	72.6	n/a	n/a
Netherlands	9,324	12,265	53.8	72	82
Portugal	5,444	7,459	n/a	49	53
Spain	29,239	41,852	n/a	28	31
United Kingdom	42,843	55,058	56.5	54	59
Total	**85,346**	**n/a**	**n/a**	**n/a**	**n/a**

[1] Based on AEA member airline traffic only.
Source: Transport Statistics GB – 1992, September 1992, and civil aviation departments – 1994.

Table 5.3 shows the importance of charter traffic for Spain and Greece, and to a lesser extent Portugal and the UK. In almost all the cases where data are available, the share of scheduled in total traffic has increased between 1990 and 1994. This could have been through the attraction of lower scheduled fares, or some switch of charter passengers to long-haul markets. Furthermore, European traffic has a somewhat higher weight in total international traffic for Denmark and France than the other countries which provided these data. To gain an idea of the largest scheduled and charter operators in EU markets, Table 5.4 shows recent annual traffic, although this refers to their system-wide operations, rather than solely intra-Community traffic.

The EU charter airline operations are almost entirely within geographical Europe and north Africa, while the scheduled airlines generate a large number of passengers on long-haul international routes (passengers rather than passenger-kms being chosen here to reduce the weight of the latter type of traffic). The largest two EU scheduled airlines in terms of European traffic are British Airways with 14.6 million and Lufthansa with 12.1 million. The next largest are SAS and Air France with 8.8 million and 8.0 million passengers respectively. This perhaps gives a better comparison of the relative sizes of scheduled and charter airlines within Europe (the latter are discussed in greater detail in Section 4.6).

Table 5.4.   Passengers carried by the largest EU scheduled and charter airlines, 1994

Scheduled airlines	Passengers ('000)	Charter airlines	Passengers ('000)
British Airways	30,201	Britannia	7,913
Lufthansa	29,956	LTU Group	6,122
SAS	18,775	Condor	5,500
Air France	15,591	Monarch	4,803
Alitalia	14,536	Air 2000	4,201
Iberia	13,356	Hapag Lloyd	4,031

Source: AEA and IACA.

Recent traffic for the European regional airlines is shown in Table 5.5, with airlines wholly or majority owned by the major airlines clearly marked.

Of the airlines in Table 5.5, only Air UK and Eurowings are independent of the large flag carriers, and of those, Air UK now has a large KLM minority (45%) holder of its shares, effectively reducing its independence. Otherwise, only Transwede (850,000) and Portugalia (516,000) remain as truly independent regional carriers with over 500,000 annual passengers.

Table 5.5.   Passengers carried by the largest EU regional airlines, 1994

Airline	Passengers ('000)
Air UK	2,605
Lufthansa City Line[1]	2,260
Binter Canarias[1]	2,000
Crossair[1]	1,970
Deutsche BA[1]	1,800
SAS Commuter[1]	1,500
KLM Cityhopper[1]	1,300
Olympic Aviation[1]	1,300
Eurowings	1,200
Delta Air Transport[1]	919
TAT (1993)[1]	911

[1] Controlled by major scheduled airline.
Source: IATA, ICAO and trade journals.

5.2.2. Air traffic trends

Because it is difficult to obtain comprehensive data on the European charter and regional airlines on a consistent basis, the analysis of traffic trends to identify the impact of EU measures focuses on the larger scheduled airlines. Association of European Airlines (AEA) members' scheduled traffic within the geographical Europe region has grown strongly over the past few years in terms of passenger numbers. The European traffic of AEA members covers a somewhat broader geographical area than intra-Community, and excludes the smaller regional airlines and airlines such as British Midland (who have only recently joined the AEA).

In the past, traffic has been driven almost entirely by economic growth, the most commonly used measure of which is gross domestic product (GDP), with a smaller contribution from yields since around 1987. In the early 1990s, European scheduled traffic increased at a faster rate than would be expected from the past relationship between real GDP and traffic, which is given by the following equation calibrated on 1965–90 data:

Passengers (no) =   - 32,510   +   68,973 Real GDP (Index)
                       (-19.0)   (+ 38.3)

Both the t-statistics were significant at the 95% level, and adjusted r^2 is 0.983. Forecasts of air traffic using 1990–94 actual European real GDP data can be seen in the next chart to fall well below the actual traffic outcome.

One possible cause of the divergence is the early 1990s recession and its effect on traffic through overcapacity and lower air fares, rather than through GDP alone. A second model was therefore calibrated on 1965–79 data, and used to predict traffic over the previous 1980–84 recession. For this model, real GDP variation again explained almost all traffic variation (adjusted r^2 was 0.995 and significant t-statistics); it also provided reasonably accurate forecasts of traffic over the 1980–84 recession period, contrary to the 1990–94 situation.

Over the previous recession European airlines managed to maintain real yields by limiting capacity increases, but over the latest recession capacity has not been restrained and real yields have had to fall to maintain seat factors. Overcapacity was also more serious in the early 1990s with AEA carriers increasing available seat-kms by 12% between 1991 and 1992, 6% in 1993 and 5% in 1994. This compares with broadly unchanged capacity offered by AEA carriers over the years 1981, 1982 and 1983, and only a 2% increase in 1984. Over both periods seat factors have been maintained at between 57% and 60%, and even increased somewhat overall in the 1990s recession (leaving aside the sharp fall immediately following the Gulf War).

Figure 5.6.   AEA European air passengers – actual vs predicted

A. 1980–84 economic recession

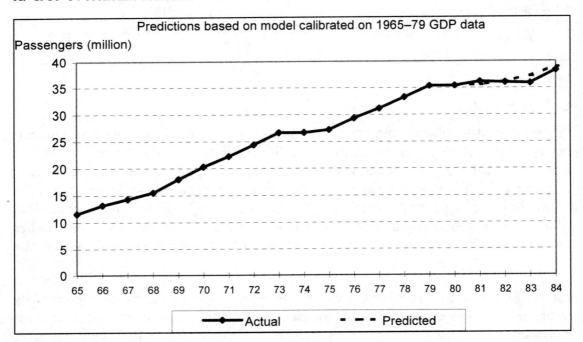

B. 1990–94 economic recession

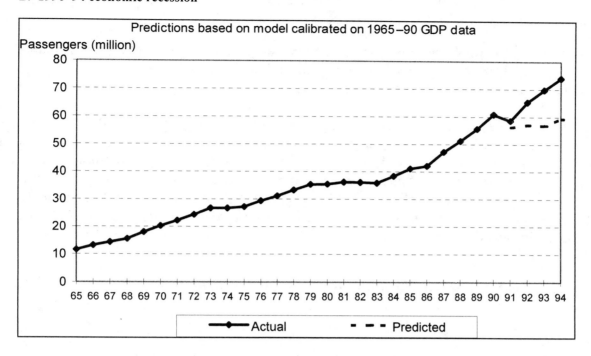

5.2.3. Impact of EU measures on air traffic

The question still remains as to how far EU measures and increased intra-EU competition might have influenced this complex mixture of traffic, capacity, yield and load factor. Real yield has become a significant determinant of passengers travelling within Europe, and this is reflected in a model calibrated on 1980–94 data (yield was not a significant explanatory variable in regression models calibrated on periods ending before 1990):

$$\text{Log (passengers)} = \begin{array}{cccc} 14.222 & + & \log(\text{real GDP}) & - & \log(\text{real yield}) \\ (+24.1) & & (+20.2) & & (-6.4) \end{array}$$

All t-statistics (shown in brackets below the equation) are significant, and the adjusted r^2 is 0.990. The Durbin-Watson statistic is 1.56, from which it can be concluded that, at the 99% level of confidence, serial correlation was not present. This suggests that almost all passenger variations were explained by variations in real GDP and real yield. Frequency competition is likely to have had little effect on the overall market size, but would have been used to increase market shares of individual carriers.

Attempts were also made to insert a competition or liberalization dummy variable into the equation from 1989 onwards, with poor results. This was hardly surprising given the gradual introduction of liberalization within Europe, starting as early as 1985 for some country pairs.

The analysis of air fares in the next section suggests that levels have risen overall with some increase in the availability of deeper discount fares. It can thus be concluded that lower yields overall in real terms (unchanged or somewhat lower in current prices) were caused largely by a change in the mix of traffic in favour of passengers travelling on promotional and discount fares; it is this that has appeared to have played a very much stronger role in generating traffic over the early 1990s, compared to the previous recession. The available evidence suggests that this came about through:

(a)   premium traffic (club and full economy fare passengers) trading down to lower available fares, possibly accepting some booking or travel time restrictions; and

(b)   more seats being available at the lower economy and discount fares.

The first effect above was the result of the general business climate, and was not dependent on the degree of competition in EU air transport. The second, however, would indicate a more competitive response by airlines, only in so far that airlines were actively promoting these lower fares to maximize revenues and raise load factors, rather than merely reacting to altered booking patterns and the external economic environment. It is also possible that the more liberal regime covering fare filing and tariff approval made it easier to offer tactical discounts to generate additional demand.

Figure 5.7.   Recent trends in European traffic, GDP and yield, 1987-93

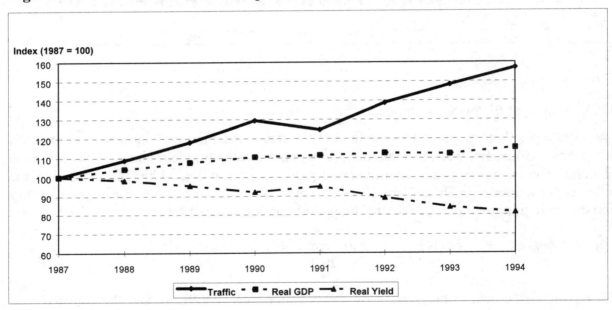

Source: AEA.

5.3.   Air cargo traffic

It has become increasingly difficult to obtain comprehensive data on intra-EU air cargo traffic. First, a large part of the fast growing air express market is carried by operators such as DHL, TNT and Fedex, who are not party to any regular exchanges of data such as through the Association of European Airlines. Second, a substantial part of the market is carried by trucks, even though it is treated as air cargo (i.e. is shipped between airports, under a flight number, and on an airway bill).

Total freight tonne-kms flown within geographical Europe by AEA member airlines increased at an average annual rate of 5.1% a year between 1976 and 1994, or by 5.3% a year between 1986 and 1994. The share of that total carried on freight-only flights within Europe declined from 20% in 1986, to 19% in 1990, to 14% in 1994 (the 1994 share for long-haul freight traffic was 33% in 1994). This trend started in the early 1980s, as airlines moved freight onto trucks, and downsized to narrow-bodied aircraft with limited lower deck capacity. On the other hand, express integrated carriers started to establish air freighter feeder services within the EU, based on hubs such as Brussels and Stansted, often using turbo-prop aircraft. No data are available on the traffic carried on these services.

According to Boeing research (based on the Official Airline Guide), the number of airport to airport truck destinations served in Europe increased from 38 in 1975 to 280 in 1990 and 386 in 1995. Thus, there was a 38% expansion over the past five years. Boeing also reported a 40% increase in frequencies offered on these routes during 1994.

How far the trends outlined above, and developments in air cargo yields, have benefited from the single market legislation is difficult to estimate. Certainly, the rapidly growing air cargo express market, which was driven by the application of systems developed in the US, could only have happened as a result of the removal of many barriers within the EU. Some of the postal authorities also made greater use of night-time flights from airports without night curfews or movement limits.

Pre-1993, most intra-EU shipments handled by express carriers such as DHL were door to door documents and dutiable parcels. Single market legislation to remove customs barriers meant that shipments no longer required customs clearance. This simplified procedures, and was reflected in a greater range of surface distribution by truck, greater punctuality and potentially lower costs to the consumer. This has resulted in a slight shift from air to road distribution within Europe. Although demand for package delivery has built up only gradually since customs regulations were relaxed, one express carrier estimates that the increase in business attributable to the wider and more reliable service developed because of the relaxation in EU customs barriers is in the order of 10%. The growth in package and larger shipments reflects the stock-keeping and warehousing strategy of international companies: for these a dependable, competitively priced overnight delivery service reduces the need for investment in regional storage centres.

There has been a rationalization of express delivery services providers on an intra-state and intra-regional level, but no true pan-European express delivery carrier has yet developed. The current major centres for European distribution of shipments from outside the continent are in Belgium and north-west Germany: from here the onward delivery is by truck, where time permits, or by air to regional distribution centres. An alternative scenario would develop the existing regional distribution centres in the UK, Spain, southern Germany and Italy to receive shipments between Europe and the rest of the world. This second scenario would reduce the volume of air shipments between the European centres.

The problem areas that still affect the air transport mode of operation are:
(a)   noise restrictions and night curfews at airports;
(b)   limited choice in ground handling agent;
(c)   air traffic control congestion (although this is minimized because most flying is by night);
(d)   slot availability (particularly London Heathrow).

5.4. Marketing innovations

5.4.1. Alliances

Some European airlines have tried to build up pan-European distribution networks through the opening up of new routes, franchise agreements, the use of hubbing, code sharing and share purchases. British Airways and more recently SAS/Lufthansa have done this, while a similar attempt by the partners in the Quality Alliance (SAS, Austrian, Swissair) failed. In examining the impact of EU measures on these and other developments, this analysis will first focus on the closest form of co-operation, namely cross-investment, before examining strategic and marketing alliances.

Table 5.6 shows the stakes held by EU airlines in airlines in other EU countries in 1985, 1990 and 1995. The main trends are as follows:

(a)   A tendency for national carriers to consolidate their position by increasing their stakes in domestic airlines, beginning in 1985–90 but intensifying during the second five-year period (e.g. Air France, KLM, SAS, Sabena). This was partly motivated by a desire to prevent foreign airlines entering the market.

(b)   Minority investments in existing regional scheduled airlines by major flag carriers in the past five years (e.g. British Airways, Lufthansa and KLM).

(c)   Some consolidation of holdings in Spanish charter airlines by EU national flag carriers between 1990 and 1995 (e.g. Aer Lingus and LTU), although the joint Iberia/Lufthansa charter airline has been discontinued. This was partly to take account of the Spanish government's concern about the low share of its airlines in the charter market, and partly because airlines elsewhere in the EU sought to take advantage of lower Spanish cost levels.

These changes should be viewed against arguably more significant world-wide trends, the most important of which were:

(a)   EU carriers investing outside the EU:
   (i)   Iberia's large stakes in South American airlines, including majority control of Aerolineas Argentinas;
   (ii)   British Airways' investments in US Air (24.6%), Qantas (25%) and Carib Express (20%);
   (iii) KLM's stake in Northwest (25%), and Kenya Airways (25%);
   (iv)   Alitalia's stake in Malev (30%);
   (v)   TAP Air Portugal's investment in Air Macao (25%);
   (vi)   SAS's stakes in South American airlines, subsequently sold (Lan Chile 42%).
(b)   Non-EU carriers investing in EU airlines:
   (i)   Swissair's stake in Sabena;
   (ii)   Swissair's and ANA's stake in Austrian.

Table 5.6. EU airline cross-border equity stakes

(omitting subsidiaries which were 100% owned throughout period)

Airline stakeholder	Partner	% stake 1985	% stake 1990	% stake 1995	
Aer Lingus	Futura (Spain)	0.0	25.0	85.0	Charter
Air Europe (ILG)	Air Europa (Spain)	25.0	25.0	0.0	Acquired by Spanish interests
	Air Europe (Italy)	0.0	100.0	0.0	Acquired by AZ/others
Air France Group	Austrian	0.0	1.5	1.5	
	EuroBerlin	0.0	51.0	0.0	Ceased operation in 1994
	Sabena	0.0	0.0	37.5	Recently sold
Alitalia	Air Europe (Italy)	0.0	0.0	27.5	
British Airways Group	Deutsche BA	0.0	0.0	49.0	
	GB Airways	49.0	49.0	49.0	Recently sold
	TAT	0.0	0.0	49.0	
KLM	Air UK	15.0	14.9	45.0	
	Air Littoral	0.0	0.0	0.0	Acquired 35% in 1991
Lauda Air (Austria)	Lauda Air (Italy)	0.0	0.0	33.0	
LTU	LTE (Spain)	0.0	25.0	100.0	
Lufthansa	Business Air	0.0	0.0	38.0	Recently sold
	Cargolux	24.5	24.5	24.5	
	EuroBerlin	0.0	49.0	0.0	Ceased operation in 1994
	Lauda Air	0.0	0.0	39.7	
	Luxair	0.0	0.0	13.0	
	Viva Air	0.0	48.0	0.0	Sold to Iberia
Luxair	Cargolux	24.5	24.5	24.5	
Maersk Air	Maersk Air (UK)/BEA	40.0	40.0	100.0	
SAS	Airlines of Britain	0.0	24.9	40.0	
	Dan Air	57.0	57.0	57.0	Ceased operation in 1995
	Groenlandsfly	25.0	37.5	37.5	
	Linjeflyg	0.0	0.0	51.0	Merged in 1995
	Scanair/Premiair	100.0	100.0	0.0	50% stake sold to Airtours (UK)
	Spanair	49.0	49.0	49.0	Charter

Source: Cranfield University research.

EU airlines also already held a number of minority stakes in non-EU airlines in 1985, many of them remaining from colonial times. These are largely still in place, for example Air France (Air Afrique, Air Comoros, Air Gabon, Air Madagascar, Air Mauritius, Air Tchad, Cameroon Airlines and Middle East Airlines), British Airways (Air Mauritius), and KLM (ALM Antillean).

Finally, many EU airlines had established 100% owned subsidiaries to operate domestic services. Some, such as British Airways and Air France, consolidated this position by buying control (BA in Brymon, AF in Air Inter and Alitalia with Avianova).

Figure 5.8.   Evolution in number of EU airline alliances, 1985, 1990, 1995

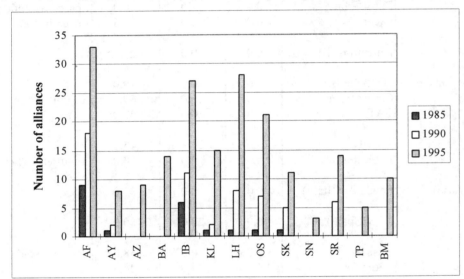

Source: Airline Business and *ABC World Airways Guide.*

Evidence that the desire to form alliances is gaining momentum can be found in the surveys undertaken by *Airline Business* (June 1994 and June 1995) which reveal partnerships in excess of 200 in the airline industry. These surveys reveal that European airlines had a total of 138 marketing alliances in 1994, and this figure increased to 171 one year later. Prior to the start of the EU liberalization process (1985), only a few airlines, namely Air France, Finnair, Iberia, KLM, Lufthansa, Austrian and SAS, had formed alliances with other international airlines. It has to be noted, however, that before 1985 many airlines operated pooling agreements, and to a certain extent recent alliances (i.e. BA and Qantas) have many features of these now illegal pools. Taken together, the total number of alliances was 20. By 1990, the total number of alliances had risen to 59, and, by the time the third package had been introduced, the total number of alliances had increased to 171 in 1995. Clearly, these alliances varied considerably in their commitment and route coverage. Many of them were also with non-EU airlines.

5.4.2.   Code sharing and franchising

Code sharing is another recent marketing change which in many cases is part of franchise agreements. But elsewhere code sharing agreements have replaced the more traditional joint ventures, such as revenue sharing pools, which have died out as a result of the first two liberalization packages. It is important to establish how widespread code sharing has become within the single market and whether it has any anti-competitive implications.

Over the past few years there has been a very rapid increase in code sharing alliances entered into by EU airlines. In 1990, the major European airlines had 20 such alliances, involving many more routes. By 1995, this number had risen to 71, of which 26 were with non-EU airlines (Figure 5.9).

Figure 5.9. Number of code sharing partners of European airlines in 1995

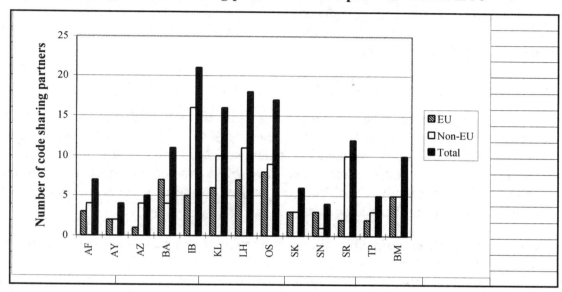

Source: Airline Business, June 1995 and *ABC World Airways Guide*, June 1995.

A more dramatic increase can be seen in terms of routes that were included in these code sharing agreements: 32 intra-EU routes in 1990 increasing to 203 in 1995. However, it is difficult to conclude that these agreements actually resulted from EU liberalization. On the contrary, their main purpose was to increase EU airlines' competitiveness in the global rather than intra-EU marketplace. In some cases, their effect would have been to reduce the degree of competition on intra-EU routes (e.g. Lufthansa/SAS).

Franchising has played a relatively minor role to date in cross-border air services in Europe. British Airways concluded their first franchise agreement in August 1993 with CityFlyer Express, followed by Brymon (which they also own) and Maersk Air, and Loganair in the following year. The latest with Manx Airlines (Europe) occurred in January 1995.

These agreements allow British Airways to offer services in thinner (mostly domestic) markets at more appropriate cost levels. The franchisee airline remains under separate ownership (with the exception of Brymon), which allows it to operate at lower cost levels than could be achieved by British Airways.

The only other airline to make similar agreements is Virgin Atlantic, which had a short-lived franchise agreement with SEEA (operating Athens-London) and Cityjet (still operating Dublin-London City). These franchises are very different from the BA ones in that no traffic feed is available to Virgin's own services, whereas BA's franchises offer a large number of traffic feed opportunities.

5.5. Productivity and competitiveness

The analysis of the last ten years in Europe should reveal the effects of transition from tight regulation to more open competition on airline productivity. Since European liberalization, one of the major areas of airline operations which productivity improvements have been directed at is labour. Labour costs are the largest single airline cost category which is relatively controllable in comparison with other operating costs. Therefore the rest of this section will concentrate on labour productivity. The analysis of airline productivity will be based on the airlines' system-wide operations as data on employee numbers and costs, specifically for European operations, are not available.

5.5.1. Trends in airline employment levels

European airlines have been under tremendous pressure to reduce labour costs as part of a range of cost-cutting activities (as discussed in Section 4.4). Such pressure has come from three sources: first, increased competition amongst European carriers due to the EU liberalization measures; second, the intensified level of international competition from major carriers outside Europe, mainly US airlines; and third, the need to recover from economic recession which resulted in financial deficits.

Amongst the many policies adopted by European carriers to reduce labour costs, one has been reduction in the number of staff. For example, Air France and its staff agreed a plan to reduce the workforce by 5,000 jobs by 1997 through early retirement and natural attrition. Alitalia also succeeded in reducing corporate (head office) staff from more than 2,300 to 300. SAS recently proposed to reduce its employee level by 3,000 through attrition, which is in addition to 3,500 jobs already eliminated since 1991. Some carriers have been more successful in reducing staff numbers than others, due partly to factors beyond management control such as cultural and social influences, the strength of labour unions and government attitudes to redundancies. For example, it has been more difficult for carriers such as Iberia to shed jobs operating from a country with over 20% unemployment. Iberia's restructuring proposal in December 1994, which included 2,120 layoffs, was met with two one-day strikes costing the carrier USD 16 million in loss of revenue.

Figure 5.10 illustrates the development in the level of employment for a sample of major EU scheduled airlines[4] from 1981 to 1994, in comparison with a group of major European scheduled carriers[5] which were not subject to the same EU liberalization measures.

It can be seen that from 1981 to 1983, the two groups of carriers had an opposing trend in their levels of employment. However, from 1983 they follow very much the same development pattern. It has been said that the 1990s were going to be characterized by staff reductions, and

---

[4]   Aer Lingus, Air France, British Airways, Iberia, KLM, Lufthansa, Olympic Airways, SAS, Sabena and TAP Air Portugal.

[5]   Swissair, Finnair and Austrian Airlines.

the trend in the above chart supports such a view. From 1989 onwards, both groups of carriers continuously reduced staff numbers.

It ought to be mentioned that the reduction in the number of employees has not always meant a worsening level of job losses to the industry as a whole. In some cases, labour moves from one organization to another. This happens when airlines outsource some of their activities, such as maintenance and catering. For example, Shannon Aerospace in Ireland carries out aircraft maintenance on behalf of a number of European carriers including its shareholders, Swissair and Lufthansa. Lufthansa has recently announced that it will transfer more maintenance work to this company, which is effectively transferring jobs to a lower wage rate country within the EU. However, in other cases airlines have moved their entire function, or part of it, to lower cost countries outside the EU, resulting in net job losses. For example, Lufthansa transferred part of the company's invoicing and revenue accounting to India.

Figure 5.10. Trends in airline employment level (annual average number of staff), 1981–93

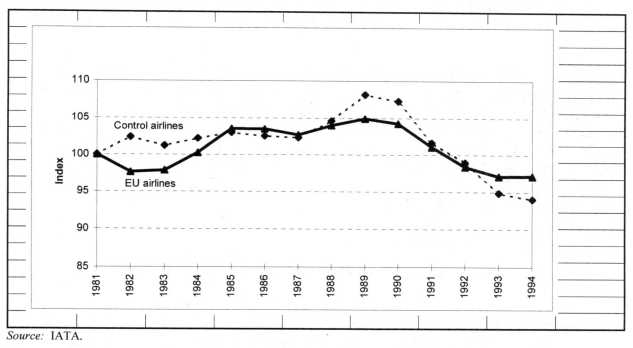

Source: IATA.

While it is difficult to quantify the impact of EU liberalization measures on the reduction in the airlines' staff levels, it is clear that the measures have encouraged such a trend. It is wrong to assume that the development in EU airlines' staff levels is entirely due to increased competition in the EU countries, as the control airlines have adopted similar strategies. While they were not subject to the same liberalization measures, they were based in states expecting to join the Community or planning a close association with it. The survey of 18 EU airlines revealed that almost two-thirds of the carriers surveyed believe that EU measures affected their staff numbers (see Appendix B). In conclusion, it could be said that EU carriers' reduction in number of staff were affected partly by EU liberalization measures, partly by international competition from carriers outside Europe and partly by the world and European economic climate, with EU liberalization measures playing the most important part.

5.5.2. Trends in labour productivity

There are a number of ways by which labour productivity can be measured, such as available tonne-kms (ATK) per employee, average labour cost per ATK, revenue per employee, and passenger-kms per cabin crew or other disaggregate measures such as aircraft hours per pilot. However, ATK per employee is a more comprehensive measure for analysing airline labour productivity.

Figure 5.11 illustrates employee productivity (ATK per employee) for a number of EU airlines from 1985 to 1994 (the airlines are ranked according to their 1994 performance). It can be seen that the majority of airlines has continued to increase their labour productivity over the years, with KLM, Lufthansa and BA at a higher rate than other carriers. The only carrier that has not achieved growth in employee productivity in recent years is Sabena, largely because of a radical reduction in capacity since 1991 (although this was largely confined to intercontinental routes). However, despite the decrease in Sabena's general employee productivity, previous research by Cranfield University shows that the airline's cockpit crew achieved the highest growth in productivity, during the period from 1983 to 1993 [Alamdari et al. 1995]. Based on the same report, EU carriers on average achieved increased productivity both in pilot and co-pilot flying hours and passenger-kms per cabin attendant in the period 1983–93.

The survey of EU airlines can show the extent to which the increase in airline labour productivity has been due to EU liberalization. 94% of the airlines surveyed believed that competition from EU airlines, which has been intensified by the adoption of EU measures, has affected airlines' improvement in efficiency (see Appendix E). It ought to be mentioned that while European carriers have increased labour productivity at a higher rate than their counterparts in the US between 1988 and 1992 [Comité des Sages, 1994], in absolute terms their productivity is still below that of the US carriers by around 28%. This gap further narrowed in 1993 [Alamdari et al. 1995].

5.5.3. Trends in labour costs

Labour costs are a major driver of overall operating costs, and show major variations between airlines.

To establish the success of carriers in reducing their labour costs, and to assess the impact of EU measures on such a strategy, a number of European carriers'[6] expenses per employee are analysed. This analyses the period 1985 to 1994.

---

6   Air France, British Airways, Iberia, KLM, Lufthansa, SAS, Sabena, TAP Air Portugal.

Figure 5.11. Available tonne-kms (ATKs) per employee, 1985/89/94

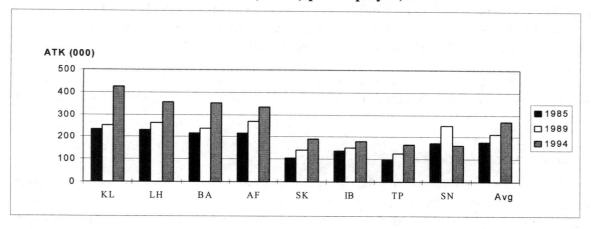

Figure 5.12. Average labour cost per employee (1994 prices), 1985/89/94, using purchasing power parity exchange rates

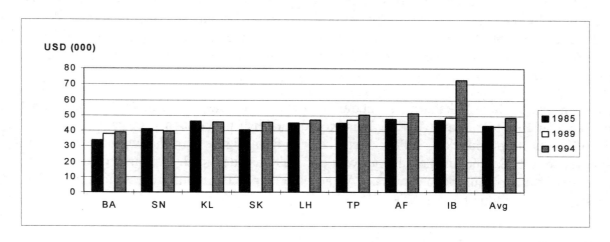

Figure 5.13. Average labour cost per ATK (1994 prices), 1985/89/94, using purchasing power parity exchange rates

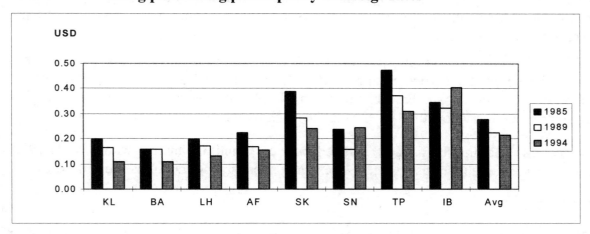

Two approaches are adopted for analysing EU carriers' labour costs. The first approach analyses labour costs per employee and labour costs per ATK in US dollars (USD) for the three years 1985, 1989 and 1994. This allows a comparison between the labour costs of different carriers, and establishes the changes in actual labour expenses.

The second approach expresses each carrier's labour expense in its local currency over the period 1985–94. This eliminates the impact of the US dollar exchange rate on the changes in labour costs of individual airlines.

Labour cost trends in US dollars

The average cost per employee for the study carriers, in 1994 US dollars, is illustrated in Figure 5.12. To take into account the differences in the cost of living of different countries the purchasing power parity (PPP)[7] exchange rates were used to convert labour costs in national currencies to US dollars. Using this rather than market exchange rates removes the cost of living variations from the comparison.

It can be seen that in most cases the airlines' average labour cost has increased, in real terms, especially in Iberia's case between 1989 and 1993. Iberia's labour costs declined in 1994 due to the wage freeze of 1993 and 1994 and reductions in number of staff as part of the airline's restructuring programme. Sabena was the only airline in the sample which experienced declining average labour costs.

Another measure which links airlines' labour costs to their employee productivity is personnel costs per available tonne-km (ATK). This would establish how much it costs an airline, in terms of labour, to produce one ATK. It can be seen from Figure 5.14 that with the exception of Iberia and Sabena, the airlines' labour cost per ATK has declined. It is interesting to note that the two southern European carriers, TAP and Iberia, pay their employees much more than other airlines for producing one ATK.

Labour cost trends in local currency

To remove the impact of exchange rates, carriers' expenses per employee are expressed in local currency, and indexed on 1985 as the base year. To establish the changes in employee expenses in real terms all the figures are adjusted by local consumer price indices (CPI) and are expressed in 1994 prices.

The airlines' expenses per employee are illustrated in Appendix E. There appears to be a mixed trend amongst the carriers with respect to their control of labour costs. While half of the eight study airlines – Air France, Lufthansa, KLM and Sabena – have maintained their labour costs around or below the 1985 level, the rest have experienced some increases.

Air France has continuously reduced average labour costs until the merger with UTA in 1992, after which average labour costs rose. For example, cost-saving measures introduced by Air

---

[7]   PPP exchange rates convert currencies on the basis of what money will buy, rather than on the basis of a market evaluation. Therefore they are the rates of currency conversion that equalize the purchasing power of different currencies. This means that a given sum of money, when converted into different currencies at the PPP rate, will buy the same basket of goods and services in all countries. Thus, PPPs are the rates of currency conversion which eliminate differences in price levels between countries.

France in September 1993 met with considerable hostility from its workforce. The resulting industrial action led to the government intervening to force the company to withdraw its proposed cuts. As the Air France case study (Appendix F.1) makes clear, this intervention led to the Chairman's resignation. Other airlines operating from countries experiencing high levels of unemployment also have found it difficult to lay off workers. Iberia experienced two days of industrial action in response to its proposed 2,120 reduction in staffing levels, leading to a revenue loss of USD 16 million.

In the last two years Lufthansa has been successful in reducing its labour costs, the main inducement being an increase in the level of competition amongst airlines and pressures to improve results prior to future privatization. Sabena has also been successful in reducing labour costs in recent years. In general, KLM has managed to maintain its labour costs below the 1985 level throughout the past decade. BA, SAS, and TAP have experienced an increase in their average labour costs. As BA has the lowest unit labour cost, such an increase has a less detrimental effect on the company compared to TAP which has the third highest unit labour cost. Iberia is the only carrier which has been faced with a continuous increase in its labour costs throughout the period 1985–92.

As mentioned earlier, the extent to which carriers are able to change working practices and expenses depends on a number of factors, such as the strength of labour unions and government and social attitudes towards redundancies and unemployment.

To provide an overall picture for trends in labour expenses of EU airlines, the study airlines' labour expenses (in an index form) are weighted by their staff numbers and summed together. This is illustrated in Figure 5.14. It can be seen that carriers overall have experienced a rise in their labour costs in real terms, though by less than 10% only over the whole period.

Figure 5.14. EU airlines' average expenses per employee (1994 prices)

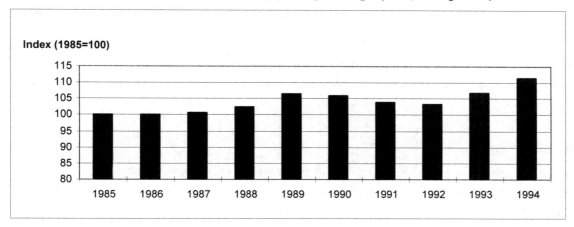

In conclusion, EU airlines have certainly reduced staff numbers and increased labour productivity both in terms of ATK per employee and labour costs per ATK. However, they have not been so successful in reducing the average labour costs per employee. Therefore, it appears that the airlines are paying their staff, on average, slightly more in return for proportionately greater productivity increases. This is possibly because the increase in outsourcing, while reducing the number of lower paid employees (e.g. cleaning and catering) and boosting productivity, has a tendency to increase average unit labour costs.

Such trends are clearly affected by EU measures, international competition from carriers outside Europe, and by the world and European economic climate. However, from the survey of 18 EU carriers it has become clear that EU liberalization measures have certainly played an important role in accelerating the reduction in staff numbers and increased labour productivity and in controlling labour costs.

5.5.4. Aircraft utilization

A key variable under direct control by management is aircraft utilization, i.e. the hours flown by each aircraft per day. Changes in such utilization since 1985 have been examined for key EU airlines.

Most airlines achieved improvements in utilization up to 1989, since when a levelling off has occurred, and in some cases a reduction.

Table 5.7 shows varying trends for the selected airlines.

Table 5.7. Aircraft utilization for European scheduled airlines

	Average daily aircraft utilization (hours) – geographic Europe[1]									
	1985	1986	1987	1988	1989	1990	1991	1992	1993	1994
Air France	6.3	6.4	8.0	8.4	9.1	8.8	8.2	7.7	7.8	8.8
British Airways	4.6	5.1	5.1	5.1	4.9	5.4	5.0	5.3	6.0	6.0
Iberia	4.5	4.2	4.1	4.5	4.7	5.0	3.9	3.5	3.6	3.4
Lufthansa	6.1	6.6	7.0	7.7	7.7	7.9	6.9	7.0	7.3	7.1
Swissair	7.5	7.7	8.1	9.6	10.2	10.8	10.2	10.3	10.6	10.8
TAP Air Portugal	3.8	4.6	5.3	6.0	6.6	7.5	7.5	7.5	6.6	6.8
AEA average	5.4	5.5	5.9	6.1	6.1	6.5	6.1	6.6	6.3	7.1

[1] Combined data for those aircraft types considered to have been operated solely within Europe.
Source: AEA.

5.6. Operating costs

As mentioned in Section 5.5, the ability for the EU airlines to control costs as a function of their marketing and competitive strategy has become crucial for their existence, especially since their unit costs are still well above their counterparts in the US and Asia/Pacific regions [Alamdari et al., 1995].

The overall cost impact depends partly on improvements in labour productivity (see Section 5.5.2) but also on other factors, such as price of fuel, route restructuring and changes in aircraft size.

Ideally, the cost analysis should be carried out for EU carriers on their intra-European routes rather than using their system-wide data. However, data in such a format are not available.

Also the carriers' cost structure and development are not only affected by their European operations, but also by competition from carriers of other regions.

However, IATA [1991-95] provides cost information on carriers' operations on intra-European routes in an aggregated form. The trend in European scheduled services costs in 1994 prices is illustrated in Figure 5.15. It can be seen that the unit cost of carriers operating on intra-European routes, in real terms, has declined in recent years.

Figure 5.15. IATA international scheduled services within Europe, 1989–94, unit costs in 1994 prices

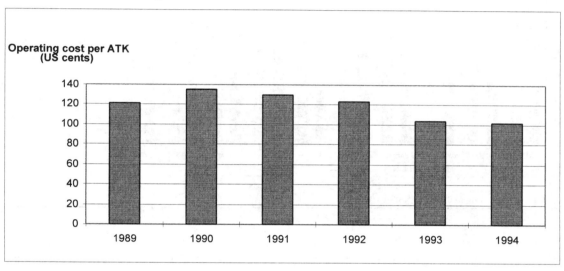

Source: IATA, *Airline Economic Results and Prospects.*

Figure 5.16 illustrates EU carriers' trends in unit costs, in real terms, for three intermediate years during the period 1983–93 (the carriers are ranked according to their 1993 performance). With the exception of Sabena and Air France, the EU airlines have been successful in reducing costs in recent years.

However, the need to reduce costs further is still important as the European carriers' unit costs of operation are still higher than those of their counterparts in the US, and the gap in the carriers' unit costs, in real terms, between the two regions has increased slightly. While the US carriers reduced their unit costs on average by 15% in 1993 compared to the 1988 level, the European carriers' unit costs declined by 12% in the same period [Alamdari et al., 1995]. This trend is also confirmed by the findings of Comité des Sages [1994] which indicated that while the US carriers reduced costs on average by 2% from 1991 to 1992, the European airlines succeeded in reducing costs by an average of 1.7%. Of the European carriers, only British Airways' and KLM's costs are comparable with those of the US airlines, with others having unit costs well above those of the US airlines. Such differences in unit costs of European and US carriers are explained partially by differences in the two regions' input costs (e.g. labour costs and airport charges), both groups operating over broadly similar average stage lengths.

A comparison of unit costs between EU carriers indicates a small (10%) reduction in variations between them. This is measured by comparing the airlines' unit costs deviation from the average in 1988 (US cents 16.2) with that of 1993 (US cents 14.5).

Figure 5.16.   Total operating costs per ATK by EU airline (1993 prices), 1983/88/93

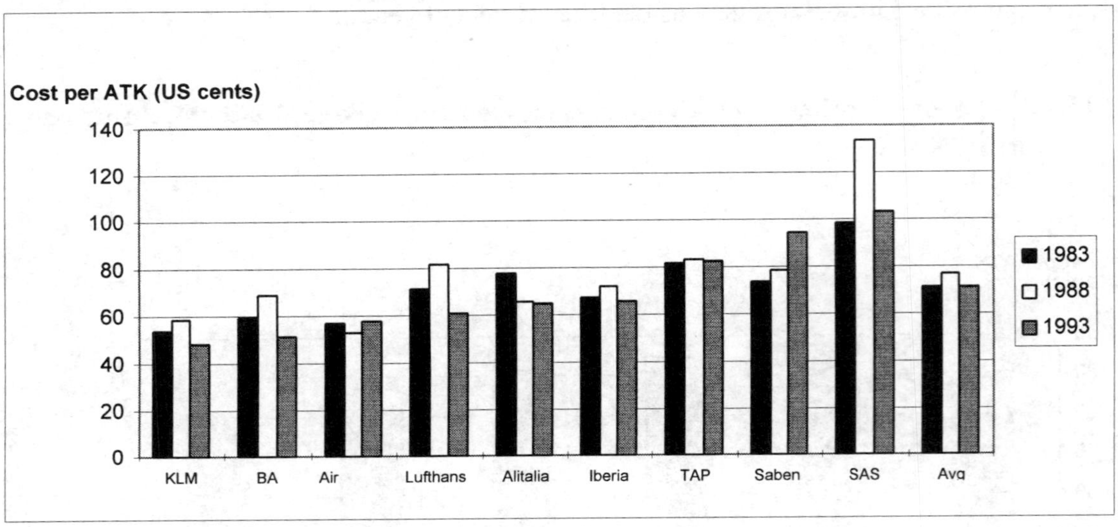

Source: ICAO, Financial Data (1983, 1988 and 1993).

Clearly the pressure on EU carriers to reduce costs has come from various sources: liberalization of European air transport markets which has resulted in a higher level of competition, international competition from airlines of other regions, economic recession and the resulting poor financial performance of airlines. Of the 18 EU airlines surveyed (see Appendix B), 65% stated that EU measures have affected their cost-cutting strategies, with 35% believing that the measures have had a significant impact on encouraging a lowering of their operating costs. Therefore, while it is not possible to quantify the impact of various factors on cost, it is clear that EU measures have had a significant effect on increasing efforts towards cost reduction.

5.7. Pricing

5.7.1. Cross-border air fares

Liberalization has offered airlines the opportunity to be much more flexible and competitive in their pricing for passenger services (though competitive, open market freight tariffs, non-scheduled arrangements and, in some cases, domestic deregulation pre-date the Community's three packages). It is important therefore to assess the extent to which they have used these freedoms and how fares and fare structures have actually developed. It is also important to investigate whether they offer greater variety and choice to users.

To do this, extensive use was made of the database of fares held by Genesis Fares Distribution, part of the Reed Travel Group. This allowed not only the quantification of the trends in the level and range of fares on routes linking EU states, but also provided data on relative fares within individual Member States. In addition, it was used to examine international fares on 72 intra-EU routes and 26 control group routes. The majority of the control group sample are fares from these countries (Austria, Switzerland and Norway) to states that have been in the EU throughout the period, the rest being between control group countries. However, it should be noted that Austria had recently adopted single market legislation whereas Switzerland had not. This control group was not ideal from a theoretical point of view, but practicalities meant that there is not a large potential population of suitable or comparable countries from which a sample could be chosen (see Appendix C.3.1 for sample size).

When the data from Genesis was combined with authoritative research from other sources [CAA, 1993 and 1995], this allowed comparisons to be made amongst individual cities within the Community.

The fares database was consistent with the database of routes used for the route and capacity studies of Section 5.1 above and this allowed other influences, like number of carriers in competition on a route and the level of concentration, to be explored. However, the published tariff is only a guide to what individual and corporate customers actually pay for their tickets. Tactical offers, special fares and discounts associated with limited seat availability are bound to be a feature of a liberalized price environment, even if this discriminates against users who do not have knowledge of and/or access to the full range of prices. The issue of special promotional fares will be analysed later. The work in this part of the report has to be read alongside the results of the study of airline yields in Section 5.6.3 which, at a macro level, does record what is paid by the average passenger. It is because of this that such results for individual airlines for individual routes are commercially confidential.

As an initial step towards evaluating trends in fares, data covering the 72 busiest intra-Community routes in each country were collected for four dates at intervals of three years (1986, 1989, 1992 and 1995). Similar data were also collected for 26 routes linking the control group of countries. These four dates were chosen because in the main they spanned the liberalization process resulting from the three packages of measures. These years also spanned an expansion period, a recession and a recovery, which in some ways made the isolation of effects resulting from the liberalization process difficult. It was felt that an examination of fares before and after the 1983 Regional Directive would not have been worthwhile because this directive was of a restricted nature and was unlikely to have had a significant influence on overall fare levels.

The data for each of the full set of 92 routes for the coming summer season were taken to be those recorded in the Genesis database for 31 March of each year of study. Although the database included a large number of fare types, it was sorted and simplified to provide four basic sets of information. These were:

(a)   the cheapest, readily available, fully flexible one-way Y class fare (calculated as half the return fare available at the origin, so that most international city pairs provided two different data entries because such fares are usually directional). In the text and figures this is called the fully flexible economy fare;

(b)   the average of all publicly available economy fares (fully flexible as well as conditioned), calculated as one-way from half the return, even if they could not be bought as one-way;

(c)   the lowest publicly available fare, calculated as one-way from half the return, even if it could not be bought as one-way;

(d)   the percentage discount offered by the lowest publicly available fare compared with the cheapest fully flexible fare.

Fares which discriminated on the basis of age were excluded from the analysis. In addition to the point that there are a large number of non-public fares (i.e. wholesale fares for tour operators, and market clearing fares only available through particular channels), it has to be recognized that in some markets there is a premium economy fare (C class) as well as a cheaper but still fully flexible fare (Y class). Where both existed, only the cheaper was included in the database if it was judged to be fully flexible and not severely capacity controlled. In cases where, at specific dates, no fare was reported for a given route, then these routes were excluded from the trend analysis.

These data were first used to obtain a broad overview of changes in fares on routes linking the 12 states which have been members of the Union throughout the liberalization period. To do this, the fares were adjusted to 1990 prices using the EU inflation rates as measured by the consumer price indices shown in Table 5.8 (the rates are based on those for the second quarter of each year).

The results in Appendices C.5 to C.8 illustrate a dynamic marketplace with significant variations amongst Member States. More specifically, they show the following:

(a)   Referring to Appendix C.5, fully flexible fares generally fell in the period 1986–89 but rose in the two periods 1989–92 and 1992–95. As far as the impact of EU liberalization is concerned, there is little evidence from these trends that EU measures had any significant impact on fully flexible fares. The particularly large increases experienced by the majority of states during the period 1989–92 can probably be explained in terms of airline attempts to maintain revenues during a period of falling demand associated with the world economic downturn at the beginning of the 1990s.

(b)   The trends in average economy fares (Appendix C.6) were more mixed in each of the three-year periods, with some states recording reductions and others recording increases. It is difficult to draw a definitive conclusion regarding average fares since the statistical derivation of average fare was in some cases based on a very small sample.

(c)   Remembering that the general effects of inflation have been removed, Appendix C.5 shows that fully flexible on-demand fares have risen over the nine years 1986–95 by a modest but significant level for the EU as a whole at around 2% per annum. As far as EU liberalization measures are concerned, the three packages have not had the effect of reducing fully flexible fares, as might have been anticipated. Liberalization has affected both the level of fares and fare structure in the discounted market.

(d)   Over the period 1986–95, average economy fares within the EU have hardly changed. Appendix C.6 shows significant reductions for Ireland and Austria, and a significant increase on UK and Belgian routes. The Irish trend can be explained by the degree of competition within the Dublin-London City pair market generated by UK-Irish bilateral deregulation which predates the first package.

(e)   With respect to control group trends over the period (Austria and Switzerland) there is little evidence of any significant divergence from the general EU trend. This suggests that whilst during most of the period none of the EU measures were adopted within the control group states, pricing strategies within those states have not differed markedly from pricing within the EU.

Table 5.8. EU consumer price index, 1986–95

Year	CPI (1990 = 100)
1986	83.9
1989	94.6
1992	109.5
1995	120.4

Source: Financial Times / Datastream.

The next step in examining overall trends was to examine changes in the range of fares on offer in Member States for international intra-EU travel, based on the sample.

The level of the deepest discounts available from the on-demand Y fare provided a measure, albeit imperfect, of the choice and variety of product/price combinations on offer to users. The analysis confirmed that the level of discounts was often in the order of 40% of the cheapest fully flexible fare, but the study showed that there were significant changes in this level of discount over time.

A review of the results illustrated in Appendix C.9 for EU states is given below:

(a)   Discounts were in general smaller in 1989 than in the other four years. Whilst EU measures may have encouraged new entry and reduced fares on some routes, the 1990–93 economic downturn will also have led to significant fare discounting at the lower end of the market.

(b)   Discounts on routes out of Germany in 1986, 1989 and 1992 were noticeably smaller compared to other EU states. This was primarily because during those periods lowest economy fares were not reported in the ABC database. By 1995, however, it appears fares were being offered in the ABC at a level of discount comparable with the general EU trend.

(c)   The UK has been unusual in that discounts tended to decline from 1986 to 1995 despite a greater degree of competition on intra-EU markets. One would have expected the level of discounts to have increased. However, one possible explanation lies in the recent decision by British Airways, the main UK operator on intra-EU routes, to cease reporting some of its lowest promotional fares on the ABC database, preferring to offer these instead through selected wholesalers and its World Offers.

(d)   The discounts on the route out of Ireland reached over 70% in 1995. Since this route refers to the Dublin-London market, one would expect to observe a greater degree of discounting, firstly because of the scale of competition, and secondly because the route has a sizeable proportion of VFR (Visiting Friends and Relatives) passenger traffic.

In order to take the analysis one step further and to allow direct comparisons to be made amongst individual routes and amongst Member States, fares had to be converted to a common currency. The ECU was chosen to be the basis for comparison and the exchange rates used are those listed in Appendix C.11. While it is recognized that there have been a number of step changes in parities, it was judged that in the majority of cases the ECU provided the best basis for overall comparisons. The ECU was also used as the basis for comparison for the control group.

The trend in the variation of fares with nominal distance in kilometres (converted from ticketed point mileages held in the Genesis database) was explored using both graphical and more mathematical techniques. In order to examine the relationship between fare and stage length, regression analysis was performed for each fare category at each time interval (1986, 1989, 1992, 1995) in order to identify the extent to which variations in fares across the sample was explained in each year by variations in stage length, and to identify, where possible, the effects of additional factors such as market concentration (see Table 5.9). The equations for each fare type and year are given in Appendix C.3.2.

The regression results indicate that:

(a)   Between 70 and 80% of the variation in fully flexible economy fare up to 1992 can be explained by stage length, whereas by 1995 it falls to 56%. This suggests that up to 1992 other potential factors on these routes based on specific market conditions had only a marginal impact on fares. However, the reduction in the r^2 statistic between 1992 and 1995 suggests that other factors increased in importance. Regressing fare against market concentration, represented by a capacity share index, did not improve the r^2 statistic. This is expected as, firstly, one would not expect significant price competition within the fully flexible fare market, and, secondly, there was insufficient variation in market concentration across routes to generate statistical significance.

(b)   Analysis of both average economy and lowest economy fares produced, as expected, a lower r^2 statistic. Lower conditional fares are unlikely to be closely related to stage length given their restrictive nature in terms of availability.

(c)   In attempting to explain the decline in r^2 with respect to fully flexible fares between 1992 and 1995, one can conclude that market concentration based on the sample of routes did not have an effect on fare. However, inclusion of percentage change in exchange rate parity 1992–95 as an additional independent variable did improve the r^2 statistic for 1995 by a considerable margin (from 0.56 to 0.75). This confirms the effects on intra-EU fares of exchange rate instability with respect to the ECU during the period 1992–95. The devaluation of the UK pound, the Spanish peseta, the Portuguese escudos and Italian lira and appreciation of the German mark, the Belgian franc, the Danish kroner against the ECU, distort the relationship between fare and stage length, producing a greater scatter of points. This can be illustrated in the more detailed scatter diagram for the 1995 fully flexible economy fare vs stage length graph (Appendix C.4).

Table 5.9.   Percentage variation in fares on intra-EU routes explained by stage length, 1986–95

	1986	1989	1992	1995
Fully flexible economy fare	70	80	77	56
Average economy fare	42	53	61	23
Lowest economy fare	14	19	33	14

Earlier studies of deregulation in the US (CAA publication CAP 654) revealed that regulated markets tend to demonstrate a clear correlation between fare and distance, while liberalized and deregulated markets show much more scatter as market-based fares become widespread. The data plotted in Appendices C.3 to C.5 show that the EU market has always had wide disparities in the fares charged. However, this has not been necessarily the result of competition. Rather, it has been the result of wide variations between the fares from individual states. Measured in terms of ECU, different national exchange rate parities distort fare differentials where one would expect on a specific route the fares set in both countries to be similar in scale. This can partly be seen from Appendix C.4 where fares of individual states can be identified.

Under a common currency regime one would expect a reduction in the difference between directional fares as a result of the increased cross-border price transparency that monetary union would be expected to bring. When questioned on the likely impact of a common currency regime on air transport, the majority of airlines expected that it will at least have some impact. One example is the Düsseldorf-Palma de Mallorca market where the difference in directional fares during 1995 was around 15%. Whilst this may have been due partially to the distorting effect of exchange rates, under a common currency environment it is likely that directional fare differentials would have been maintained, given differences in price and income elasticities at both points.

There is unlikely to be any significant convergence in directional fares over the medium term, given that airlines will continue to exploit variation in price and income elasticities at both ends of a cross-border route, and to place barriers in the way of cross-border ticketing. This practice, generally known as arbitrage, involves travel agents purchasing tickets for a specific cross-border route in the cheaper directional market. The *Ahmed Saeed* case (Case 66/86 [1989] ECR 803, [1990] 4 CMLR 102) in the European Court of Justice in 1987 found this practice to be legal, but despite this ruling, the majority of airlines do not accept flight coupons obtained under this practice.

The fact that the scatter is caused by variations between countries rather than variety from any one country, or on any one route, was confirmed by the recent study conducted by the UK CAA (CAP 654). The study used a different sample of routes in 1995 to make inter-country comparisons. Appendix C.10 highlights the UK CAA's findings.

In its report, the CAA notes:

'On international routes the lowest fully flexible fares remain lower from London than from other EU capitals, with four fairly distinct country groupings being evident. London is the cheapest; then Athens, Lisbon and Madrid; next Copenhagen, Dublin, Paris, Rome and Stockholm; and, finally, Amsterdam, Brussels, Frankfurt, Helsinki, Luxembourg and Vienna the most expensive. At most distances these fares range upwards from 25% above the London levels.'

The question of choice and variety on any given route can only be addressed by a more micro-level study. Examination of November 1995 promotional fares issued by British Airways, Lufthansa and British Midland can provide an example of pricing strategies used by airlines during off-peak periods. Tables 5.11 to 5.13 present the promotional fare as a percentage of the published lowest economy return fare (*ABC 1995*) using the British Airways 'World

Offers', Lufthansa 'Buy and Fly' and British Midland 'Diamond Deals' promotional return fares.

From Table 5.10, it can be seen that the promotional fare offered by British Airways on the London to Paris and Amsterdam routes matches the lowest available economy return fare. This should be expected, since generally speaking both these city pair markets are associated with significant fare differentials due to first, higher levels of discretionary traffic and second, the relatively high levels of competition. On the other hand, the World Offers fare for London-Zurich represents a significant discount from the lowest published available economy fare. This suggests an attempt by the airline to attract additional leisure traffic on what is generally considered to be a predominantly business-orientated route.

Analysis of Lufthansa's Buy and Fly promotion on selected routes out of Germany again appears to suggest that on services from Frankfurt and Düsseldorf to London, special offers are not much lower than the lowest published fare, because there is already considerable competition and attractive fare discounts. On those routes to Madrid and Athens which are generally low frequency markets, however, the Lufthansa promotional fare appears as a significant discount on what are generally considered to be non-fare discount routes.

Table 5.10.   British Airways' World Offers as a percentage of lowest published economy return fare

Origin-Destination	World Offers as a % of lowest economy fare	Number of operators
London-Amsterdam	100	6
London-Paris	100	5
London-Cologne	87	2
London-Lyon	86	3
London-Malaga	84	2
London-Faro	79	2
London-Düsseldorf	76	4
London-Frankfurt	74	5
London-Rome	64	3
London-Berlin	63	2
London-Hamburg	62	3
London-Bremen	61	2
London-Munich	61	3
London-Barcelona	59	2
London-Zurich	59	4
London-Toulouse	56	2
London-Venice	49	2
London-Brussels	45	4
London-Athens	41	3

Source: BA World Offers leaflet.

Table 5.12 refers to the promotional fares offered by UK carrier British Midland, an airline which tends to operate in highly competitive markets. One would expect therefore that the margin between its promotional fare and the lowest published economy fare would be relatively insignificant.   This is indeed confirmed through observation of Table 5.13, particularly with respect to its promotional fares on the London-Amsterdam, London-Paris and London-Dublin routes. On the other hand, the margin appears greater on the London-Prague and Zurich routes were traffic is predominately business related and, hence, generally characterized by the absence of a large number of discount fares.

A very recent form of special offer related to air fares is the 20% reduction offered on British Airways World Offers (and 30% off other BA fares) to those paying with a NatWest Bank credit card. This offer has a limited duration of about one month.

The above analysis was carried out using published fares, which in some countries are subject to travel taxes, security or airport charges, while in other countries they are included in the fare. As Table 5.13 shows, these have been increasing in importance over the period.

Table 5.11. Lufthansa's promotional return fare as a percentage of lowest published economy return fare

Origin-Destination	Buy and Fly as a % of lowest economy fare	Number of operators
Frankfurt-London	85	4
Cologne-London	79	2
Düsseldorf-London	79	4
Berlin-London	73	2
Hamburg-London	73	3
Düsseldorf-Birmingham	72	2
Frankfurt-Birmingham	64	2
Munich-London	63	3
Munich-Athens	57	2
Berlin-Athens	50	2
Düsseldorf-Athens	50	2
Frankfurt-Athens	50	2
Düsseldorf-Madrid	42	2
Frankfurt-Madrid	42	2
Munich-Madrid	42	3

Source: Lufthansa Buy and Fly Promotion leaflet.

Table 5.12. British Midland's promotional return fare as a percentage of lowest published economy return fare

Origin-Destination	Diamond Deal as a % of lowest economy fare	Number of operators
London-Amsterdam	100	6
London-Paris	100	5
London-Dublin	100	5
London-Frankfurt	74	5
London-Prague	62	2
London-Zurich	59	4

Source: British Midland Diamond Deal Promotion, *Sunday Observer* 26.11.95.

In conclusion, the analysis of pricing at this stage using fare data from a sample of routes suggests that no definitive conclusion can be drawn with respect to the impact of specific EU liberalization measures. However, the fares analysis can confirm that:

(a)   As expected, trends over the period 1986–95 in fully flexible fares appeared more responsive to airline yield requirements in that operators were seeking to maintain and recoup revenue in the aftermath of the world recession from the price inelastic business segments of the market. EU liberalization measures have not had a significant impact on fully flexible fares.

(b)   Analysis of lowest economy fare trends over the period indicates that the level of discounting has intensified after 1989. This was primarily because of prevailing economic circumstances where airlines were striving to fill excess capacity brought on by the deterioration in world economic conditions; this has tended to exaggerate any impact of the second and third EU packages.

Overall, the results suggest that the impact of growing competition was observed in the lower economy fares, with deeper discounts and special offers pitched below the lowest available published fare. Airlines have continued to seek revenue increases from the business market segments by increasing these fares, and in this respect it can be concluded that the EU measures have not produced the desired effect. These findings are based only on published information, but were largely confirmed during the airline and aviation authority interviews (Appendix B).

5.7.2. Domestic air fares

Developments in air fares within EU countries do not have the same implications for the completion of the single market as cross-border fares. However, recently there have been some significant changes in domestic air services and air fares for certain countries which are closely related to sector-specific EU measures, in particular in France, Germany, Italy and Spain. In all cases except perhaps Germany, the domestic airline networks of these countries have been regarded by their respective governments until very recently as essential public services that were best served on a monopolistic basis by their respective flag carriers (or their subsidiaries). In response to policy measures contained in the third package, however, this situation has been radically transformed. Over the past two years, new entrants, predominantly former charter carriers, have been allowed access to many domestic trunk routes, transforming them into highly competitive city-pair markets.

In order to compare the domestic fares charged in different EU countries, the one-way fully flexible and lowest economy return fares charged on routes of varying stage length from a sample of five countries were taken and converted into a common currency. To assess the impact of increased competition, fare data were taken for three years spanning the period 1989–95. The results of this analysis are contained in Appendix D.4.

Reference to the six graphs (lines of best fit) contained in Appendix D.4 reveals that one-way fully flexible economy fares are most expensive in Germany and least expensive in Spain. This remains the case for each of the three years investigated. A very different picture emerges for the lowest return fares, with Spain having the most, and Italy the least, generous discount prices in 1989. France replaces Spain in having the lowest return fares by 1992, whilst Italy retains its earlier position. The situation changes again in 1995, with German discounted fares being the most expensive and UK fares the least. It should be noted that French, Italian and Spanish domestic fares have until very recently been tightly controlled by their respective governments. (The above comparisons should be treated with caution given that no account has been taken of the different standards of living evident in the five countries.)

Table 5.13.   Passenger and airport taxes levied on fares (intra-EU and EU control group routes in ECU)

Country	1986	1989	1992	1995
Austria	0	0	0	3.08
Belgium	0	0	7.13	13.31
Denmark	0	0	8.24	9.00
France	0	0.71	2.17	2.63
Germany	5.22[1]	5.30[1]	2.94	3.52
Greece	4.45	3.93	0	10.02/20.05 [2]
Ireland	6.67	6.42	6.51	6.17
Italy	0	6.64	6.47	6.50
Luxembourg	0	0	0	3.16
Netherlands	0	2.78	2.82	3.14
Portugal	0.50%[3]	0	0	7.86
Spain	0	0	0	0
Switzerland	0	0	0	9.24
United Kingdom	0	0	0	5.99/11.99[4]

[1]   Passenger tax levied on fares from West Berlin.
[2]   Lower rate applicable on flights associated with sector distance between 100 km and 750 km. Higher rate refers to flights over 750 km distance.
[3]   Stamp duty levied as a % of fare.
[4]   5.99 applies to UK domestic routes and services to EU states, Iceland, Norway, Basel and Geneva; 11.99 applies to all other international routes.
    Source: ABC World Airways Guide.

A further comparative analysis contrasts the fares charged on French, German, Italian, Spanish and UK domestic routes with the prices levied in each country for intra-EU journeys of similar distance routes in 1986, 1989, 1992 and 1995. As for the above analysis, two fare categories have been selected (one-way fully flexible and lowest return economy fares). Appendix D.5 contains eight graphs (lines of best fit) contrasting French domestic fares with their intra-EU equivalents for routes of varying sector length. It is apparent that intra-EU fares for journeys originating in France are considerably more expensive than domestic trips of an equivalent length. This situation has not changed to any significant degree over the past ten years. Appendix D.6 contains a similar set of graphs for German domestic and intra-EU routes. A very different pattern is revealed, with the margin between the two sets of fares being very much less. German intra-EU fares are shown to rise more sharply with sector length than their French equivalents.

Appendix D.7 provides a similar graphical analysis for Italian domestic and intra-EU fares. Whilst there is a marked difference between the two markets for one-way fully flexible economy fares, there is little separation between the lowest return fares in 1986 and 1989. An increasing gap does, however, begin to emerge in 1992.

Spanish domestic and intra-EU fares are contrasted in Appendix D.8. A wide gap is seen to have existed throughout the study period between the two fare groups. Increased competition in both markets would appear to have had a strong impact in 1995, as is evident from the graph showing the one-way fully flexible fares. The final appendix, D.9, contains information on UK fares. Whilst there is a clear margin between the one-way fully flexible fares in the two markets throughout the ten-year period, there has been little difference between the lowest return fares. The high degree of competition on UK domestic trunk routes would go some way to explaining this outcome.

The above analysis has been enhanced by a more detailed examination of three countries where notable changes have occurred over the past year, namely France, Germany and Italy. In France, Air Inter was authorized by the government in 1985 to continue operating its domestic route network on an exclusive basis for a further 15 years. Air France's acquisition of UTA in 1990, however, had the effect of amending this arrangement. To gain the approval of the European Commission for the take-over, the French government had to concede the opening up of eight major domestic routes to competition. In reality though, only one of the routes identified became subject to any significant degree of entry. Minerve, renamed AOM after its merger with Air Outre Mer, began operating between Orly and Nice in 1991. This particular carrier's policy has been to compete with Air Inter on in-flight service and ground handling, but not on price. Air Inter's response has been to increase frequency on the route, whilst maintaining its policy of providing a no frills, single class service utilizing aircraft configured with a high density seating layout. Interestingly, the entry of AOM did not lead to a large increase in capacity on the route. Whilst Air France (operating Paris CDG-Nice) and Air Inter increased the number of flights they operated between 1990 and 1994 by some 12%, the total number of seats supplied by them fell by 6%. This was achieved by reducing the size of aircraft employed on the route.

The French government had intended that its domestic routes should be opened to competition only gradually, but pressure from the Commission and a ruling by the European Court ensured that other trunk routes became available at the beginning of 1995. (Appendix D.2 provides details of entry dates and the number of seats supplied by the respective carriers.) Air Liberté, unlike AOM, has actively engaged in fare competition with Air Inter. A good example of this competitive activity is provided by the Paris-Toulouse route, on which, after some initial aggressive discounting of the lowest fares available, prices have stabilized with Air Liberté undercutting Air Inter by some 21% for a fully flexible Y class return journey, and claiming a 30% share of the market and profits. (Appendix D.3 provides a summary of fares charged by the four carriers operating the route during the first year of competition.) On this particular route, consumers have benefited from both lower fares and a wider choice of fares, in-flight meals and drinks, a substantial increase in service frequency, and the introduction of business class by the new entrants.

Competition on domestic routes in Germany, the second largest home market in Europe, remains confined to the five trunks served by Deutsche BA and Lufthansa. At present, only DBA and Eurowings have the potential to provide any serious challenge to Lufthansa. Eurowings, however, has assiduously avoided challenging the flag carrier, seeking instead to act in a complementary manner. Earlier incursions into the domestic sector by charter carriers (Aero Lloyd (1988–92) and German Wings (1989–90)) have not been repeated, although LTU does provide low frequency services at unattractive departure times on a number of routes.

DBA has competed with Lufthansa on four trunk routes since 1992, having taken over the Internal German Services of British Airways. Its further expansion into the domestic market has so far been limited to the Düsseldorf-Munich route which it entered in April 1994. Lufthansa's response to DBA was to introduce a differentiated product on seven of its domestic trunk routes in the autumn of 1994 under the name Lufthansa Express. Aside from improved in-flight service and reduced check-in times, the carrier adopted a uniform peak/off-peak pricing structure for its Express operations. The effect of this innovation was to reduce Lufthansa's one-way business class fare on the Düsseldorf-Munich route by as much as 38% at off-peak times. DBA by comparison did not distinguish between peak and off-peak periods. Its equivalent fare was set some 29% lower than Lufthansa's peak price, but slightly more than its off-peak rate. By February 1995 however, Lufthansa had raised its off-peak fare to DM 299, some 15% higher than that charged by DBA.

Lufthansa abandoned its Express product in October 1995, citing difficulties in attracting sufficient passengers at off-peak times and problems associated with a confused branding image. The price war between DBA and Lufthansa had the effect of depressing yields by around 20% on the contested routes, whilst increasing the volume of traffic. It would appear that neither carrier has generated profits from these operations, but it would seem likely that Lufthansa is profitable on its monopolistic trunk routes, on which it charges higher fares. Table 5.15 contrasts the fares charged on the contested Düsseldorf-Munich route with those levied on the monopolistic Berlin-Frankfurt sector. The UK Civil Aviation Authority identified four such monopolistic trunk routes in Germany as presenting amongst the best opportunities for entry in Europe [CAA, 1995]. Difficulties in gaining access to sufficient slots at Frankfurt would appear to be a key factor in preventing competition.

Table 5.14. Düsseldorf-Munich and Berlin-Frankfurt one-way fares (DM), 1994–95

	Düsseldorf-Munich						Berlin-Frankfurt	
	Lufthansa				Deutsche BA		Lufthansa	
	C class		Y class		C class	Y class	C class	Y class
	peak	off-	peak	off-				
July 1994	401	401	401	401	-	-	381	381
Sept 1994	369	249	299	199	260	180	381	381
Feb 1995	369	299	259	199	260	180	381	381
Jun 1995	369	319	259	229	290	220	381	381

Source: *ABC World Airlines Guide* and CAA CAP 654.

Prior to 1995, Italian domestic services were operated on a concession basis, with Alitalia contracted to provide the vast majority. Given that the flag carrier had this arrangement renewed in 1991 for a ten-year period, it would follow that its termination in 1995 was as a direct result of the third package. Domestic fares have been regulated throughout by the government and were capped at 1985 levels for over five years. Overall profits on domestic services have been small, partly as a consequence of the contractual requirement placed on Alitalia and its subsidiary ATI to operate loss-making services. Alitalia absorbed its domestic subsidiary ATI in 1994. Avianova, a regional formed in 1986 and jointly owned by ATI and Meridiana (known as Alisarda until 1991), became a wholly owned subsidiary of Alitalia in 1995.

The Milan-Rome route, the fifth busiest city-pair in Europe, has recently been transformed as a result of the entry of two new carriers. Since the early 1990s, Alitalia and Meridiana have operated on the route charging identical fares. It would appear that Meridiana had provided services using Alitalia's concession. In March 1991, Alitalia operated 23 services each weekday between Fiumicino and Linate and Meridiana three per weekday between Fiumicino and Malpensa. By November 1995, Alitalia was operating 30 flights each weekday and Meridiana four.

In November 1995, Air One began operating six daily flights between Fiumicino and Linate. Frequency was increased to 13 services per day from January 1996. Air One operates a single class cabin configuration on the route providing a 'quality service including meals and free drinks'. Noman Charter began operating six flights daily between Linate and Ciampino in December 1995. By mid-January 1996, capacity on the Rome-Milan city-pair had increased by over 50% in less than three months. Air One's one-way fully flexible fare is 24% lower than the equivalent tariff with Alitalia and Meridiana. Noman provides an even greater discount of 37% with its fully flexible single fare. At present, all operators would appear to be offering a single class of service. A listing of the fares currently charged by the four carriers operating between Milan and Rome is given in Table 5.16. The prices levied by Alitalia and Meridiana in 1991 are also included in this table.

Table 5.15.   Rome-Milan fare development, 1991 and 1996

		March 1991 (LIT)	January 1996 (LIT)
Alitalia / Meridiana	Y one-way	196,000	230,000
	Y return (Mon-Fri)	392,000	460,000
	Y return (Sat-Sun)	392,000	230,000 (AZ only)
	Y day return (Sat-Sun)	275,000	230,000
	Y excursion return	-	322,000 (IG only)
Air One	Y one-way (Mon-Fri)	-	174,000
	Y one-way (Sat-Sun)	-	130,000
Noman	Y one-way	-	144,000
	Y weekend return	-	225,000
	Y day return (Sun)	-	225,000

Source: ABC World Airlines Guide and airlines.

5.7.3. Domestic vs cross-border air fares

Overall, it is apparent that cross-border fares are more expensive than those levied on domestic routes of a similar distance. This is particularly the case for fully flexible fares and less so for those that are conditional. There are three key factors which explain these disparities. First, differences in the nature and extent of regulatory control between intra-EU and domestic markets, second, the effects of rail competition on domestic air services, and third, carriers operating on intra-EU routes incur higher costs.

It has been only very recently that measures designed to liberalize air transport have affected domestic services. For most of the past 12 years, the focus of attention has been on cross-border routes. Until recently, with the exception of the UK, domestic air services in the Member States have been subject to a greater degree of economic control than intra-EU operations. A key feature of this domestic regulatory regime has involved the control of air fares. In many countries, governments have used price controls on domestic air services in furtherance of various social and regional economic development policy objectives. Cross-subsidization has been an intrinsic element of this strategy, with the profits earned on domestic trunk routes and international services being used to cover losses incurred on thinner regional operations. In the cases of Air Inter, Alitalia and Iberia, a condition of their monopoly status has been the requirement to operate loss-making, low density inter-regional services. Significant differences exist, therefore, between fully flexible fares levied on domestic and intra-EU routes in both Italy and Spain. Disparities between domestic and intra-EU fares are, on the other hand, less significant in the UK where there has been a longer experience of domestic deregulation. In light of the UK experience and the removal of cabotage restrictions in 1997, one would anticipate a general reduction in the divergence between domestic and intra-EU fares in other Member States over the medium term.

The effect of competition from rail will also have had an impact on the level of domestic air fares relative to those fares levied on comparable intra-EU routes. In Germany and France, for example, subsidized rail services are generally considered to be both modestly priced and highly efficient, hence functioning as an effective substitute to air travel. On the other hand, cross-border EU air services, with the exception of some routes between France, Belgium, the Netherlands and Germany have not been subject to the same degree of competitive pressure from surface transport. This is primarily because of the fact that air transport continues to maintain a relative speed and service convenience advantage over rail arising from the relatively poor cross-border integration of many national rail networks. The development of a fully integrated city centre to city centre cross-border high speed rail network therefore can be expected to exert a significant degree of competitive pressure on intra-EU air services. One recent example has been the reduction in passenger traffic on air services between London and Paris because of the Channel tunnel.

The third explanation for the disparity in fares is the higher costs incurred by carriers operating intra-EU services. Additional costs are incurred by cross-border operators in offering superior levels of service such as catering and airline lounge facilities which are generally not supplied on domestic flights. Furthermore, cross-border services are also subject to higher airport user charges. At many major airports, there is a significant difference between passenger charges levied on domestic and cross-border traffic. For example, the current passenger charges levied on EU cross-border passengers at London Heathrow and Paris Charles de Gaulle are respectively 195% and 267% higher than those levied on domestic traffic. These differentials have been justified in order to cover the additional costs to the airport operator associated with the provision of passport control and customs facilities for cross-border traffic. They have been reduced in some countries like Germany, and would be expected to narrow further in the future. Indeed, the Commission is currently drafting a policy designed to regulate airport charges.

5.7.4. EU air fares vs other world regions

The average local European economy class normal air fare increased from USD 462 in September 1992 to USD 500 in September 1994 [ICAO, 1992 and 1995]. Using these ICAO data from a large sample of routes, the 1994 level was compared to international fares in 16 other world regions, adjusting for variations in average city-pair distance by a simple regression of fare against distance. This gave a good fit (r^2 of 0.91), with the actual 1994 local European fare being 42% above the level predicted by the regression equation. By contrast, air fares between Canada, the US and Mexico were 14% below their predicted levels. The

September 1992 actual local European fare level was 45% above the level predicted by a similar regression equation. Thus, the local European normal economy fare levels, when adjusted for sector distance, have fallen somewhat in relation to international air fares in other world regions. Over the same period, air fares between Canada, the US and Mexico, a region that was also recently liberalized, moved higher in relation to their predicted levels.

Local European normal economy air fares in September 1985 were only 8% above the level predicted by the fare vs distance model for that year [ICAO, 1985]. The apparent deterioration in European fares between 1985 and 1992 was caused largely by a strengthening of the ECU against the USD (by 41%), which did not reflect changes in differential growth rates in consumer prices in the US and Europe. After allowing for this distortion, European air fares would be significantly higher than those of comparable sector length in North America.

The conclusion from this analysis is that European fare levels appear significantly higher in recent years than would be expected given their average sector distance and international nature, but this is largely due to the overvalued European exchange rates. Other reasons for the differences could be variations in traffic density, which would determine the potential for competition, and variations in costs such as airport charges or fuel prices.

5.7.5. Airline yields

The trend in average total yield (passengers plus cargo) on intra-European routes is shown in Figure 5.17. The yield, expressed in real terms, has clearly declined since 1991. This is due to a number of factors including an increase in the level of fare competition among carriers (see Section 5.7), a change in traffic mix, lower unit costs and the effects of the economic recession.

Figure 5.17.   IATA international scheduled services within Europe, 1989–94 (yield in 1994 prices)

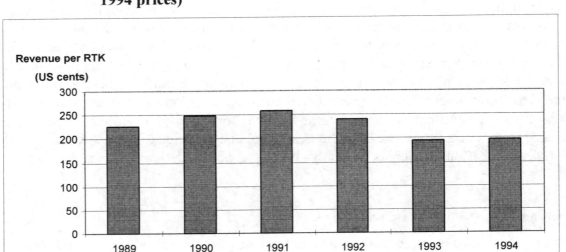

Source: IATA, *Airline Economic Results and Prospects.*

To focus the analysis of yield on EU carriers' intra-European passenger operations, yield data reported to the AEA were used for more detailed analysis. However, such data are available up to 1992 only, and include the European operations of some airlines based outside the EU such as Swissair. After 1992, certain member airlines of the AEA decided that yield information should be withheld as being commercially sensitive, particularly for those that were governed by strict stock exchange reporting requirements.

Figure 5.18 illustrates the trend in the EU for three intermediate years over the period from 1985–92. There appear to be mixed trends amongst carriers: overall yields increased in real terms from 1985 to 1988, and just kept pace with inflation between 1988 and 1992. However, since 1992, the AEA indicates that average passenger yields per passenger (and not per passenger-km) for all their members have declined in constant price terms by 5.7% in 1993 and 3.1% in 1994.

Figure 5.18.   Passenger yields per passenger-km, geographic Europe, by EU airline, 1985/88/92 (in 1985 prices)

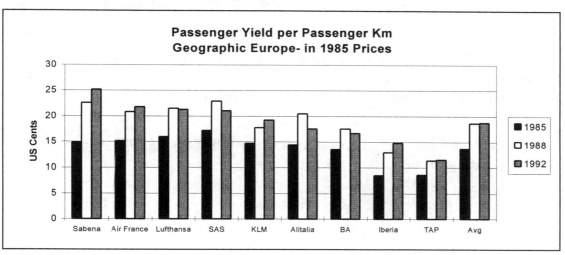

Source: AEA (geographic Europe includes all international routes originating and terminating within Europe (including Turkey and the CIS up to 55°E), the Azores, the Canary Islands and Madeira.

Table 5.16.   Trends in European promotional fare usage and discounts

Year	Promotional fare as % of full fare	Promotional passengers as % of total passengers
1985	58.0	60.5
1986	56.5	61.0
1987	57.0	61.5
1988	57.0	62.0
1989	57.0	62.0
1990	54.0	63.0
1991	54.0	64.0
1992	51.0	67.0
1993	48.6	70.1
1994	48.3	71.7
1995 (provisional)	49.2	70.9

Source: AEA Yearbooks.

As mentioned above, declining yields in recent years are caused partly by a change in traffic mix, and also by changes in fare structure.

Table 5.16 reveals that in addition to the dilutionary effect of an increased share of passengers travelling on promotional fares, the average discount increased, both developments accelerating in the period since 1990. A small reversal of these trends was evident in 1995, although this is based on preliminary data.

Yields appear to have declined in recent years in Europe mainly as a result of changes in fare structure, initiated by increased competition in European liberalized markets. This is supported by the survey of 18 EU carriers of which a large proportion (77%) indicated that EU measures affected their pricing (see Appendix B).

5.8. Profitability and sources of finance

The factors affecting airline profitability are complex and many are unrelated to liberalization. However, it may be possible to draw some conclusions about the effect on airline profitability of the moves towards the creation of the single market from the analyses of unit costs and revenues (see Sections 5.5 and 5.6).

Figure 5.19 shows the worsening profit situation on intra-European routes, following a profitable year in 1989. A return to profit at the operating level occurred in 1994 (although an overall loss was reported after interest charges), a trend which has continued.

Figure 5.19.   IATA international scheduled services within Europe, 1989–94: operating ratio

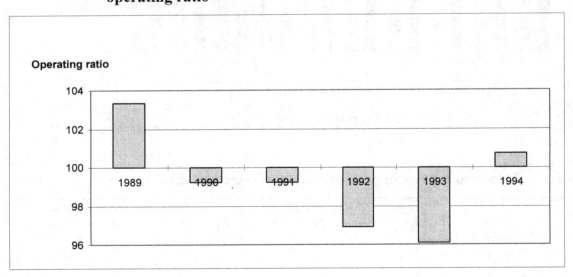

Source: IATA, *Airline Economic Results and Prospects.*

The financing of airlines and aircraft acquisitions may also be affected by liberalization, quite apart from the increased cost of finance resulting from privatization. The US deregulation experience has shown that airline earnings have become more volatile, which in turn increases risk and the expected returns from investors in the industry. However, for the European industry there are still few airlines which are not controlled by governments, and few years of data upon which to base an analysis of the effects of liberalization on finance, privatization and liberalization.

A recent report concluded that there were huge differences within Europe from country to country with regard to the regulatory environment for airline finance [Jet Finance SA, 1994]. Their recommendations included the harmonization of such areas as accounting standards, taxation, leasing regulations, as well as actions such as setting up an EU-wide aircraft and aircraft mortgage register.

5.9. Environmental impact

Environmental issues concerning air transport and government-imposed regulations covering these issues concern noise and pollution. While noise has a local impact, aircraft pollution has a more long-term global impact, not least because most of the products of combustion are distributed higher in the atmosphere where the effects are less well understood. However, it ought to be mentioned that the transitory contribution of air transport industry operations to total global air pollution, based on the existing knowledge, is very small, producing for example around 3% of the global carbon dioxide (CO_2). Other emissions such as oxides of nitrogen (e.g. NO_x) are perhaps more of a problem for the industry, and measures to reduce NO_x (for example with CFM's new A320 engines ordered by Swissair) tend to increase fuel burn and CO_2 emissions.

As discussed in Section 5.7.5, the reduction in yield caused by the changes in the mix of traffic in favour of passengers travelling on promotional and discount fares, played an important role in generating a higher number of passengers than would have been the case if European markets had not been liberalized.   It was also argued that such an increase in the level of demand was met by an even faster growth in capacity. Such an increase in capacity coupled with trends in aircraft downsizing have clearly resulted in a greater number of aircraft movements in the European liberalized markets than would have been the case under the previous regulatory regimes. A larger number of aircraft movements probably means more aircraft emissions and noise, although operations by two new fuel efficient smaller aircraft such as the Fokker 100 or Airbus 320 may be roughly equivalent to a single Airbus A300 or Lockheed Tristar.

However, regulatory bodies both at regional and international level have responded to the environmental impact of aircraft operations by imposing regulations on aircraft noise and, to some extent, emissions. In conjunction with discussions on more stringent noise rules than ICAO Annex 16 Chapter 3, the European Commission has been considering requiring aircraft to meet NO_x standards that are 20% lower than those recommended by ICAO in November 1993. At the same time the airlines appear to have responded to the environmental impact of their operation by adopting quieter aircraft with more fuel efficient engines which take greater account of emission standards. Replies to the questionnaire distributed to airlines as part of this study revealed that 16 of the 18 EU carriers responding have seen their operations affected by environmental considerations.

5.10. Summary of the impact of EU measures

The aim of this chapter was to examine the impact of the sector-specific EU measures on the development of air services, traffic, fares and economics. These developments were evaluated over a period from the mid-1980s up to 1995 (or the most recent year for which data were available), principally:

(a)   number of cross-border routes operated;
(b)   average frequencies and seats offered;
(c)   average carriers per route and capacity concentration;
(d)   passenger and cargo traffic;
(e)   airline alliances and code sharing;
(f)   productivity and costs;
(g)   air fares and yields.

While it may be too early to evaluate the full impact of EU measures, particularly the third package, since 1992 there has been an increase in the growth of new routes operated within the EU. This was due both to the introduction of non-stop connections between such regional points as Billund and Birmingham, as well as the redesignation as scheduled of a number of German charter services to Spain. It seems likely that there was some net benefit in terms of choice of non-stop destinations, taking into account developments for the control group of countries.

The number of seats offered also expanded over the period, and the average frequencies operated increased between 1989 and 1992, although declining between 1992 and 1995. However, they will still be higher in 1995 than in 1989. It can be concluded from this that some frequency competition occurred in the first period, but more recently average frequencies have been diluted by the introduction of the below average frequency (around two departures a day) air services described in the previous section.

The number of carriers per route, and carrier concentration have implications for consumer choice and competition. Here the picture is not particularly encouraging, partly because of the introduction of single carrier regional routes, and also because the entry of new competitors to the denser routes has been limited to particular cases (e.g. British Midland and EBA in Belgium). On the other hand, the consumer did gain from the availability of more non-stop services between regional cities.

Passenger traffic has increased over the period of recession of the early 1990s at a much faster pace than would be expected from the GDP growth in EU countries. Overall, European air traffic was around 20% higher over the period 1992–94 than it would otherwise have been. This was due largely to more passengers being attracted by discount fares, and larger discounts being offered compared to the full fare, as well as greater availability and awareness of such offers. Airlines were able to manage yields and seat inventories better through computer driven revenue management systems, but the more competitive European environment gave them greater incentive to do this.

Comprehensive air cargo traffic, including traffic carried by integrated carriers, was not available, and a significant amount of cargo now travels between airports by truck. However, there is evidence that the measures have encouraged strong growth in air cargo, particularly in express parcels.

Alliance and code sharing activity also increased over the period, but this was more to improve economies of scope and global network coverage than to compete in intra-EU markets.

EU carriers have made some progress in reducing costs, although the gap between EU and US carriers is not narrowing. Labour costs have been reduced by many airlines, mainly through a reduction in staff numbers and productivity gains, rather than through salary reductions. Some outsourcing has probably helped this trend. These efforts have been helped by reduced fuel prices in real terms, but many infrastructure costs such as en-route navigation charges remain high – and increasing – relative to other world regions. In addition to the liberalization of European air transport markets, international competition from airlines of other regions, economic recession and the resulting poor financial performance of airlines have all applied pressure on airlines to reduce costs. While it proved impossible to evaluate the contribution from each, the results of the airline survey indicated that EU measures had played an important part in efforts towards cost reduction.

Intra-EU air fare developments show contrasting trends: fully flexible and club class fares have increased, while promotional and conditional fares have fallen. Thus airlines have pursued strategies of price discrimination, as was the early experience in both US [Meyer et al. 1981] and Australian [Bureau of Transport and Communications Economics, 1995] air transport markets following deregulation. The overall benefit of this has been larger numbers of people benefiting from lower fares; the effect on full fares suggests that there has been limited competition for the business passenger, with a notable absence of price wars for this market segment, for whatever reason. It could be concluded that EU measures have encouraged airlines to compete more vigorously for leisure passengers, but competition for full fare passengers has been more through level of service and product innovation.

There are still significant variations in intra-EU fares on a directional basis, and between intra-EU and domestic fares. The first difference will only disappear if airlines allow cross-border ticketing, while the second should fall over time.

6. Airline case studies

Case studies were carried out on five EU airlines, each representing in broad terms a type of carrier, defined in terms of ownership and range of operations. The airlines selected were:

(a)   Air France,
(b)   British Airways,
(c)   Eurowings,
(d)   Maersk Air,
(e)   TAP Air Portugal.

The case study reports can be found in Appendix F. Summaries of the reports follow in this section: these focus on the airlines' responses to the single market. Table 6.1 summarizes the use made by the five carriers of opportunities opened by the liberalization packages in Europe, as well as other tactics not directly facilitated by the three packages, but which carriers have used to establish markets on new routes and to increase or maintain their share on established routes.

Table 6.1.   Case study airlines: methods of increasing or maintaining market share

	Use of liberalization packages					Other tactics	
	New routes				Protection		
	Consecutive cabotage	Third & Fourth Freedoms	Fifth Freedom	Pricing	Public service obligation	Code sharing	Airline acquisitions
Air France *state-owned major*	Very limited	Limited	Limited	Limited	None	Extensive	Yes
British Airways *privatized major*	Limited	Limited	Limited	Extensive	None	Very extensive	Yes
Eurowings *small regional*	None	Moderate	None	Moderate	None	Extensive	No
Maersk Air *charter → scheduled*	None	Extensive	None	Moderate	None	Extensive	Yes
TAP Air Portugal *smaller national carrier*	Limited	Moderate	Moderate	Limited	Yes	Limited	No

6.1. Air France

Air France is a state-owned major carrier. The basis of the carrier's response to the single European market has been expansion to ensure that it maintains a strategic European and world position prior to an eventual consolidation of the European airline industry, considered inevitable by Air France. Network expansion was achieved by a mixture of organic growth, alliances, and acquisitions. At the same time the fleet grew rapidly with the addition of new aircraft. This took place in spite of worsening finances and at a time when the economic recession and the Gulf War were adversely affecting the company's traffic and yields. Drastic cost-cutting exercises were needed to rescue the carrier, creating labour unrest and demoralizing the workforce. The airline has been unable to combine in a cohesive strategy the airline resources it acquired, and has been forced to divest itself of a number of them. Air

France finds it difficult to take advantage of its extensive world network to build a Paris hub because of the lack of domestic feed into Paris Charles de Gaulle.

Air France took only limited advantage of the opportunities opened by the third package. Some Fifth Freedom routes were initiated. Pricing freedom has been used, but the airline's relatively poor yield management system has meant that this has not had a positive effect on yield.

State aid was required to rescue the company, approved by the Commission subject to conditions, some of which have prevented the carrier from integrating fully and marketing successfully the operations of Air Inter.

6.2. British Airways

British Airways was privatized almost ten years before the adoption of the first package. It thus passed through a major restructuring process well in advance of the introduction of the three packages of liberalization, and wider economic events have had a greater impact on its operations and strategy than the EU single market process. The airline has striven to maintain its competitive position not only within the European context, but also among North American and Asian airlines. The passenger feed from the non-European markets through London into the airline's European network gives British Airways a particular advantage over most of its European competitors. The three packages have had little effect on the airline outside the freedom to price its product competitively, providing it with the opportunity to employ its yield management system to great success. British Airways has responded to the more competitive environment with a search for size and the development of new marketing strategies. Network expansion has resulted from organic growth, major shareholdings in EU carriers and in airlines elsewhere, franchising and other forms of alliance.

British Airways is profitable and confident. It sees as anti-competitive the infusion of state aid to the weaker EU airlines.

6.3. Eurowings

Eurowings is a privately owned regional airline, formed by the merger between two regional carriers in 1992. The initial focus was on the German domestic market, but high costs and increasing intermodal competition made the market less attractive. The airline has since switched its attention to cross-border services in niche markets where yields are higher. Alliances with major carriers have been a key to success on these routes. Eurowings has increased its activity in the charter market, again as a niche operator from regional German airports.

The airline has found pricing flexibility made possible in the third package an important marketing tool. Network expansion did not generally benefit from the EU liberalization process, but the freedoms opened by the process will be important in establishing routes to and from Austria. In fact consecutive cabotage of EU carriers in Germany has had a significant, and negative, impact on Eurowing's operations on some domestic routes.

6.4. Maersk Air

Maersk is a privately owned carrier based in Denmark. The airline began scheduled international operations between Copenhagen and London in 1984, under the 1983 Regional Directive. Prior to this, operations had been mainly charter services. The airline prepared for the single market, expanding its network by buying a shareholding in a UK carrier, which also facilitated the moving of its UK operation from Southend airport to London Gatwick. Maersk now fully owns a UK subsidiary which operates under a franchise agreement with British Airways.

The airline continues to operate a substantial charter programme: it is not clear if the development of its international services is made possible by cross-subsidization from the charter side of the business.

Maersk's strategy in scheduled operations appears to be that of establishing niche operations away from the SAS dominated hub of Copenhagen. Thus, most growth in terms of international destinations has been from Billund. Obviously, this strategy has been assisted by the third package. Although regulatory barriers have been removed, the airline has found that other barriers such as slot availability at major airports are effective constraints.

6.5. TAP Air Portugal

TAP is a state-owned carrier operating intercontinental and European routes from a base on the periphery of Europe. It has been technically bankrupt, and, in a normal commercial world without government ownership, by now would have ceased operations. The airline has not made extensive use of the opportunities offered by the three packages. The only direct benefit gained from the initial relaxation of constraints was the opening of Fifth Freedom routes to serve thin markets which could not otherwise be served in an economical way from Lisbon. Very limited use has been made of consecutive cabotage opportunities, in common with most other carriers. Code sharing, a marketing tactic increasingly used by TAP, appears to be an evolutionary product of the market rather than a direct result of European liberalization. TAP did not have a cost base low enough, or a yield management system sufficiently sophisticated, to allow it to make profitable use of free pricing.

The airline divested itself of the obligation to operate unprofitable domestic services to the Azores and Madeira, but then successfully re-applied to serve the routes under public service obligation rules, with a subsidy from the Portuguese state.

Throughout the 1980s, rather than follow the more reasonable road of reducing the cost burden, the airline pursued a course of route expansion, in Europe and elsewhere. The reasoning appears to have been to spread costs: the additional seat-kilometres generated, however, could not be filled in a profitable way. The airline was overstaffed, and flew a fleet of inadequate composition across a network that was too ambitious. The Portuguese state recognized that its national carrier, already technically bankrupt, was not going to recover without radical restructuring which would address the need to cut costs and rationalize the network. The European Commission approved this action, subject to some conditions. The airline is making progress towards the performance objectives it set itself, but these may not be achieved within the specified period.

7. Conclusions and policy implications

The purpose of this review has been to examine developments in the EU air transport market structure and performance which can be traced back to Community initiated or Community inspired changes in the regulatory framework for Community air transport. These were discussed in Chapter 3 of the study, with the three packages introduced between January 1988 and January 1993 being the most significant measures. These have opened up access to, and freed pricing for, cross-border services and led to the liberalization of domestic markets, a process which will be completed in 1997.

It would have been unrealistic to expect the degree of competition now apparent in the US domestic air transport market to be evident in Europe in such a short space of time, given the US's long history of social and cultural integration, and the fact that it deregulated its air transport markets over 15 years ago. Secondly, a large part of intra-EU air travel is carried out by charter airlines, and this was already liberalized on a bilateral basis before the single market measures. This leisure or price-sensitive segment of the industry would perhaps have been expected to benefit most from such measures. This chapter summarizes the progress towards a single market in air transport by reviewing the impact of the measures in terms of changes in airline strategies and market structure, focusing mainly on the scheduled sector. It also highlights the remaining barriers to the full exploitation of the single market, concluding with the implications of such barriers for EU air transport policy, as well as the implications for consumers.

7.1.   Progress towards a single market in air transport

Progress towards a single market in air transport has been assessed by a review, supported by case studies, of airline strategic developments following from, and in anticipation of, the three EU air transport packages and other sector-specific measures. It has also been evaluated through an analysis of developments in air services, traffic, productivity, air fares and costs and profitability.

Three types of strategic response were identified, which could be summarized as first, the blocking strategy, second, going for expansion and greater economies of scope, and third, aiming for a more focused competitive stance. Airlines in northern Europe, for example KLM, Lufthansa and British Airways, have all made a successful transition from state-owned public utility to market-orientated enterprise by pursuing a combination of these strategies. All three, particularly KLM, have responded very much to global competition, with BA and Lufthansa also active in protecting home and, to a lesser extent, EU markets. EU measures have contributed to these strategies, but have not played a major role. For other, smaller airlines, such as two of the airlines studied in greater detail in the case studies, Maersk Air and TAP, EU markets are much more important. For these airlines the measures have played a larger part.

Examples of less successful strategies have been Iberia's global strategy of South American airline investments, and Air France's Sabena and CSA share purchases which were subsequently unwound. Air France, however, did undertake some fairly vigorous blocking strategies through its acquisition of UTA, which gave it control of Air Inter, although this does not so far appear to have been very effective. An increasing number of alliances and code sharing agreements were concluded by European airlines, but many of these were more global that intra-EU in scope. Two that did have an impact on intra-EU competition were those between Lufthansa and SAS, which was allowed after the European Commission imposed conditions, and between Swissair, Austrian and Sabena. While both were again more global in nature, they tended to restrict competition on routes between their respective countries, without adding significant competition in other EU markets.

Charter airlines have been somewhat cautious in entering scheduled markets in head-to-head competition with flag carriers in northern Europe, possibly because of some of the earlier experiences with this strategy. But they have converted some of their charter routes to scheduled routes and put more emphasis on direct sales of seat-only products. Southern European experience, however, indicates recent entry into scheduled domestic markets by a number of charter carriers. Overall, there has also been some tendency for these markets to become dominated by vertically integrated travel groups.

It was concluded from the analysis of the impact of EU measures on airline operations that from 1993 there was an increase in the growth of new routes operated within the EU. This was due both to the introduction of non-stop connections between regional points, as well as the redesignation as scheduled of a number of German charter services to Spain. It seems likely that there was some net benefit for consumers in terms of choice of non-stop destinations, taking into account developments for the control group of countries.

The new direct air services that were introduced between 1992 and 1994 were generally of relatively low frequency. This meant that the average frequencies operated per route declined over this period. However, the earlier period, 1989 to 1992, was characterized by greater frequency competition, as well as an increase in the number of effective competitors per route. Over the more recent period, the latter trend was reversed, with adverse implications for consumer choice and competition. Here the picture is not particularly encouraging, partly because of the introduction of single carrier regional routes mentioned above, but also because the entry of new competitors to the denser routes has been limited in number (e.g. British Midland at Heathrow, and EBA at Brussels).

Passenger traffic has increased in the early 1990s, in spite of the economic downturn. Growth rates were higher than would be expected from the GDP growth of EU countries, and higher than had been experienced over the previous (early 1980s) recession. It can be concluded that European air traffic was approximately 20% higher over the period 1992 to 1994 than it would otherwise have been. This was principally due to the greater use made of reduced air fares and special offers, and through the more effective use of computer driven revenue management systems, encouraged by the more competitive European environment.

In the early 1990s, EU carriers have been relatively successful in reducing costs, helped by stable or declining fuel costs. Reductions in staff numbers and productivity gains have led to lower staff costs for many EU airlines. However, airlines have been less successful in reducing salaries to sustainable market levels, and infrastructure costs in Europe remain high relative to other world regions. It is difficult to conclude that the liberalizaton of European air transport was solely responsible for these cost trends; international competition from airlines of other regions also played a part, as did the economic recession and the resulting poor financial performance.

There has been a greater emphasis on price discrimination by EU airlines, with the resulting trend of increased fully flexible fares, and declining promotional and conditional fares. It can be concluded that EU measures have encouraged airlines to compete more vigorously for leisure passengers through price, but competition for full fare passengers has been more through level of service (especially frequency) and product innovation (for example, airport lounges).

7.2.   Remaining single market barriers in air transport

7.2.1.   Sector-specific measures and related barriers

Any remaining barriers were identified in the light of the industry developments analysed in Chapters 4 and 5, which suggested that, in addition to legal and administrative barriers, there could also be problems for new entrant airlines attempting to reach a large enough size to benefit from economies of scale and scope.   Barriers have also been identified from questionnaire responses from 18 EU airlines and seven EU air transport administrations, as well as interviews with German, French and UK aviation experts, and the UK Air Transport Users Council (see Appendix B).

Taking action to prevent EU airlines becoming too large relative to EU markets, however, may limit the degree to which EU airlines can compete on a global scale against the larger US and Asian carriers.   In fact, many EU airlines see themselves competing in a global marketplace, and form alliances or code sharing arrangements to increase their effectiveness in this respect. Code sharing, on the one hand, allows airlines to serve markets that legal barriers might prevent them serving, and, on the other hand, helps to remove those barriers on a world, rather than just an EU scale.   As with franchising, code sharing can work both to increase competition, by allowing smaller airlines some benefits of economies of scope, but also to reduce competition by combining the services of two potential competitors.

The following list summarizes the barriers that remain, ranked according to the importance given to them by both airlines and aviation authorities (expressed in the questionnaire responses shown in Appendix B, and summarized in Figure 7.1), from most important to least important:

(a)   The lack of peak hour slots at many major airports makes the entry of new carriers on the densest routes, where competition would be most viable, almost impossible. It also inhibits niche carriers from serving regional routes. The regulation on slot allocation, in accepting grandfather rights, has done little to alleviate this.

(b)   Frequent flyer programmes (FFPs) give large carriers a major competitive advantage over small new entrants. This is reinforced by franchising agreements which tie many smaller carriers into one or other larger airline's FFP.

(c)   Approval by the Commission of state aid with inadequate conditions has enabled high cost and unprofitable airlines to continue to operate in markets from which they might otherwise have withdrawn. This has distorted competition.

(d)   The marketing and administrative costs of entering international airline markets on any significant scale are high, and pose significant barriers to effective market entry. Some smaller carriers also experience administrative costs in bringing potential problems to the Commission's attention, and have suffered disproportionately from delays in taking corrective action.

(e)   The reluctance of some states to implement the existing regulations, particularly in the early stages of the liberalization process, has hindered carriers from taking advantage of opportunities that are intended to be available, e.g. Italian resistance to Lufthansa consecutive cabotage operations, or Greek delays in processing applications for licences and aircraft operator's certificates.

(f)   Airline alliances make it more difficult for smaller airlines or new entrants successfully to enter established city-pair markets. However, they are an essential means for EU carriers to maintain or enhance their global competitive position.

(g)   The use of override commissions (i.e. high extra commission usually based on sales volumes) or other incentives by large carriers gives new entrants a competitive disadvantage in selling through travel agents.

(h)   Vertical integration between charter airlines and major tour operators within the same country makes new entry into that country's charter market difficult for other Community airlines or indeed start-up airlines from that country. Such markets are, however, already highly competitive.

Often the barriers are more powerful in combination: for example, frequent flyer programmes and override commissions, taken together, can be a strong deterrent to entry by new airlines.

Only four of the 18 airline respondents mentioned user charges as a barrier. This might have concerned the level of airport and ATC charges in Europe, which for regional operators amount to a high percentage of costs per passenger. They may also have had in mind airport pricing policies which offer volume discounts only achievable by the national flag carrier (e.g. Brussels and Lisbon), or involve high flat rate charges for runway use (e.g. Heathrow) which raise user charges for new entrants, who typically operate with smaller aircraft than incumbents. These discourage new entry, but are not very significant over the EU as a whole.

Only one airline out of 18 specifically mentioned ground handling monopolies as a barrier to entry; these distort competition through discriminatory pricing, discriminatory quality of service and make sensitive information available to the handling agent, who may be an airline competitor. Such issues are being addressed in the forthcoming Commission Directive, albeit on a gradual basis. (Council Directive 96/67/EC came into force following the completion of this study.)

None of the respondents to the questionnaires mentioned pricing as a barrier, with many stressing the positive impact of the flexibility and lack of administrative requirements. However, open pricing has enabled incumbent airlines to match selectively or undercut any low fares introduced by new entrant airlines, and could be considered to make market entry by the latter more difficult. The question of whether such selective pricing is predatory has been defined by the Commission with reference to variable costs, but would be difficult to enforce in practice. From the questionnaires received, five administrations had referred such predatory pricing cases to the European Commission, while two had not.

Other distortions to the single market are related to the interdependence of the EU air transport markets with world-wide markets. First, bilaterals with third countries do not allow for ownership of designated airlines by nationals of other Community countries (i.e. the concept of a Community Air Carrier is not accepted). This limits the scope for competition on routes to third countries and for cross-border mergers.

Second, differences in bilaterals with third countries distort competition between carriers within the single market, as some carriers have access to profitable, protected markets, whilst other carriers face competition in all their major markets.

Figure 7.1.   Importance of various barriers to entry

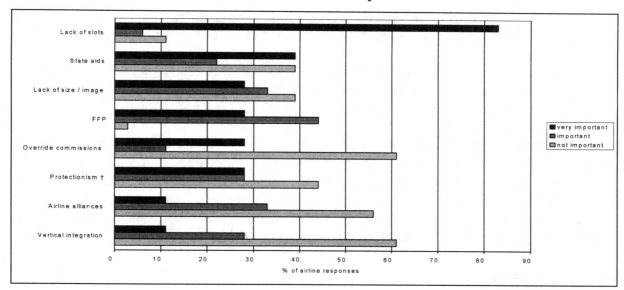

† Reluctance of some states to enforce EU measures.
Source: Airline questionnaire responses (Appendix B).

7.2.2. Horizontal measures and related barriers

Very significant progress has been made towards the completion of the single market in the Community, and this has had both a real and a psychological effect on trade and commerce in general. It was impossible, however, to quantify such impact on intra-EU air transport. Estimates have been made of the boost that all measures have had on Community GDP, and even if this were as low as an incremental effect of 1% a year, this would have generated an additional million or so scheduled passengers a year. In addition, this would have generated a substantial number of additional charter passengers.

In many of the more specific areas, however, such as the rate of VAT charged on domestic air travel, or social conditions and charges, EU harmonization measures have yet to be introduced. In these areas, benefits are still to come, but in the meantime certain distortions will be present in air transport as in other industries.

Views as to the importance of EU horizontal measures on the air transport industry were obtained from airline and aviation authority questionnaire responses.   The following summarizes the importance that respondents attached to them, ranked from most important to least important:

(a)   **Differences in social costs between Member States:** these have a significant distorting effect on labour costs and differences in taxation can distort costs more generally. Seventeen out of 25 airlines attached some importance to this, with 11 of these reporting a significant impact.

(b)   **The single EU currency:** Sixteen out of 25 respondents would expect the introduction
        of a single currency in Europe to have at least some impact, with nine suggesting a
        significant impact.

(c)   **Corporate taxation:** Fifteen out of 25 attached some importance to differences in
        corporate taxation within the EU, five of them reporting these differences as being very
        significant.

(d)   **Barriers to trade:**   Fourteen out of 25 thought that the removal of trade barriers,
        customs formalities etc. would have some impact, with eight reporting a significant
        impact.

(e)   **Variations in rates of indirect taxation:** Eleven cited this as having some impact, and
        six a significant impact; this applies specifically to the large variation in VAT applied to
        domestic air travel, ranging from zero to 15%.

Other related areas mentioned were company law and accounting system variations (three
giving this a high importance, and eight some importance), and public procurement (with three
and six respectively). Not mentioned in the survey, but of potential importance, are the
benefits that other competitive modes of transport receive from subsidies and EU funding.
These effects can be felt in some domestic markets (e.g. Spain and France), where private
airlines compete with heavily subsidized rail services.

7.3.   Consumer impacts

An alternative way of looking at the impact of the EU air transport measures is to see what
effect they have had on consumers. Economic theory would suggest that improvements in the
single market for air transport would lead to benefits to consumers in terms of service levels
(including more direct services), choice of airline and air fares. These benefits have been
assessed mainly for the scheduled intra-EU markets, rather than the charter markets which had
already been largely liberalized (although charter carriers have more recently been catering
increasingly for the seat-only market, giving consumers greater flexibility). After examining
the service level and fare impacts, the benefits from increased air travel are assessed, followed
by some discussion of other issues such as denied boarding and CRSs.

Passengers clearly benefited from access to a larger number of destinations by scheduled non-
stop flights. This was due to more flights between regional cities, but also because of a
change of designation to scheduled of a number of charters, particularly out of Germany.

EU measures did not have any downward effect on fully flexible fares which tended to
increase even faster than the consumer price index over the whole period of liberalization
measures; however, they reduced the level and increased the range of promotional fares. Both
the level of discount from the fully flexible fare and the number of passengers taking
advantage of such discounts have increased between 1985 and 1994, with a small reversal of
this trend being evident in 1995.

A combination of service level improvements and greater use of deeper discount promotional
fares had the combined effect of increasing the number of European scheduled passengers in
1994 above the level predicted purely by GDP by 25%, or by an additional 14.6 million
passengers (see model in Section 5.2.3). Some of this traffic might have been diverted from
surface transport or air charters, but a significant part would have been additional traffic
generated.

The evidence set out above suggests that users appear to have benefited from the strategic responses of incumbent carriers and from market entry which have resulted in greater variety and choice. The EU liberalization process was designed to avoid as much as possible some of the instabilities that occurred in the US, although there were some larger airline failures (e.g. German Wings, Dan Air, and Air Europe) which occurred in the earlier days of liberalization. But new entrants have provided, and continue to provide, a stimulus to innovation. Demand has been stimulated, particularly on French, Italian and Spanish domestic services, on the Ireland-UK market, and where airlines with more appropriate cost structures have opened up previously non-viable low-density services.

There is little evidence that pre-existing economic benefits have been lost (i.e. through the large-scale permanent withdrawal of services, or disproportionate increases in fares). The one benefit which has declined is the automatic acceptance by one airline of another airline's tickets (especially for promotional fares), but this needs to be viewed in the light of overall choice of carrier and the increased network scope offered by many airlines, and lower fares. Discussions with one air transport consumer body did not reveal any increase in the level of complaints from air transport users.

7.4. Policy implications

Given that by the end of 1997 the one remaining restriction on intra-EU operations will have been removed, the most important barrier remaining to the completion of the single market in air transport is access to airport slots, which inhibits entry both from new airlines, and larger airlines that already operate some services from an airport. This is being addressed currently by the Commission, but it is difficult to see a solution that does not involve either confiscation or some form of auction (or better still where possible investment in expanding airport capacity). An auction has the advantage of not requiring procedures for confiscation, and may not be the barrier to new entrants that has often been claimed.

The second most important problem has been the very large sums of money going to some airlines in the form of state aid. This has clearly distorted the single market and presents considerable potential problems of unfair price competition. So far this has not happened on a very significant scale in intra-EU markets as a whole. Cross-subsidization could be a problem also, and this is being addressed within the EU by the phasing out of monopoly rights such as ground handling concessions. Cross-subsidization of EU services from profits earned on protected long-haul markets could only be dealt with by increasing competition on these routes, something that can be done now only on an individual country basis. More rigorous monitoring of state aid conditions is thus recommended, as well as changing those conditions where necessary as the market situation changes.

A similar approach to cross-subsidization would be necessary in areas such as alliances, code sharing and FFPs. These can be grouped together as tending to reduce competition and increasing barriers to entry in intra-EU markets, but increasing competition in global markets. Addressing this on a purely single market basis might not lead to the best overall outcome.

Many of the other benefits that have yet to accrue from the single market are related to horizontal measures. These include the harmonization of taxation and social policies in member countries. This would ensure that the key airline input markets such as labour, capital and goods and services were more competitive, a position that some of them do not yet approach.

Greater efficiency and the lower cost provision of air transport infrastructure, such as airport and air traffic services, would also reduce the cost of operating air services. The Commission involvement in these areas has so far been limited, but future action might be inevitable to encourage cross-border travel and commerce.

APPENDIX A

Definitions of air transport terms

Aircraft hours are the total number of aircraft block hours in revenue service, block hours being calculated from the moment the aircraft moves under its own power for purpose of flight until it comes to rest at the next point of landing.

Aircraft kilometres are the sum of products obtained by multiplying the number of flights performed on each flight stage by the stage distance.

Aircraft utilization is the average number of block hours that each aircraft is in use. Generally this is measured on a daily or annual basis.

Average aircraft capacity is obtained by dividing available tonne-kilometres by aircraft kilometres flown.

Available seat-kilometres (ASKs) are obtained by multiplying the number of seats available for sale on each flight stage by flight stage distance.

Average passenger haul is obtained by dividing revenue passenger kilometres flown by the number of passengers.

Average stage length is obtained by dividing aircraft kilometres flown by number of aircraft departures for each airline; it is the weighted average of stage/sector lengths flown by an airline.

Available tonne-kilometres (ATKs) are obtained by multiplying the number of tonnes of capacity available for carriage of passengers and cargo on each sector of a flight by flight stage distance.

Block time (hours) is the time for each flight stage or sector, measured from when the aircraft leaves the airport gate or stand (chocks off) to when it arrives on the gate or stand at the destination airport (chocks on).

Operating costs per ATK is a measure obtained by dividing total operating costs by ATKs. It includes flight operating expenses, sales ticketing and promotional costs, ground operations costs and general and administration costs. It usually excludes interest payments, but includes aircraft lease rentals.

Operating ratio is the operating revenue expressed as a percentage of operating costs.

Passenger load factor is passenger-kilometres expressed as a percentage of available seat-kilometres.

Revenue passenger-kilometres (RPKs) are obtained by multiplying the number of fare paying passengers on each flight stage by flight stage distance.

Revenue tonne-kilometres (RTKs) are obtained by multiplying the total number of tonnes of passengers and cargo carried on each flight stage by flight stage distance. Passenger tonne-kilometres are normally calculated on standard basis of 90 kg average weight, including free and excess baggage.

Scheduled freight yields are obtained by dividing total revenue from scheduled freight by RTK from freight.

Scheduled passenger yields are obtained by dividing the total scheduled passenger revenue by RTK from passengers.

Seat factor or passenger load factor on a single sector is obtained by expressing the passengers carried as a percentage of the seats available for sale; on a network of routes it is obtained by expressing the total passenger-kms as a percentage of the total seat-kms available.

Seat pitch is the standard way of measuring seat density on an aircraft. It is the distance between the back of one seat and the same point on the back of the seat in front.

Unit costs are obtained by dividing total operating costs by ATKs.

Weight load factor is revenue tonne-kilometres performed expressed as a percentage of available tonne-kilometres.

Yields are obtained by dividing the total operating revenue by RTKs.

Market access

The 1944 Chicago Convention provided a framework within which states could negotiate bilaterally the provision of air services. Except for Fifth Freedom, whose applicability has always been heavily restricted, these bilateral agreements referred to traffic between two contracting countries.

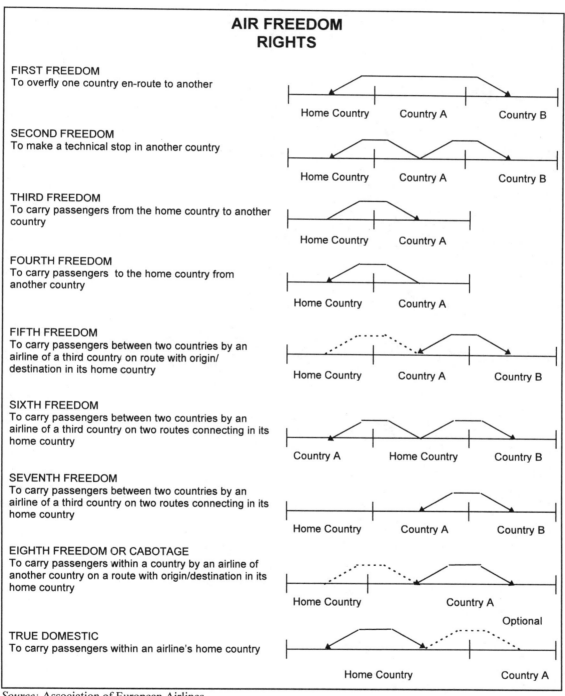

Source: Association of European Airlines.

The term 'Sixth Freedom' was coined to describe the combination of Third and Fourth, reflecting the reality of hub-and-spoke networks. More recently, Seventh and Eighth Freedoms have been quoted as potential opportunities for liberalization.

APPENDIX B

Air transport industry survey

B.1. Approach to industry survey

To fill the gaps in the data and information required to evaluate the 'effectiveness of single market integration in air transport', key officials of airlines and relevant civil aviation authorities were surveyed. The survey involved both postal questionnaires and interviews. The latter were also used since it is believed that the quality of data and information gathered would be richer, and a better insight into the developments of airlines and policies adopted by authorities would be gained.

The questionnaire: The questionnaire structure and questions are shown on the following pages. The length and depth of the questionnaire was determined by data requirements and the need to limit the time needed to complete it. The questionnaire responses are shown in Appendix B.2.

The interviewer: the interviews were carried out by members of the research team who are specialized in their field, and have particular knowledge of the countries and airlines concerned.

The interview approach: once the appointment with the industry officials were made, a copy of the list of information required and any points that were to be discusseed in the course of the interview were sent to the interviewees (see following pages). This enabled the officials to give the matter some thought, arrange for appropriate staff to be present at the interview, and possibly gather the information and data required before the actual interview.

B.1.1. Civil aviation authorities

Questionnaires were sent to Belgium, Denmark, France, Germany, Greece, Ireland, Italy, the Netherlands, Portugal, Spain and the UK.

Interviews were conducted with the UK, Germany and France.

B.1.2. Airlines

Questionnaires were sent to Aer Lingus, Air France,* Air Liberté, British Airways,* British Midland, Eurowings,* EBA, Finnair, Iberia, KLM, Lauda Air, LTU/LTE, Lufthansa, Maersk,* Meridiana, Olympic, Ryanair, Sabena, SAS, Spanair and TAP.*

Interviews were conducted with British Airways, British Midland, Air France, Maersk, Eurowings and SAS (by phone).

---

*   Case study airlines.

B.1.3. Interview checklist – Airlines

For each of the questions the interviewer will try (a) to establish the impact of EU measures on any development as opposed to other factors such as competition from international carriers outside EU and the economy, and (b) where possible, distinguish between the impact of the three liberalization packages.

The following questions are to ensure that the interviewer will cover all the major areas. However, in the course of the interview other areas may also be explored.

Search for size

How important do you think the size of your airline is to allow you to compete effectively in EU markets and in global markets?

Do you see concentration increasing on any part of your network? If yes, on which type of routes has concentration increased, and why?

In your opinion, have the three EU packages encouraged airlines to adopt the following strategies? If yes, which package has had the most significant impact?

(a)   code sharing;
(b)   alliances;
(c)   franchising;
(d)   establishment of low-cost subsidiary.

Have you experienced or do you encounter any conflict of interest between charter and scheduled operation, and why? Has the third EU package had any impact?

Route developments

What are the main factors driving your airline route strategy in Europe (e.g. competition, profitability, market share, long-haul feed, etc.)?

Has your airline policy in relation to European route development changed since 1985? What are the reasons for these changes, if any?

To what extent did the entry to or exit from any European market happen as a direct result of the EU three packages? If so, which package?

Have you made use of consecutive cabotage rights so far, and would you use the unrestricted freedom available after 1997?

Do you see cabotage right as a threat to your own airline's domestic services?

Product developments

Has your airline introduced changes in any of its products on European services (e.g. check-in facilities, in-flight services, baggage handling, airport lounges)?

What have been the major changes?

What are the main reasons for these changes? Are they driven by the EU liberalization or other factors?

Pricing strategies

What are the developments in your airline pricing strategies with respect to European services? What has affected such developments?

Are your domestic pricing strategies different from those applied to European cross-border services? If yes, specify how they differ.

Are your European price strategies different from those of international routes outside the EU? If yes, specify how they differ.

Would you say that in recent years your airline has increased fully flexible fares to compensate for low revenues from discounted fares? If yes, why? Have EU measures encouraged that? If yes, which measure has made the most significant impact?

What is your relationship with wholesalers? Has your relationship strengthened in recent years? If yes, why?

Who would you say are the price leaders in any of your European markets, and if so, which markets?

What are the main factors driving your airline yields? What is the role of EU measures in that? Any specific measure?

Would you or have you considered a simpler fare structure as a response to greater competition? If yes, on which European routes?

Do you see the pricing freedoms that the third package has allowed in Europe as advantageous or not? What are the implications?

Cost cutting

What are the cost reduction policies adopted by your airline?

Would you say that you have been successful in reducing operating costs? If so, in which areas?

When did you start implementing your cost reduction policies? What obstacles did you meet?

How has aircraft utilization developed in recent years and why?

To what extent have cost reduction policies been driven by EU measures (specify which measure and on which costs category)?

Are there any EU measures that you think have actually increased your costs? If so, specify the measure(s) and the cost category affected.

Labour issues

How have staff numbers in your airline developed over the past few years: have there been any reductions? If yes, which categories of staff have been more affected?

Have you increased the percentage of part-time staff employed?

Have you increased the percentage of non-EU personnel?

Have you implemented any changes in working conditions/rules? What are they?

Have you implemented any changes in salary/wage levels? Can you explain?

To what extent have EU liberalization packages encouraged the above? Specify which package/measures.

What is the airline management view about unions? Do unions create obstacles?

Has labour productivity increased? If yes, in which areas?

Distribution

Have your distribution policies been affected by EU liberalization packages? If yes, which package and how?

Has your relationship with travel agents changed since 1985? If yes, in what way?

Are the changes caused by EU liberalization packages? If so, which one(s)?

Financial performance

To what extent do you think EU liberalization measures have been responsible for your airline financial performance? Which measures have had an impact, and why?

Barriers to entry

Are there any markets/routes that your airline wished to enter but could not?

If yes, which route or market, and what have been the barriers?

Environmental impact

Have environmental issues (noise, engine emissions, etc.) restricted your operation?

Explain in what way.

B.1.4. Airline questionnaire

Individual completing this questionnaire

Name:................... ....

Job title:........... ....

Phone/fax:..

(1)   The list attached contains non-stop routes British Airways introduced in the periods June 1989–June 1992 and June 1992–June 1995. We should like to know how important EU legislation was in your decision to begin operating these sectors.

Please indicate below those routes you consider introduced largely because of changes in the regulatory environment created by the three packages of EU air transport measures.

(2)   Please indicate the importance of the following barriers to entry for both new airlines and existing airlines wishing to enter any cross-border routes within the EU.

(Score each barrier by ticking a box from 1 to 10: 1 indicates no effect and 10 maximum effect).

	1	2	3	4	5	6	7	8	9	10
Lack of airport slots										
State aids										
Other government protectionism *(please specify)*										
....										
....										
Reluctance of some states to enforce three packages of EU air transport measuress										
Vertical integration of charter airlines, tour operators and travel agents										
Use of override commissions										
Frequent flyer programmes										
Airline alliances										
Small airlines' lack of size and image compared to established airlines										
Any other barriers *(please specify)*										

(3)   Please indicate the effect of the three packages of EU air transport measures on your strategies, since 1985, in relation to the following.

(Score by ticking a box from 1 to 10:   1 indicates no effect and 10 maximum effect).

	1	2	3	4	5	6	7	8	9	10
Alliances										
Product development										
Distribution										
Pricing										
Marketing innovations										
Cost cutting										
Staff numbers										
Route rationalization										
Others *(please specify)*										

(4)   To what extent have any recent improvements in efficiency been affected by the following factors?

(Score the importance of each factor from 1 to 10: 1 indicates no effect and 10 maximum effect).

	1	2	3	4	5	6	7	8	9	10
Three packages of EU air transport measures										
Competition from EU airlines										
Competition from US carriers										
Competition from Asian carriers										
Other factors *(please specify)*										

(5)   To what extent has recent financial performance (profits/losses) been affected by the following factors?

(*Score the importance of each factor from 1 to 10: 1 indicates no effect and 10 maximum effect*).

	1	2	3	4	5	6	7	8	9	10
Three packages of EU air transport measures										
Economic climate										
Competition from EU airlines										
Competition from US carriers										
Competition from Asian carriers										
Other factors (please specify)										

(6)   Are you likely to make use of the opportunity opened up by the removal of cabotage restrictions in 1997?

(*Indicate the likelihood on a scale of 1 to 10, with 1 indicating not likely at all and 10 definitely*).

	1	2	3	4	5	6	7	8	9	10
Usage of cabotage rights										

(7a)   Do you see environmental pressures making an impact on your operations?

(*Indicate the extent on a scale of 1 to 10, with 1 indicating no impact and 10 maximum impact*).

	1	2	3	4	5	6	7	8	9	10
Impact of environmental pressures										

(7b)   To what extent is this due to the three packages of EU air transport measures?

(*Indicate the extent on a scale of 1 to 10, with 1 indicating not significant and 10 highly significant*).

	1	2	3	4	5	6	7	8	9	10
Impact of EU air transport measures										

(8)   Although not specifically aimed at air transport, some EU legislation may have an impact on the air transport industry. Please indicate the importance to the industry of the following EU measures (current or proposed).

(Score each measure from 1 to 10, with 1 indicating not important and 10 very important).

	1	2	3	4	5	6	7	8	9	10
Removal of physical barriers to trade										
Indirect taxation										
Public procurement *										
Social legislation										
Corporate taxation										
Single currency										
Company law and accounting legislation										
Any other measures *(please specify)*										

*Public procurement: government policy on the procurement of goods and services for official use

B.1.5. Interview checklist – Department of Civil Aviation

Bilaterals with other EU countries: elaborate where necessary on answer to question 1 in the questionnaire.

Could you identify new airlines and any problems in relation to the development of applications for commercial air services licences, and more recently AOCs (intra-EU)?

Have you imposed any public service obligations? Have arrangements been made with airlines following tender procedures? If so, elaborate.

In your opinion, have the three EU packages encouraged airlines to adopt the following strategies? If yes, which package has had the most significant impact?

(a)   code sharing;
(b)   alliances;
(c)   franchising;
(d)   establishment of low-cost subsidiary.

Are there any markets/routes that an airline wished to enter but could not? If yes, which route or market, and what have been the barriers?

Have you received any complaint about predatory behaviour from airlines? What have been the nature of complaints? Has there been an increase in the number of such cases?

In your monitoring of air fares since the introduction of the third package, can you give examples of air fares that you considered either too high or too low, and was (or will there be) further action taken?

Has there been any problem relating to implementation and enforcement of the three packages? If so, specify regulations and directives, and the nature of problems.

Are there any EU measures which you believe have had a negative impact on airlines or the industry as a whole? If so, which measure and what has been the impact?

Have environmental issues (noise, engine emissions, etc.) restricted airlines operation? If so, explain in what way.

B.1.6. Department of Civil Aviation questionnaire

Individual completing this questionnaire

Name:..

Job title:...

Phone/fax:...

(1)   Please tick the following boxes if the bilateral agreement between Austria and each of the other EU Member States were unrestricted in terms of designation, capacity and fare on the three dates below.

Unrestricted designation: double (two airlines from each state) or
                               multiple (any number of airlines from each state)
Unrestricted capacity: no restriction on capacity or frequency share
Unrestricted fare: double disapproval (fares in effect unless both
                               governments disaprove), or no government intervention

	December 1986			December 1988			December 1990			December 1992		
	Designation	Capacity	Fares	Designation	Capacity	Fares	Designation	Capacity	Fare	Designation	Capacity	Fare
Belgium												
Denmark												
France												
Germany*												
Greece												
Ireland												
Italy												
Luxembourg												
Netherlands												
Portugal												
Spain												
UK												

* Assume West Germany until reunification

(2)   Please indicate the importance of the following barriers to entry for both new airlines and existing airlines wishing to enter any cross-border routes within the EU.

(Score each barrier by ticking a box from 1 to 10: 1 indicating no effect and 10 maximum effect).

	1	2	3	4	5	6	7	8	9	10
Lack of airport slots										
State aids										
Government protectionism										
Other government protectionism *(please specify)*										
....										
....										
Reluctance of some states to enforce three packages of EU air transport measures										
Vertical integration of charter airlines, tour operators and travel agents										
Use of override commissions										
Frequent flyer programmes										
Airline alliances										
Small airlines' lack of size and image compared to established airlines										
Any other barriers *(please specify)*										

(3)   Please list any air services (with the operators) that come under public service obligation rules.

(4a)   Do you monitor predatory behaviour in the following areas?

	Yes	No	Comments
Pricing			
Frequency			
Capacity			
FFP incentives			
Others *(please specify)*			

(4b)   Have you received any formal complaints in the following areas?

	Yes	No	Comments
Pricing			
Frequency			
Capacity			
FFP incentives			
Others *(please specify)*			

(4c)   Have you made formal complaints to the EU in any of the following areas?

	Yes	No	Comments
Pricing			
Frequency			
Capacity			
FFP incentives			
Others *(please specify)*			

(4d)   In monitoring air fares since the introduction of the third package, have there been air fares you considered either too high or too low, and was further action taken?

(5)   Do you consider the following airline strategies as anti-competitive?

	Yes	No	Comments
Mergers/alliances			
Code-sharing			
Franchising			
Others *(please specify)*			

(6a)   Do you see environmental pressures making an impact on airline operations?
(Indicate the extent on a scale of 1 to 10, with 1 indicating no impact and 10 maximum impact).

	1	2	3	4	5	6	7	8	9	10
Impact of environmental pressures										

(6b)   To what extent is this due to the three packages of EU air transport measures?
(Indicate the extent on a scale of 1 to 10, with 1 indicating not significant and 10 highly significant).

	1	2	3	4	5	6	7	8	9	10
Impact of EU air transport measures										

(7)   Although not specifically aimed at air transport, some EU legislation may have had an impact on the EU air transport industry. Please indicate the importance to the industry of the following EU measures.

(*Score each measure from 1 to 10, with 1 indicating not important and 10 very important*).

	1	2	3	4	5	6	7	8	9	10
Removal of physical barriers to trade										
Indirect taxation										
Public procurement										
Social legislation										
Corporate taxation										
Single currency										
Company law and accounting legislation										
Any other measures *(please specify)*										

B.1.7. Department of Civil Aviation questionnaire - statistical information

Could you please supply air traffic data between Austria and each of the following EU countries for **1994**.

To/From:	Passengers (000)	
	Scheduled	Charter
To Belgium		
From Belgium		
To Denmark		
From Denmark		
To France		
From France		
To Germany		
From Germany		
To Greece		
From Greece		
To Ireland		
From Ireland		
To Italy		
From Italy		
To Luxembourg		
From Luxembourg		
To Netherlands		
From Netherlands		
To Portugal		
From Portugal		
To Spain		
From Spain		
To UK		
From UK		

B.2.   Results of industry survey

Questionnaire responses – Airlines

Airline response rate

	Number of airlines	%
Total questionnaires	21	100
Total responses	18	86
No responses	3	14

Type of airline

	Number of airlines	%
National flag carriers	12	67
Regional airlines	5	27
Charter	1	6

Questionnaire responses – National civil aviation authorities

DCA responses

	Number of airlines	%
Total questionnaires	12	100
Total responses	7	58
No responses	5	42

B.2.1. Airlines

Q1   New routes introduced 1989–92 and 1992–95 due to 1990 and 1992 packages

	1989–92		1992–95	
Aer Lingus	BRS-BRU BRS-DUS	MAN-PAR	None	
Air France	BLQ-PAR BRU-PAR CWL-PAR	LIS-MAD LON-SXB AMS-CPH	BER-SXB ‡ HAM-SXB MUC-SXB	
Alitalia	BCN-TRN BLQ-BRU DUB-MAN FRA-PSA	LYS-ROM MIL-SVG MIL-VLC ROM-SCQ	BRU-DUB	
British Airways			BRU-ROM † PAR-ROM †	SKG-TRN †
British Midland	BFS-CDG EDI-CDG LHR-BRU	LHR-CDG LHR-NCE	AGP-EMA BRU-BHX BRU-EMA CPH-EDI	CPH-GLA EMA-NCE EMA-PMI FRA-LHR
Finnair			HEL-STO-BER HEL-STO-STR HEL-STO-MIL HEL-STO-MAN	HEL-STO-MUC HEL-STO-LGW HEL-DUS-BCN
Iberia	AGP-AMS † AGP-DUB † ALC-AMS † BCN-DUB	LON-OVD † LON-ZAZ † PAR-ZAZ † ROM-VLC	BRU-AGP † BRU-PMI † EDI-MAD† DUB-ALC†	DUB-PMI † FRA-ZAZ † PAR-VLL†
KLM	AMS-BER AMS-BFS AMS-BHX AMS-BOD AMS-BRE AMS-BRU AMS-CWL AMS-GCI AMS-HAJ AMS-JER	AMS-LUX AMS-MRS AMS-NUE AMS-ORK AMS-SOU AMS-STR AMS-SVQ AMS-TLS AMS-TRN AMS-VCE	AMS-BLL AMS-MLH AMS-SXB	
Lufthansa	MUC-AGP BER-ATH DUS-ATH HAM-ATH STR-ATH CGN-BCN BER-MIL	BER-ROM FRA-BIO FRA-BRI MUC-BRI MUC-CAG CGN-MAD	HAJ-BCN LIS-BCN BCN-MIL+ BCN-LIS + BRU-MIL+ CGN-ROM	DUB-MIL + HAM-ROM HAM-VCE MAN-MIL+ PAR-MIL+ MUC-OLB CGN-VCE
Maersk Air	BLL-AMS BLL-BRU BLL-LGW	BLL-ARN CPH-LGW	CPH-KRS BLL-FRA	
Ryanair	none		DUB-LGW STN-PIK	ORK-STN NOC-STN
Sabena	BRU-BRS BRU-GLA BRU-HAM	BRU-LBA BRU-VCE	BRU-HAJ BRU-EDI BRU-NCL BRU-FIR BRU-NAP BRU-BIO	BRU-ORY BRU-BLL BRU-BER BRU-BLG BRU-SXB

† Services operated by partner or franchise airlines
+ Operated under code sharing agreement
‡ Operated under Public Services Obligation Rules

Q2   Importance of the following barriers to entry

Lack of airport slots

	Number of airlines	%
Very important	15	83
Important	1	6
Not important	2	11

Use of override commissions

	Number of airlines	%
Very important	5	28
Important	2	11
Not important	11	61

State aids

	Number of airlines	%
Very important	7	39
Important	4	22
Not important	7	39

Frequent flier programmes

	Number of airlines	%
Very important	5	28
Important	8	44
Not important	5	28

Reluctance of some states to enforce three packages of EU air transport measures

	Number of airlines	%
Very important	5	28
Important	5	28
Not important	8	44

Airline alliances

	Number of airlines	%
Very important	2	11
Important	6	33
Not important	10	56

Vertical integration of charter airlines, tour operators and travel agents

	Number of airlines	%
Very important	2	11
Important	5	28
Not important	11	61

Small airlines' lack of size and image compared to established airlines

	Number of airlines	%
Very important	5	28
Important	6	33
Not important	7	39

Other barriers to entry

	Number of airlines	%
User charges	4	28
GH monopoly	1	6
Skilled staff costs	1	6

Q3   Effect of EU measures on following strategies

Alliances

	Number of airlines	%
Significant effect	5	28
Some effect	8	44
Little effect	5	28

Product development

	Number of airlines	%
Significant effect	9	50
Some effect	4	22
Little effect	5	28

Distribution

	Number of airlines	%
Significant effect	5	28
Some effect	5	28
Little effect	8	44

Pricing

	Number of airlines	%
Significant effect	11	61
Some effect	3	17
Little effect	4	22

Marketing innovations

	Number of airlines	%
Significant effect	5	28
Some effect	9	50
Little effect	3	17
No response	1	6

Cost cutting

	Number of airlines	%
Significant effect	7	39
Some effect	5	28
Little effect	6	33

Staff numbers

	Number of airlines	%
Significant effect	7	39
Some effect	5	28
Little effect	6	33

Route rationalization

	Number of airlines	%
Significant effect	11	61
Some effect	2	11
Little effect	4	22
No response	1	6

Major impact on other strategies

	Number of airlines	%
Hub strategy	1	6
Fleet composition	1	6
Restructuring	1	6
No response	15	82

Q4   Effect of following factors on recent improvements in efficiency

1987,1990 and 1993 EU packages

	Number of airlines	%
Significant effect	7	39
Some effect	7	39
Little effect	3	17
No response	1	6

Competition from EU airlines

	Number of airlines	%
Significant effect	12	66
Some effect	5	28
No response	1	6

Competition from US airlines

	Number of airlines	%
Significant effect	3	17
Some effect	6	33
Little effect	8	44
No response	1	6

Competition from Asian airlines

	Number of airlines	%
Significant effect	2	11
Some effect	3	17
Little effect	12	67
No response	1	6

Other factors

	Number of airlines	%
1991-1993 recession	3	17

Q5   Effect of following factors on recent financial performance

1987, 1990 and 1993 EU packages

	Number of airlines	%
Significant effect	5	28
Some effect	7	39
Little effect	6	33

Economic climate

	Number of airlines	%
Significant effect	14	76
Some effect	3	18
Little effect	1	6

Competition from US airlines

	Number of airlines	%
Significant effect	3	17
Some effect	6	33
Little effect	9	50

Competition from Asian airlines

	Number of airlines	%
Significant effect	1	6
Some effect	4	22
Little effect	13	72

Competition from EU airlines

	Number of airlines	%
Significant effect	10	56
Some effect	6	33
Little effect	2	11

Q6   Removal of cabotage restrictions

Likely to make use of removal of cabotage restrictions in 1997

	Number of airlines	%
Definitely	2	11
Likely	6	33
Not likely	9	50
No answer	1	6

Q7   Environmental impact

Impact of environmental measures on operations

	Number of airlines	%
Significant impact	5	28
Some impact	11	61
Little impact	2	11

Q8   Impact of various items of EU legislation on air transport

Removal of physical barriers to trade

	Number of airlines	%
Significant impact	7	39
Some impact	6	33
Little effect	1	6
No response	4	22

Corporate taxation

	Number of airlines	%
Significant impact	4	22
Some impact	9	50
Little effect	4	22
No response	1	6

Indirect taxation

	Number of airlines	%
Significant impact	5	28
Some impact	6	33
Little effect	6	33
No response	1	6

Single currency

	Number of airlines	%
Significant impact	8	44
Some impact	6	33
Little effect	4	22

Public procurement

	Number of airlines	%
Significant Impact	2	11
Some impact	6	33
Little effect	8	44
No response	2	11

Company law and accounting legislation

	Number of airlines	%
Significant impact	2	11
Some impact	7	39
Little effect	8	44
No answer	1	6

Social legislation

	Number of airlines	%
Significant impact	10	56
Some impact	5	28
Little effect	3	17

B.2.2. National civil aviation authorities

Q1   Form of unrestricted bilateral agreements between Member States prior to 1993

	December 1986			December 1988			December 1990			December 1992		
	Design'n	Capacity	Fares	Design'n	Capacity	Fares	Design'n	Capacity	Fares	Design'n	Capacity	Fares
Belgium	UK PRT	UK	UK	UK PRT	UK	UK	UK PRT GRC	UK	UK	UK PRT GRC	UK	UK
Denmark	PRT			PRT			PRT GRC			PRT GRC		
France	UK PRT GRC			UK PRT GRC			UK PRT GRC			UK PRT GRC		
Germany	UK PRT			UK PRT			UK PRT GRC			UK PRT GRC		
Greece	FRA ITA UK			FRA ITA UK			FRA ITA UK DEU BEL DNK			FRA ITA UK DEU BEL DNK		
Ireland	PRT BEL DNK FRA DEU LUX NLD PRT UK	DNK NLD		PRT BEL DNK FRA DEU LUX NLD UK	DNK UK NLD	UK	PRT BEL DNK FRA DEU LUX NLD PRT UK	DNK NLD UK	UK	PRT BEL DNK FRA DEU LUX NLD PRT UK	DNK NLD UK	UK
Italy	PRT			PRT			PRT			PRT		
Luxem'g	UK PRT	UK	UK	UK PRT	UK	UK	UK PRT	UK	UK	UK PRT	UK	UK
Nethe'ds	UK	UK	UK	UK	UK	UK	UK	UK	UK	UK	UK	UK
Portugal	BEL DNK FRA DEU IRL ITA LUX NLD UK ESP			BEL DNK FRA DEU IRL ITA LUX NLD UK ESP			BEL DNK FRA DEU IRL ITA LUX NLD UK ESP			BEL DNK FRA DEU IRL ITA LUX NLD ESP UK		
Spain	BEL DNK DEU ITA LUX NLD PRT		BEL DNK GRC DEU ITA LUX NLD PRT	BEL DNK DEU ITA LUX NLD PRT		BEL DNK GRC DEU ITA LUX NLD PRT	BEL DNK DEU ITA LUX NLD PRT		BEL DNK GRC DEU ITA LUX NLD PRT	BEL DNK DEU ITA LUX NLD PRT		BEL DNK GRC DEU ITA LUX NLD PRT
UK	BEL NLD LUX FRA DEU	BEL NLD LUX	BEL NLD LUX	BEL NLD LUX IRL FRA DEU	BEL NLD LUX IRL	BEL NLD LUX IRL	BEL NLD LUX IRL FRA DEU	BEL NLD LUX IRL	BEL NLD LUX IRL	BEL NLD LUX IRL FRA DEU	BEL NLD LUX IRL	BEL NLD LUX IRL

* Assume West Germany until reunification

Q2 Importance of following barriers to entry

Lack of airport slots

	Number of DCA	%
Very important	1	14
Important	3	43
Not important	2	29
No response	1	14

Use of override commission

	Number of DCA	%
Very important	0	0
Important	1	14
Not important	5	71
No response	1	14

State aids

	Number of DCA	%
Very important	0	0
Important	2	29
Not important	4	57
No response	1	14

Frequent flier programmes

	Number of DCA	%
Very important	1	14
Important	1	14
Not important	4	57
No response	1	14

Reluctance of some states to enforce three packages of EU measures

	Number of DCA	%
Very important	0	0
Important	0	0
Not important	6	86
No response	1	14

Airline alliances

	Number of DCA	%
Very important	1	14
Important	3	43
Not important	2	29
No response	1	14

Vertical integration of charter airlines, tour operators and travel agents

	Number of DCA	%
Very important	0	0
Important	1	14
Not important	5	71
No response	1	14

Small airlines' lack of size and image compared to established airlines

	Number of DCA	%
Very important	3	43
Important	3	43
Not important	0	0
No response	1	14

Q3   Routes designated under public service obligation status

Belgium	None			
Denmark	None			
France	PAR-AUR PAR-CCF	BER-SXB PAR-LPY	RHE-LYN LRH-PIS	PAR-MCU LIL-DIJ
Germany	None			
Greece	None			
Ireland	DUB-KIR DUB-GWY	DUB-SXL DUB-CPN	-	-
Italy	None			
Netherlands	None			
Portugal	LIS-FNC LIS-PXO OPO-FNC	OPO-PXO LIS-PDL LIS-TER	LIS-TER LIS-HOR TER-HOR	FNC-PDL FNC-PXO
Spain	None			
UK	SYY-BEB BEB-BRR	SYY-BRR	-	-

Q4   Monitoring of predatory behaviour

(a)   Monitoring of predatory behaviour in following areas

	Number of DCA		%	
	Yes	No	Yes	No
Pricing	5	2	71	29
Frequency	5	2	71	29
Capacity	5	2	71	29
FFP incentives	2	5	29	71

(b)   Complaints received in following areas

	Number of DCA		%	
	Yes	No	Yes	No
Pricing	2	4	29	57
Frequency	1	5	14	71
Capacity	1	5	14	71
FFP incentives	0	6	0	86

(c)   Are complaints referred to EU of predatory behaviour in following areas?

	Number of DCA		%	
	Yes	No	Yes	No
Pricing	5	2	71	29
Frequency	5	2	71	29
Capacity	5	2	71	29
FFP incentives	5	2	71	29

(d)   Air fares considered too high or too low

	Number of DCA	%
Too high	1	14
Too low	1	14
Neither	3	42
No response	2	28

Q5   Anti-competitive airline strategies

Do you consider the following to be anti-competitive strategies?

	Number of DCA			%		
	Yes	No	Yes/No	Yes	No	Yes/No
Code sharing	2	3	1	28	42	14
Franchising	1	5	1	14	71	14
Mergers	2	3	1	28	42	14

1 DCA did not respond
Yes/no refers to cases where DCA considered a strategy to be both anti-competitive and not anti-competitive.

Q6   Impact of environmental pressures

	Number of DCA	
	Little impact	No response
Q6 (a)	4	3
Q6 (b)	4	3

Q7   Impact of various items of EU legislation on air transport

Removal of physical barriers to trade

	Number of DCA	%
Significant impact	1	14%
Some impact	0	0%
Little impact	4	57%
No response	2	29%

Single currency

	Number of DCA	%
Significant impact	1	14
Some impact	1	14
Little impact	3	43
No response	2	29

Indirect taxation

	Number of DCA	%
Significant impact	1	14
Some impact	0	0
Little impact	4	57
No response	2	29

Company law and accounting legislation

	Number of DCA	%
Significant impact	1	14
Some impact	1	14
Little impact	3	43
No response	2	29

Public procurement

	Number of DCA	%
Significant impact	1	14
Some impact	0	0
Little impact	4	57
No response	2	29

Social legislation

	Number of DCA	%
Significant impact	1	14
Some impact	1	14
Little impact	3	43
No response	2	29

Corporate taxation

	Number of DCA	%
Significant impact	1	14
Some impact	1	14
Little impact	3	43
No response	2	29

Scheduled traffic between Member States 1994 ('000)

	B	DK	F+	D†	GR†	IRL	I	LUX	NL	P	E	UK
B		N/A	736	736	232	109	N/A	N/A	307	239	754	1,870
DK			451	588	296	71	N/A	N/A	390	0	237	1,238
F+				2,460	518	281	2,702	71	1,111	959	1,896	6,663
D†					2,414	268	2,400	N/A	1,586	570	4,017	6,090
GR†						38	600	21	507	12	98	689
IRL							81	0	134	0	59	4,959
I								N/A	932	356	1,595	2,916
LUX									44	36	129	160
NL										258	797	3 992
P											582	965
E												2,752
UK												

Charter traffic between Member States 1994 ('000)

	B	DK	F+	D†	GR†	IRL	I	LUX	NL	P	E	UK
B		N/A	74	N/A	N/A	7	N/A	N/A	0.234	102	942	10
DK			26	N/A	N/A	0.817	N/A	N/A	0.469	61	500	44
F+				96	N/A	148	473	5	14	249	1,167	596
D†					N/A	76	251	N/A	7	868	8,595	99
GR†						78	N/A	N/A	736	4	72	4,273
IRL							56	0.021	9	85	435	34
I								N/A	32	52	1,159	1,272
LUX									0.384	27	104	0.04
NL										280	1,107	21
P											97	1,657
E												14,758
UK												

† Traffic flows to Belgium, Denmark, France and Italy: 1993 data.
‡ All data include charter traffic except for UK, Ireland, Netherlands, Spain and Portugal.
+ Traffic flows to Belgium, Denmark, Italy and Luxembourg: 1993 data.

Cross-border capacity and air fares

C.0. The development of carriers per route by seats, flights and routes: intra-EU services in June 1989, 1992, 1994 and 1995

Carriers per route	1995			1994			1992			1989		
	seats	flights	route	seats	flights	routes	seats	flights	routes	seats	flights	routes
12										50,057	336	1
11										81,956	529	3
10							112,945	701	2	22,525	124	2
9				23,927	148	1	39,375	210	3	32,331	195	2
8	111,232	768	2	25,265	153	1	31,648	164	2	36,836	318	2
7	40,922	240	3	32,450	219	2	91,671	651	4	67,011	472	5
6	122,863	900	6	102,727	663	6	61,600	481	5	110,422	942	6
5	251,164	1,754	20	248,421	1,787	10	101,071	724	10	47,502	323	5
4	231,541	1,686	29	261,510	1,986	34	205,560	1,435	25	144,614	1,074	24
3	349,344	2,449	67	298,338	2,356	67	305,485	2,528	49	165,755	1,365	48
2	884,436	7,251	420	783,107	6,621	353	716,625	6,740	374	559,555	5,242	318
1	456,410	6,102	903	402,777	5,663	836	284,608	4,180	680	233,131	3,559	625

NB: Routes are directional (i.e. Madrid-Rome and Rome-Madrid are two routes). Non-EU Fifth Freedom carriers are included.

C.1. 100 busiest EU cross-border routes, June 1995

Ranking by		Between		and		Weekly			Carriers	Percentage total weekly			Cumulative percentage total weekly		
Seats	ASK	State	City	State	City	Seats	ASK million	Flights	operating	Seats	ASK	Flights	Seats	ASK	Flights
1	3	UK	LON	F	PAR	111,232	38.5	768	8	4.5%	1.7%	3.6%	4.5%	1.7%	3.6%
2	5	IRL	DUB	UK	LON	77,925	35.6	622	5	3.2%	1.5%	2.9%	7.7%	3.2%	6.6%
3	18	N	AMS	UK	LON	55,224	20.0	457	6	2.3%	0.9%	2.2%	10.0%	4.1%	8.7%
4	7	D	FRA	UK	LON	48,312	31.2	275	7	2.0%	1.3%	1.3%	12.0%	5.4%	10.0%
5	25	B	BRU	UK	LON	47,080	16.1	422	4	1.9%	0.7%	2.0%	13.9%	6.1%	12.0%
6	16	I	MIL	F	PAR	32,448	20.8	196	3	1.3%	0.9%	0.9%	15.2%	7.0%	12.9%
7	9	UK	LON	I	MIL	31,268	30.5	176	3	1.3%	1.3%	0.8%	16.5%	8.3%	13.8%
8	2	UK	LON	I	ROM	30,279	43.5	147	5	1.2%	1.9%	0.7%	17.7%	10.2%	14.4%
9	4	E	MAD	UK	LON	29,803	36.8	203	5	1.2%	1.6%	1.0%	18.9%	11.8%	15.4%
10	39	F	PAR	N	AMS	29,581	11.9	211	6	1.2%	0.5%	1.0%	20.1%	12.3%	16.4%
11	8	I	ROM	F	PAR	28,009	30.8	189	6	1.1%	1.3%	0.9%	21.3%	13.7%	17.3%
12	11	D	CPH	UK	LON	27,632	26.9	196	5	1.1%	1.2%	0.9%	22.4%	14.8%	18.2%
13	36	D	FRA	F	PAR	26,930	12.2	178	5	1.1%	0.5%	0.8%	23.5%	15.3%	19.1%
14	6	D	DUS	E	PMI	26,492	35.5	87	3	1.1%	1.5%	0.4%	24.6%	16.9%	19.5%
15	12	E	MAD	F	PAR	25,496	26.7	200	5	1.0%	1.2%	0.9%	25.6%	18.0%	20.4%
16	14	UK	LON	D	MUC	24,828	23.2	168	4	1.0%	1.0%	0.8%	26.7%	19.0%	21.2%
17	41	UK	LON	D	DUS	23,048	11.3	164	4	0.9%	0.5%	0.8%	27.6%	19.5%	22.0%
18	1	GR	ATH	UK	LON	19,524	47.0	100	3	0.8%	2.0%	0.5%	28.4%	21.6%	22.4%
19	10	P	LIS	F	PAR	18,892	27.3	136	4	0.8%	1.2%	0.6%	29.2%	22.7%	23.1%
20	19	UK	LON	F	NCE	18,710	19.4	130	4	0.8%	0.8%	0.6%	29.9%	23.6%	23.7%
21	84	F	PAR	B	BRU	18,014	4.6	151	2	0.7%	0.2%	0.7%	30.7%	23.8%	24.4%
22	55	I	MIL	D	FRA	17,134	8.7	125	2	0.7%	0.4%	0.6%	31.4%	24.2%	25.0%
23	15	E	MAD	I	ROM	16,848	22.4	91	5	0.7%	1.0%	0.4%	32.1%	25.1%	25.4%
24	71	NL	AMS	D	FRA	16,556	6.0	102	7	0.7%	0.3%	0.5%	32.7%	25.4%	25.9%
25	21	GR	ATH	I	ROM	16,194	17.3	70	2	0.7%	0.7%	0.3%	33.4%	26.1%	26.2%
26	51	UK	MAN	F	PAR	15,674	9.2	116	4	0.6%	0.4%	0.5%	34.0%	26.5%	26.8%
27	62	E	MAD	P	LIS	15,529	8.0	132	3	0.6%	0.3%	0.6%	34.7%	26.9%	27.4%
28	47	D	MUC	F	PAR	15,366	10.4	128	3	0.6%	0.5%	0.6%	35.3%	27.3%	28.0%
29	13	P	LIS	UK	LON	15,030	23.5	84	2	0.6%	1.0%	0.4%	35.9%	28.3%	28.4%
30	38	NL	AMS	I	MIL	14,602	12.1	98	2	0.6%	0.5%	0.5%	36.5%	28.9%	28.9%
31	44	D	HAM	UK	LON	14,406	10.7	110	3	0.6%	0.5%	0.5%	37.1%	29.3%	29.4%
32	88	IRL	DUB	UK	MAN	14,401	3.8	132	2	0.6%	0.2%	0.6%	37.7%	29.5%	30.0%
33	22	E	MAD	I	MIL	14,350	16.9	84	2	0.6%	0.7%	0.4%	38.3%	30.2%	30.4%
34	31	D	CPH	FR	PAR	14,146	14.2	110	3	0.6%	0.6%	0.5%	38.9%	30.8%	30.9%
35	23	B	BRU	I	ROM	14,090	16.5	106	4	0.6%	0.7%	0.5%	39.4%	31.6%	31.4%
36	20	D	FRA	E	PMI	13,938	17.4	68	5	0.6%	0.8%	0.3%	40.0%	32.3%	31.8%
37	86	UK	BHX	IRL	DUB	13,870	4.4	134	2	0.6%	0.2%	0.6%	40.6%	32.5%	32.4%
38	68	NL	AMS	UK	MAN	13,814	6.7	126	4	0.6%	0.3%	0.6%	41.1%	32.8%	33.0%
39	33	D	FRA	I	ROM	13,600	13.0	86	4	0.6%	0.6%	0.4%	41.7%	33.3%	33.4%
40	28	E	BCN	UK	LON	13,588	15.6	84	2	0.6%	0.7%	0.4%	42.2%	34.0%	33.8%
41	59	NL	AMS	DK	CPH	12,760	8.1	98	3	0.5%	0.3%	0.5%	42.8%	34.4%	34.2%
42	70	UK	BHX	F	PAR	12,700	6.2	108	2	0.5%	0.3%	0.5%	43.3%	34.6%	34.8%
43	24	B	BRU	E	MAD	12,452	16.3	82	4	0.5%	0.7%	0.4%	43.8%	35.3%	35.1%
44	56	B	BRU	I	MIL	12,012	8.4	112	3	0.5%	0.4%	0.5%	44.3%	35.7%	35.7%
45	60	D	CPH	D	FRA	11,884	8.1	94	2	0.5%	0.3%	0.4%	44.8%	36.1%	36.1%
46	52	B	BRU	DK	CPH	11,821	8.9	113	2	0.5%	0.4%	0.5%	45.3%	36.4%	36.6%
47	54	UK	LON	F	LYS	11,804	8.8	108	2	0.5%	0.4%	0.5%	45.7%	36.8%	37.2%
48	43	D	BER	UK	LON	11,656	11.0	82	2	0.5%	0.5%	0.4%	46.2%	37.3%	37.5%
49	85	D	DUS	F	PAR	11,496	4.5	86	2	0.5%	0.2%	0.4%	46.7%	37.5%	37.9%
50	50	E	BCN	FR	PAR	11,354	9.6	102	2	0.5%	0.4%	0.5%	47.1%	37.9%	38.4%

C.1. 100 busiest EU cross-border routes, June 1995 (continued)

Ranking by		Between		and		Weekly			Carriers	Percentage total weekly			Cumulative percentage total weekly		
Seats	ASK	State	City	State	City	Seats	ASK million	Flights	operating	Seats	ASK	Flights	Seats	ASK	Flights
51	58	E	BCN	I	MIL	10,958	8.1	80	3	0.4%	0.3%	0.4%	47.6%	38.3%	38.8%
52	67	D	DUS	I	MIL	10,446	7.0	74	2	0.4%	0.3%	0.3%	48.0%	38.6%	39.2%
53	96	DK	CPH	D	HAM	10,204	2.8	70	3	0.4%	0.1%	0.3%	48.4%	38.7%	39.5%
54	37	P	OPO	F	PAR	10,102	12.1	70	3	0.4%	0.5%	0.3%	48.8%	39.2%	39.8%
55	95	B	BRU	D	FRA	10,042	3.1	84	2	0.4%	0.1%	0.4%	49.3%	39.3%	40.2%
56	74	IRL	ORK	UK	LON	9,941	5.7	88	3	0.4%	0.2%	0.4%	49.7%	39.6%	40.6%
57	32	D	FRA	E	MAD	9,900	14.0	68	3	0.4%	0.6%	0.3%	50.1%	40.2%	40.9%
58	42	I	MIL	D	CPH	9,569	11.0	70	2	0.4%	0.5%	0.3%	50.5%	40.7%	41.3%
59	35	NL	AMS	I	ROM	9,548	12.4	70	2	0.4%	0.5%	0.3%	50.8%	41.2%	41.6%
60	94	UK	LON	NL	RTM	9,504	3.1	156	3	0.4%	0.1%	0.7%	51.2%	41.3%	42.3%
61	61	E	BCN	I	ROM	9,453	8.0	69	2	0.4%	0.3%	0.3%	51.6%	41.7%	42.7%
62	27	E	AGP	UK	LON	9,410	15.7	68	3	0.4%	0.7%	0.3%	52.0%	42.4%	43.0%
63	77	UK	LON	IRL	SNN	9,282	5.5	63	1	0.4%	0.2%	0.3%	52.4%	42.6%	43.3%
64	100	NL	AMS	B	BRU	9,076	1.4	110	2	0.4%	0.1%	0.5%	52.8%	42.7%	43.8%
65	34	E	MAD	NL	AMS	8,776	12.8	70	2	0.4%	0.6%	0.3%	53.1%	43.2%	44.1%
66	63	D	BER	F	PAR	8,742	7.4	74	2	0.4%	0.3%	0.3%	53.5%	43.5%	44.5%
67	82	B	BRU	UK	MAN	8,726	4.7	76	2	0.4%	0.2%	0.4%	53.8%	43.7%	44.8%
68	66	F	PAR	I	VCE	8,540	7.1	56	2	0.3%	0.3%	0.3%	54.2%	44.0%	45.1%
69	73	D	HAJ	UK	LON	8,460	5.9	56	2	0.3%	0.3%	0.3%	54.5%	44.3%	45.4%
70	48	E	BCN	NL	AMS	8,315	10.3	69	2	0.3%	0.4%	0.3%	54.9%	44.8%	45.7%
71	53	E	BCN	D	FRA	8,106	8.8	56	2	0.3%	0.4%	0.3%	55.2%	45.1%	46.0%
72	29	D	FRA	P	LIS	8,036	15.1	54	2	0.3%	0.7%	0.3%	55.5%	45.8%	46.2%
73	83	F	PAR	I	TRN	8,012	4.6	62	2	0.3%	0.2%	0.3%	55.9%	46.0%	46.5%
74	79	NL	AMS	D	MUC	8,008	5.4	76	2	0.3%	0.2%	0.4%	56.2%	46.2%	46.9%
75	30	UK	ATH	D	FRA	8,006	14.5	52	4	0.3%	0.6%	0.2%	56.5%	46.8%	47.1%
76	92	NL	AMS	UK	BHX	7,994	3.5	102	2	0.3%	0.2%	0.5%	56.8%	47.0%	47.6%
77	76	D	HAM	F	PAR	7,788	5.7	76	2	0.3%	0.2%	0.4%	57.2%	47.2%	48.0%
78	99	UK	GLA	IRL	DUB	7,775	2.1	80	2	0.3%	0.1%	0.4%	57.5%	47.3%	48.3%
79	72	F	PAR	IRL	DUB	7,673	6.0	59	2	0.3%	0.3%	0.3%	57.8%	47.6%	48.6%
80	91	F	PAR	D	STR	7,572	3.7	66	2	0.3%	0.2%	0.3%	58.1%	47.8%	48.9%
81	26	UK	ATH	F	PAR	7,560	15.8	28	2	0.3%	0.7%	0.1%	58.4%	48.4%	49.1%
82	57	E	BCN	B	BRU	7,533	8.1	65	3	0.3%	0.4%	0.3%	58.7%	48.8%	49.4%
83	80	D	DUS	UK	MAN	7,344	4.8	60	2	0.3%	0.2%	0.3%	59.0%	49.0%	49.6%
84	90	NL	AMS	D	STR	7,292	3.7	66	2	0.3%	0.2%	0.3%	59.3%	49.2%	50.0%
85	46	UK	ATH	I	MIL	7,173	10.5	30	2	0.3%	0.5%	0.1%	59.6%	49.6%	50.1%
86	97	NL	AMS	D	HAM	7,148	2.7	66	1	0.3%	0.1%	0.3%	59.9%	49.7%	50.4%
87	49	D	DUS	E	IBZ	7,026	10.1	22	2	0.3%	0.4%	0.1%	60.2%	50.2%	50.5%
88	75	I	BLQ	F	PAR	6,860	5.7	52	2	0.3%	0.2%	0.2%	60.5%	50.4%	50.8%
89	40	P	LIS	BE	BRU	6,616	11.4	59	3	0.3%	0.5%	0.3%	60.7%	50.9%	51.0%
90	64	UK	LON	I	VCE	6,456	7.3	42	2	0.3%	0.3%	0.2%	61.0%	51.2%	51.2%
91	93	UK	LON	D	CGN	6,426	3.4	39	2	0.3%	0.1%	0.2%	61.3%	51.4%	51.4%
92	65	E	PMI	D	STR	6,372	7.3	28	2	0.3%	0.3%	0.1%	61.5%	51.7%	51.5%
93	69	E	BCN	PT	LIS	6,311	6.3	53	3	0.3%	0.3%	0.3%	61.8%	52.0%	51.8%
94	17	D	DUS	E	LPA	6,310	20.1	18	2	0.3%	0.9%	0.1%	62.0%	52.8%	51.9%
95	98	I	MIL	D	MUC	6,230	2.2	76	2	0.3%	0.1%	0.4%	62.3%	52.9%	52.2%
96	45	D	DUS	UK	SKG	6,120	10.6	30	5	0.3%	0.5%	0.1%	62.5%	53.4%	52.4%
97	81	UK	BHX	D	FRA	6,114	4.7	50	2	0.2%	0.2%	0.2%	62.8%	53.6%	52.6%
98	89	D	NUE	F	PAR	6,104	3.8	62	2	0.2%	0.2%	0.3%	63.0%	53.7%	52.9%
99	78	UK	LON	I	TRN	5,966	5.5	40	2	0.2%	0.2%	0.2%	63.3%	54.0%	53.1%
100	87	UK	LON	D	STR	5,853	4.4	43	2	0.2%	0.2%	0.2%	63.5%	54.2%	53.3%

	Weekly		
	Seats	ASK million	Flights
Total EU interstate services:	2,447,496	2,312	21,200

C.2. Capacity index for routes from Spain representing 50% of total capacity

From city	state	To city	Carrier shares of capacity June 1995 (%)					Index (%)
MAD	UK	LON	AR 5%	BA 42%	FV 12%	IB 36%	UK 5%	33%
MAD	FR	PAR	AF 31%	AR 12%	IB 42%	IT 10%	RN 5%	30%
PMI	D	DUS	DE 21%	LT 77%	YP 2%			64%
MAD	I	ROM	AR 5%	AZ 37%	IB 41%	KU 3%	TG 14%	33%
MAD	P	LIS	IB 42%	NI 21%	TP 36%			36%
MAD	I	MIL	AZ 45%	IB 55%				50%
PMI	D	FRA	DE 49%	FV 14%	LH 14%	LT 14%	YP 9%	30%
BCN	UK	LON	BA 57%	IB 43%				51%
MAD	B	BRU	BQ 16%	IB 45%	MU 5%	SN 33%		35%
BCN	F	PAR	AF 58%	IB 42%				51%
BCN	I	MIL	AZ 54%	IB 40%	LH 6%			45%
MAD	D	FRA	IB 44%	LA 12%	LH 44%			40%
BCN	I	ROM	AZ 68%	IB 32%				57%
AGP	UK	LON	BA 41%	FV 42%	ZB 16%			38%
MAD	NL	AMS	IB 38%	KL 62%				53%
BCN	NL	AMS	IB 36%	KL 64%				54%
BCN	D	FRA	IB 54%	LH 46%				50%
BCN	B	BRU	BQ 26%	IB 37%	SN 37%			34%
IBZ	D	DUS	DE 22%	LT 78%				66%
BCN	P	LIS	IB 24%	LH 27%	TP 49%			37%
PMI	D	STR	DE 84%	LT 16%				73%
LPA	D	DUS	DE 37%	LT 63%				54%

From city	state	To city	Carrier shares of capacity June 1992 (%)					Index (%)
MAD	UK	LON	BA 46%	DA 11%	FV 9%	IB 34%		35%
MAD	F	PAR	AF 45%	AR 3%	AV 7%	IB 45%		41%
BCN	F	PAR	AF 42%	IB 32%	IW 16%	RH 10%		32%
BCN	UK	LON	BA 42%	DA 7%	FV 12%	IB 40%		35%
MAD	I	ROM	AM 6%	AR 10%	AZ 30%	IB 39%	TG 15%	28%
MAD	D	FRA	AV 7%	IB 42%	LA 8%	LH 44%		38%
AGP	UK	LON	BA 38%	BD 11%	FV 38%	ZB 12%		32%
MAD	NL	AMS	IB 43%	JL 7%	KL 50%			44%
MAD	P	LIS	AF 15%	IB 57%	TP 27%			43%
MAD	I	MIL	AZ 51%	IB 49%				50%
BCN	D	FRA	IB 45%	LH 43%	RH 12%			40%
BCN	NL	AMS	IB 45%	KL 55%				51%

From city	state	To city	Carrier shares of capacity June 1989 (%)					Index (%)
MAD	FR	PAR	AF 42%	AM 8%	AR 8%	AV 8%	IB 35%	31%
MAD	GB	LON	BA 40%	DA 6%	IB 54%			45%
MAD	IT	ROM	AR 7%	AZ 32%	IB 47%	TG 14%		35%
BCN	GB	LON	BA 43%	IB 57%				51%
MAD	PT	LIS	AC 20%	IB 44%	TP 36%			36%
BCN	FR	PAR	AF 47%	IB 53%				50%
MAD	IT	MIL	AZ 45%	IB 55%				51%
AGP	GB	LON	BA 52%	IB 40%	ZB 8%			43%
BCN	IT	MIL	AZ 40%	IB 60%				52%
MAD	DE	FRA	AV 11%	IB 57%	LH 32%			44%
BCN	PT	LIS	TP 17%	TW 83%				72%
MAD	BE	BRU	IB 56%	SN 44%				51%

C.3. Cross-border air fares

C.3.1. Sample size for air fare analysis

Origin State	EU cross-border routes	Control group routes
Austria	4	5
Belgium	4	1
Denmark	3	1
France	5	3
Germany	15	2
Greece	3	-
Ireland	1	-
Italy	7	-
Luxembourg	2	-
Netherlands	4	1
Norway	-	1
Portugal	3	-
Spain	8	-
Switzerland	8	9
United Kingdom	5	3
TOTAL	**72**	**26**

Appendix C - Cross-border capacity and air fares

C.3.2. Cross-border air fare regression results

In order to identify the extent to which fare is influenced by variation in stage length, linear regression was performed on the sample of intra-EU city-pair fare data. The process involved regressing fare against stage length for three different fare types at four time intervals set between 1986 and 1995. In the regression model below for each city-pair ij, Y and SL represent fare and stage length (in km) whilst α functions as a model constant and β represents the stage length (SL) coefficient. As fare generally increases with stage length, the parameter β would be expected to have a positive sign:

$$Y_{ij} = \alpha + \beta\, SL_{ij}$$

The statistical significance of such a relationship is measured by the t-statistics and the coefficient of determination r^2. The value of the β t-statistic and r^2 should be above 1.96 and 0.60 respectively to guarantee significance. Regression equations covering each individual fare type for each time interval are outlined below. Y, YAVG and YLOW refer to one-way fully flexible economy fare, average economy fare and lowest economy fare respectively. The t-statistics are expressed in italics below their respective parameters and n represents the sample size.

$Y1986_{ij} = 121 + 0.19\, SL_{ij}$ $r^2 = 0.70, n = 57$
11.54

$Y1989_{ij} = 107 + 0.20\, SL_{ij}$ $r^2 = 0.80, n = 57$
15.42

$Y1992_{ij} = 126 + 0.19\, SL_{ij}$ $r^2 = 0.77, n = 57$
15.87

$Y1995_{ij} = 144 + 0.16\, SL_{ij}$ $r^2 = 0.56, n = 57$
8.63

$YAVG\,1986_{ij} = 113 + 0.12\, SL_{ij}$ $r^2 = 0.42, n = 63$
6.80

$YAVG\,1989_{ij} = 103 + 0.13\, SL_{ij}$ $r^2 = 0.53, n = 63$
8.44

$YAVG\,1992_{ij} = 98 + 0.14\, SL_{ij}$ $r^2 = 0.61, n = 63$
9.93

$YAVG\,1995_{ij} = 129 + 0.07\, SL_{ij}$ $r^2 = 0.26, n = 63$
4.32

$YLOW\,1986_{ij} = 97 + 0.07\, SL_{ij}$ $r^2 = 0.14, n = 61$
3.30

$YLOW\,1989_{ij} = 111 + 0.09\, SL_{ij}$ $r^2 = 0.19, n = 61$
3.89

$YLOW\,1992_{ij} = 68 + 0.11\, SL_{ij}$ $r^2 = 0.33, n = 61$
3.61

$YLOW\,1995_{ij} = 101 + 0.04\, SL_{ij}$ $r^2 = 0.14, n = 61$
3.29

C.3.3. Fully flexible fares against stage length, 1986–95

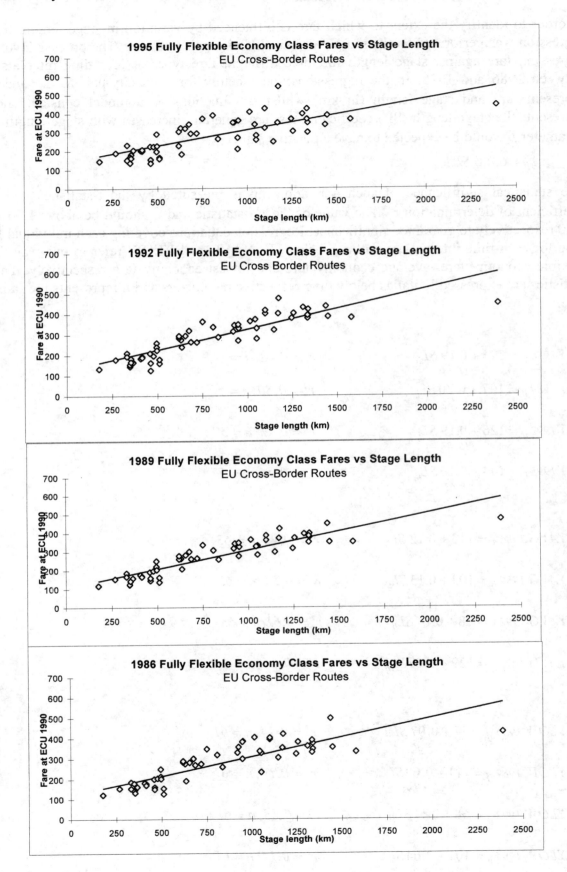

C.3.4. Lowest economy fares against stage length, 1986–95

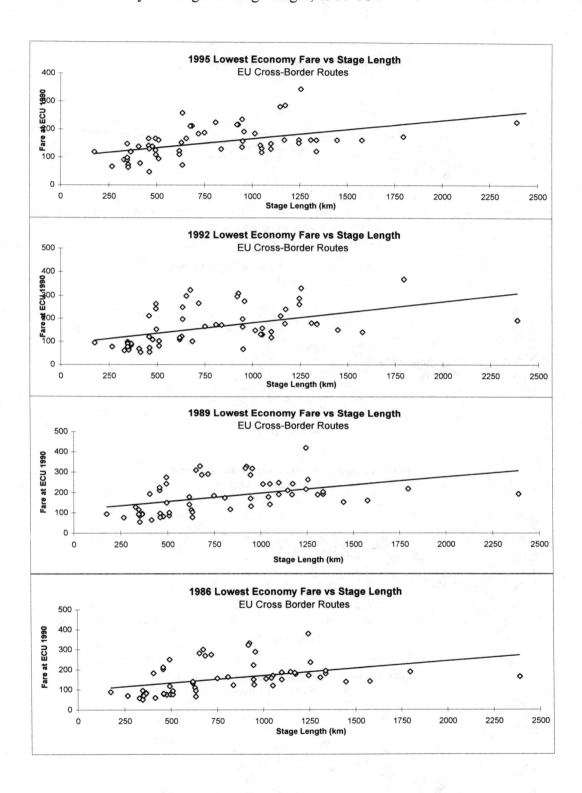

C.3.5. Average economy fares against stage length, 1986–95

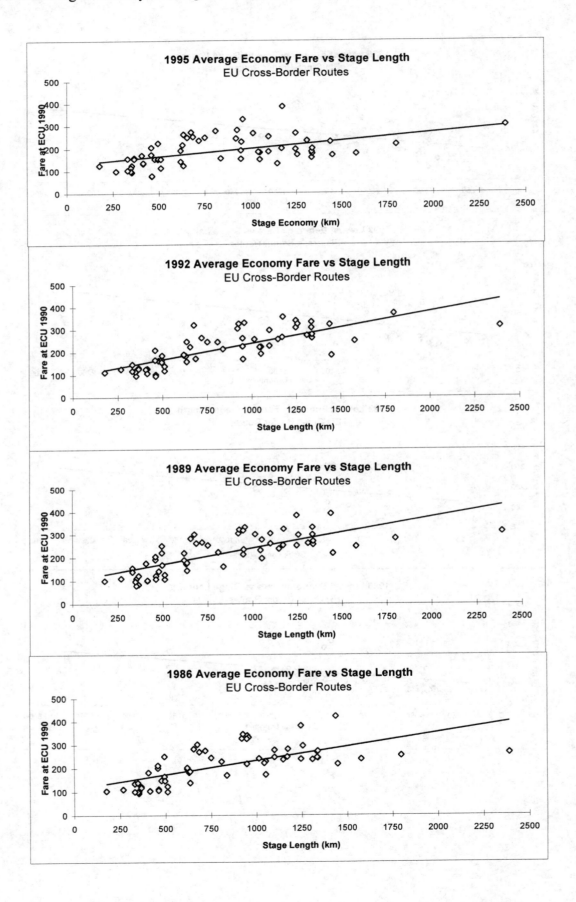

C.4. Fully flexible fares against stage length by EU state, 1995

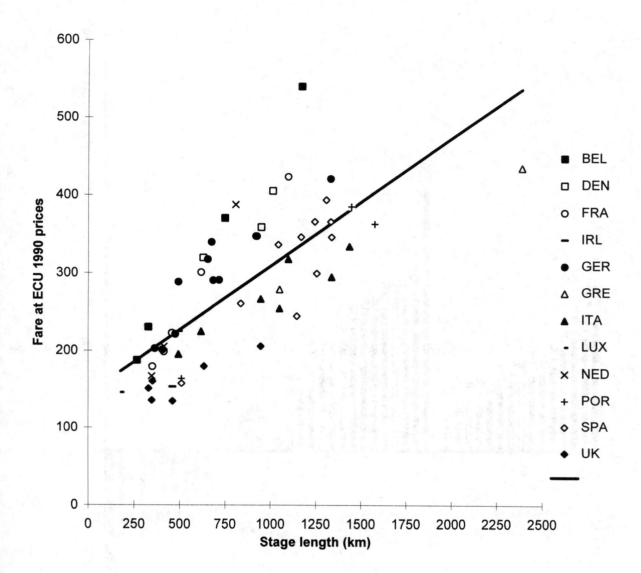

C.5. Average annual fully flexible economy fare trends, 1986–89, 1989–92 and 1992–95

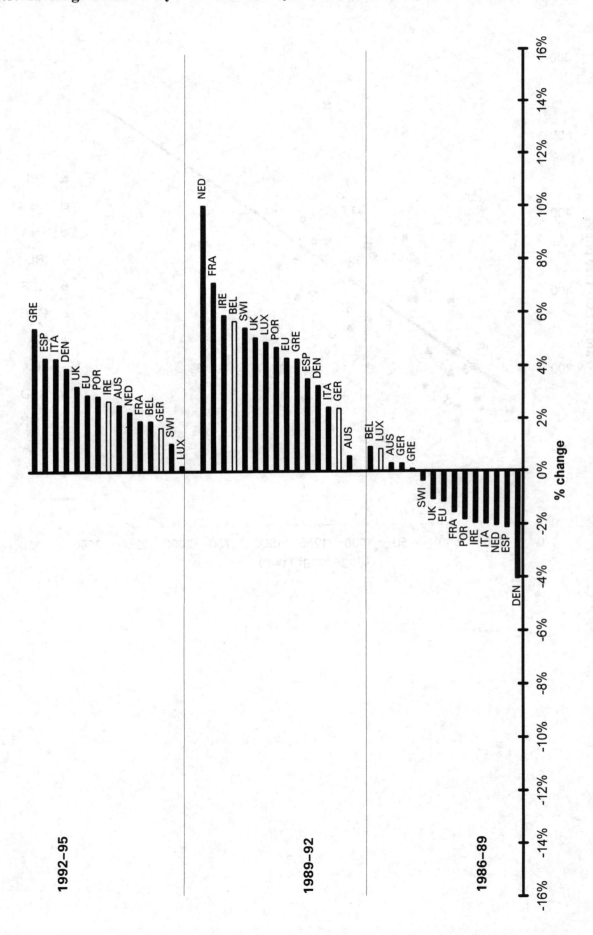

C.6. Average economy fare trends, 1986–89, 1989–92 and 1992-95

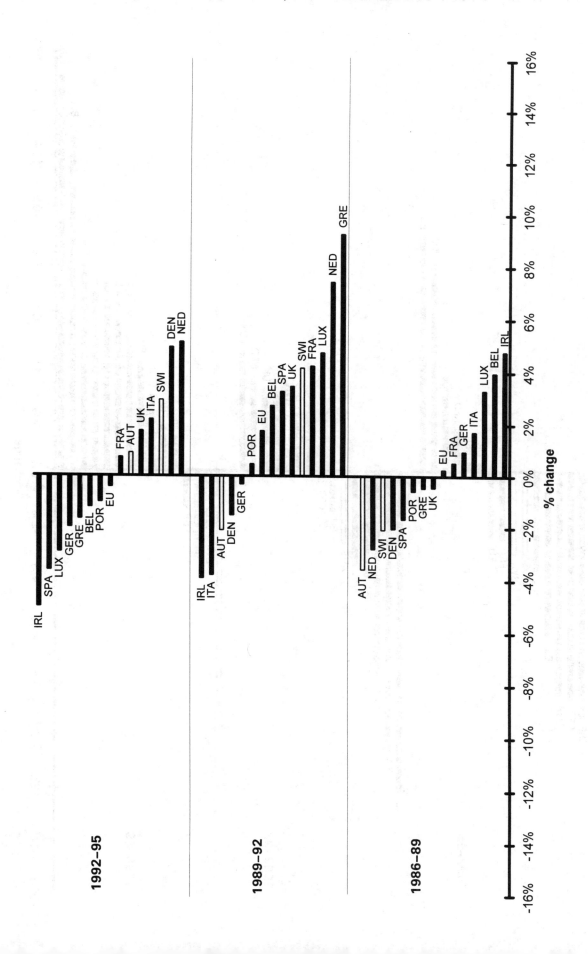

C.7. Average annual lowest economy fare trends, 1986–89, 1989–92 and 1992–95

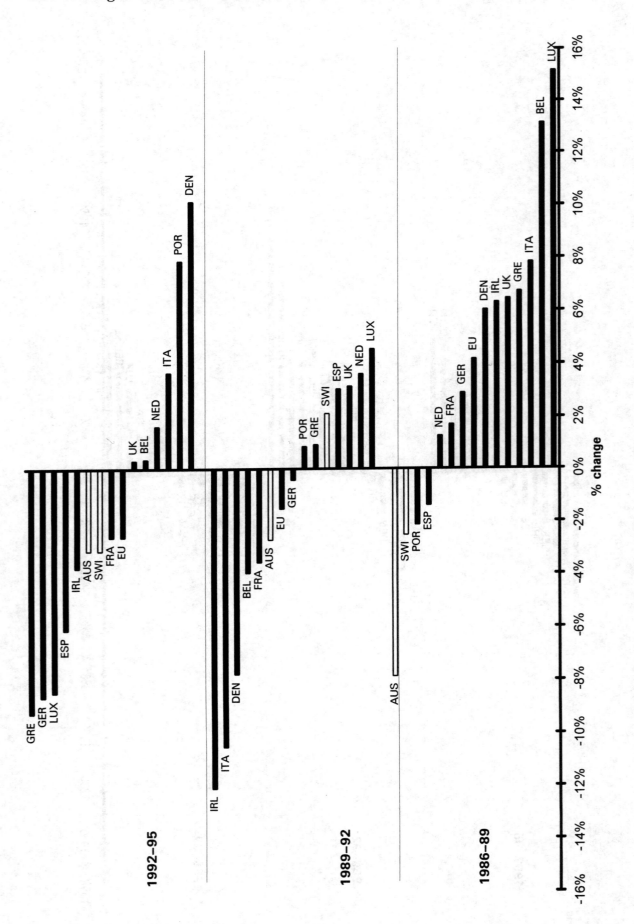

C.8. Average annual fare trends, by fare type, 1986–95

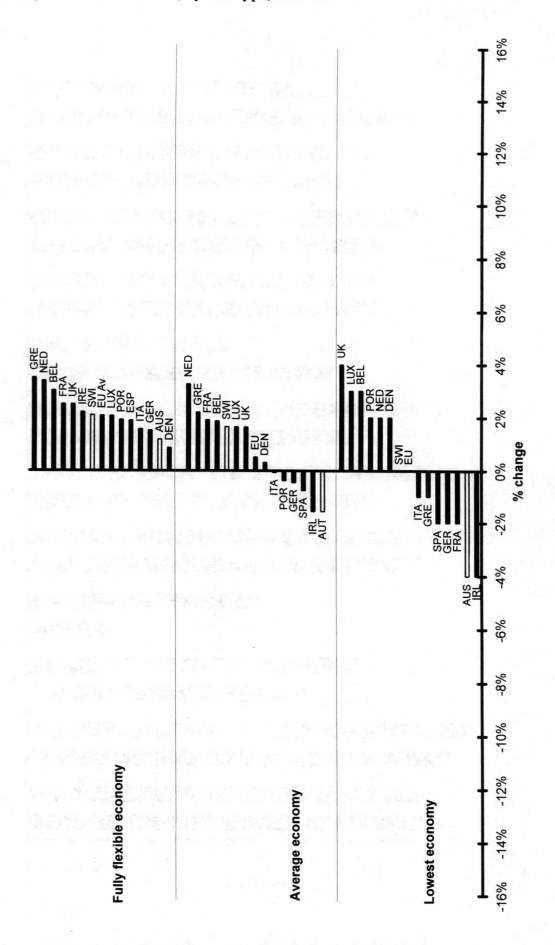

C.9. Lowest economy class fare as % discount from fully flexible economy fares, 1986, 1989, 1992, 1995

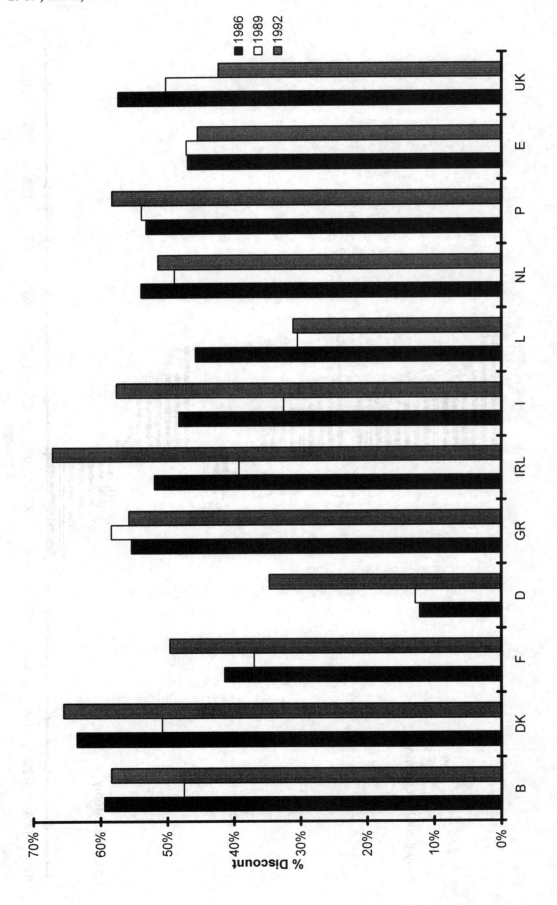

C.10. Return fares against stage length for selected cities, 1995 (from CAA CAP 654)

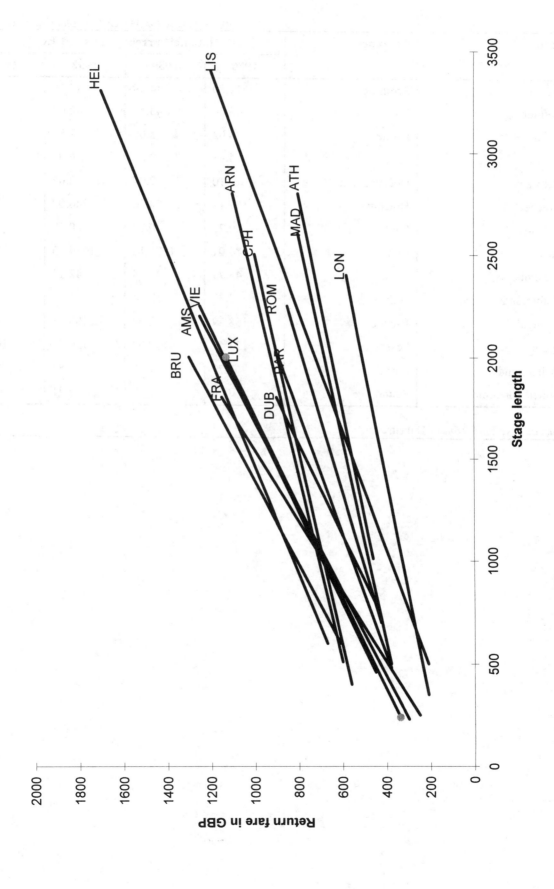

C.11. Exchange rate parities (ECU conversion rate), 1986–95

Average rate for March to September in each year

State	Currency	National currency units to 1 ECU			
		1986	1989	1992	1995
Austria	Schilling	14.80	14.59	14.36	12.98
Belgium	Franc	43.60	43.47	42.09	38.32
Denmark	Kroner	8.02	8.07	7.89	7.22
France	Franc	6.93	7.02	6.90	6.45
Germany	Deutschmark	2.10	2.07	2.04	1.84
Greece	Drachma	157.17	178.16	246.08	299.26
Ireland	Punt	0.75	0.78	0.77	0.81
Italy	Lira	1486.01	1506.18	1544.75	2166.47
Luxembourg	Franc	43.75	43.58	42.12	37.94
Netherlands	Guilder	2.37	2.34	2.30	2.06
Portugal	Escudos	158.89	172.69	188.53	194.06
Spain	Peseta	133.47	130.00	129.45	162.07
Switzerland	Franc	1.77	1.80	1.84	1.51
United Kingdom	Pound	0.65	0.67	0.71	0.83

Source: Financial Times / Datastream.

APPENDIX D

Domestic capacity and air fares

D.1. The three densest domestic routes, 10 EU states, June 1995

State	Between	and	Weekly			A/L	% National domestic			% national share of EU domestic		
			Seats	ASK million	Flights		Seats	ASK	Flights	Seats	ASK	Flights
Portugal	LIS	OPO	19,498	5.40	162	3	31%	14%	24%			
	LIS	FNC	15,176	14.63	163	1	24%	38%	18%			
	LIS	FAO	6,772	1.48	57	2	11%	40%	8%			
	PORTUGAL TOTAL		62,745	38.02	684					2%	3%	3%
Netherlands	AMS	MST	1,980	0.33	66	1	36%	48%	24%			
	AMS	EIN	1,376	0.14	35	1	25%	20%	13%			
	RTM	EIN	855	0.07	45	1	16%	10%	17%			
	NETHERLANDS TOTAL		5,461	0.70	272					0%	0%	100%
Italy	ROM	MIL	12,317	2.40	63	1	15%	16%	5%			
	ROM	PMO	5,597	1.30	63	1	11%	11%	5%			
	ROM	CTA	1,434	0.37	26	1	8%	12%	5%			
	ITALY TOTAL									5%	3%	6%
Ireland	DUB	SNN	12,317	2.40	63	1	56%	54%	21%			
	DUB	ORK	5,597	1.30	63	1	25%	29%	21%			
	DUB	KIR	1,434	0.37	26	1	6%	8%	9%			
	IRELAND TOTAL		22,160	4.43	298					1%	0%	1%
Greece	ATH	SKG	18,412	5.49	82	1	15%	16%	5%			
	ATH	HER	12,718	3.97	80	1	11%	11%	5%			
	ATH	RHO	9,666	4.04	74	1	8%	12%	5%			
	GREECE TOTAL		120,820	34.78	1,554					5%	3%	6%
UK	LON	EDI	51,937	27.79	371	3	12%	16%	6%			
	LON	GLA	46,871	26.17	348	3	10%	15%	5%			
	LON	BFS	46,140	24.11	394	5	10%	14%	6%			
	UK TOTAL		448,975	176.89	6,505					17%	14%	25%
France	PAR	MRS	76,526	48.26	418	4	12%	14%	7%			
	PAR	NCE	70,671	47.84	405	4	11%	14%	7%			
	PAR	TLS	60,448	34.98	336	3	9%	10%	6%			
	FRANCE TOTAL		651,224	345.42	5,827					25%	28%	22%
Spain	MAD	BCN	63,897	30.86	459	3	14%	12%	14%			
	BCN	PMI	27,961	5.62	197	3	6%	2%	6%			
	MAD	PMI	19,522	10.66	128	3	4%	4%	4%			
	SPAIN TOTAL		450,372	260.09	3,227					17%	21%	13%
Denmark	CPH	AAR	19,222	3.21	132	1	28%	24%	17%			
	CPH	AAL	14,360	3.42	98	1	21%	25%	13%			
	CPH	KRP	11,914	2.76	86	1	17%	20%	11%			
	DENMARK TOTAL		68,292	13.63	756					3%	1%	3%
Germany	BER	FRA	29,102	12.54	122	1	7%	8%	3%			
	FRA	HAM	27,045	11.14	126	1	7%	7%	3%			
	BER	MUC	25,587	12.92	215	3	6%	8%	5%			
	GERMANY TOTAL		400,123	159.19	4,225					15%	13%	16%

TOTAL EU SERVICES			2,610,827	1,225.94	26,195

D.2. Entry and capacity on French domestic trunk routes

Route	Pre-entry Carriers	Seats per weekday	Entry date	Carriers	Seats per weekday	Entry date	Carriers	Seats per weekday	Entry date	Carriers	Seats per weekday
PAR-TLS	IT/AF	908	1/1995	IT/AF	908	4/1995	IT/AF	908	10/1995	IT/AF	908
	IT	3690		IT	3518		IT	3011		IT	2967
		4598		VD	676		VD	1014		VD/RN	2267
					5102		RN	520		IJ	612
								5453			**6754**
PAR-NCE	AF	2414	4/1991	AF	1188	1/1996	AF	853			
	IT	2856		IT	3574		IT	2580			
		5272		IW	620		IW	1860			
					5382		VD	845			
								6138			
PAR-MRS	IT/AF	939	1/1995	IT/AF	939	3/1995	IT/AF	939			
	IT	4416		IT	4122		IT	3349			
		5355		IW	1085		IW	1395			
					6146		IJ	612			
								6295			
PAR-MPL	IT/AF	390	10/1995	IT/AF	390	1/1996	IT/.AF	390			
	IT	1488		IT	1488		IT	1660			
		1878		IW	620		IW	620			
					2498		VD	390			
								3060			
PAR-BOD	IT/AF	594	5/1995	IT/AF	594						
	IT	2552		IT	2552						
		3146		VD	1014						
					4160						
PAR-SXB	IT/AF	422	9/1995	IT/AF	422						
	IT	2454		IT	2380						
		2876		VD	676						
					3478						
PAR-TLN	IT	1032	2/1996	IT	1174						
		1032		IW	1639						
					2813						
PAR-PGF	IT	688	2/1996	IT	688						
		688		IW	998						
PAR-PUF	IT	830	2/1996	IT	723						
		830		IW	1033						
PAR-LYS	AF	409									
	IT	1345									
		1754									
PAR-BIQ	IT	860									
PAR-BES	IT	788									
PAR-FNI	IT	797									
PAR-EAP	IT	1232									
PAR-NTE	IT	730									
PAR-AJA	IT	390									
PAR-GNB	IT	797									

Airline and airport three letter codes

Airlines		Airports	
AF	Air France	PAR	Paris
IJ	TAT	TLS	Toulouse
IT	Air Inter	NCE	Nice
IW	AOM	MRS	Marseilles
RN	Euralair	MPL	Montpellier
VD	Air Liberté	BOD	Bordeaux
		SXB	Strasbourg
		TLN	Toulon
		PGF	Perpignan
		PUF	Pau
		LYS	Lyon
		BIQ	Biarritz
		BES	Brest
		FNI	Nimes
		EAP	Mulhouse
		NTE	Nantes
		AJA	Ajaccio
		GNB	Grenoble

D.3. Air fares on the Paris-Toulouse route

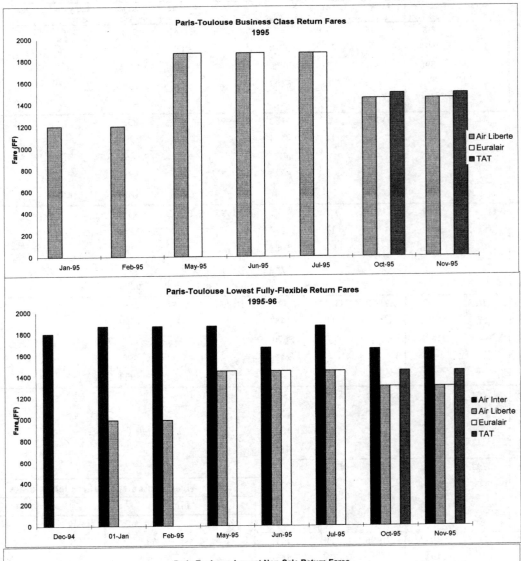

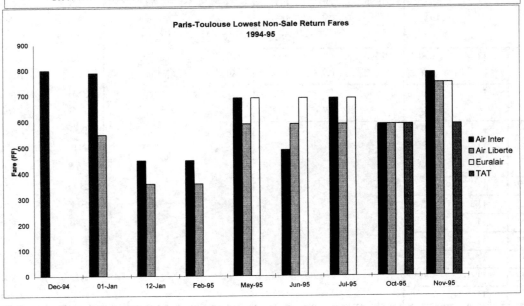

D.4. Comparison of domestic fares in France, Germany, Italy, Spain and the UK, 1989, 1992 and 1995

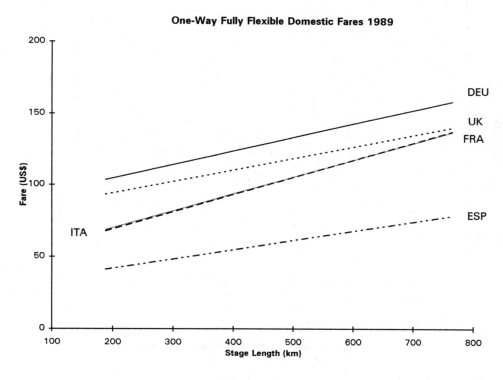

One-Way Fully Flexible Domestic Fares 1989

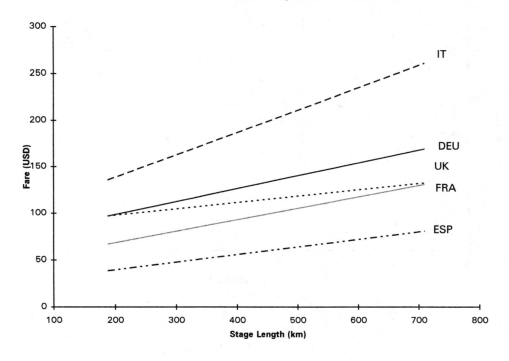

Lowest Return Economy Domestic Fares 1989

One-Way Fully Flexible Domestic Fares 1992

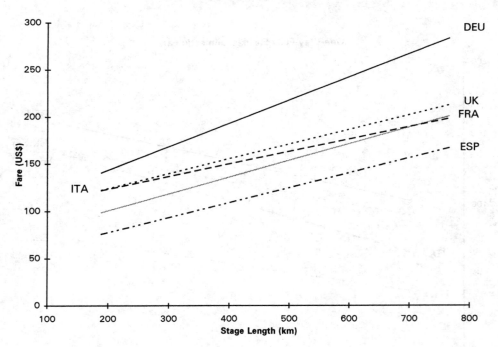

Lowest Return Economy Domestic Fares 1992

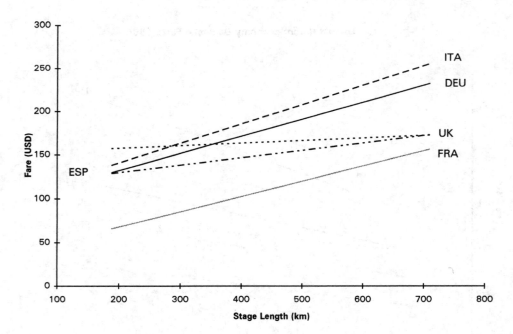

One-Way Fully Flexible Domestic Fares 1995

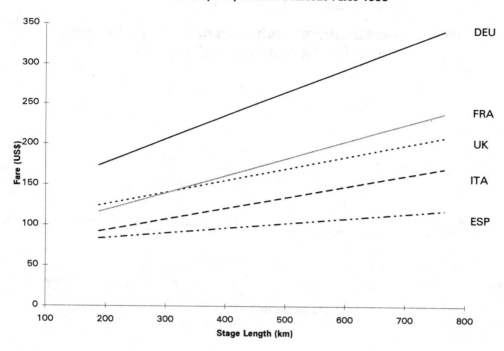

Lowest Return Economy Domestic Fares 1995

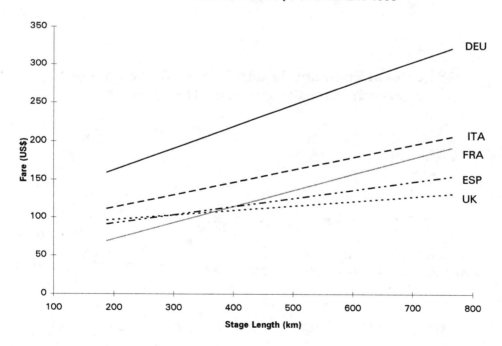

D.5. Comparison of French domestic and intra-EU air fares

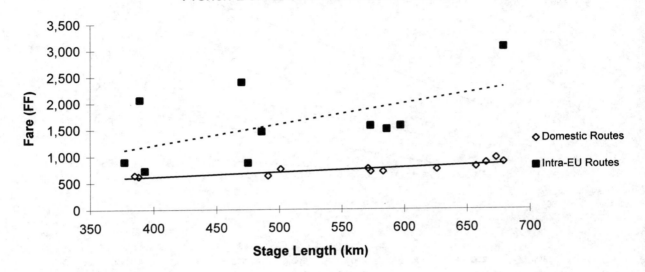

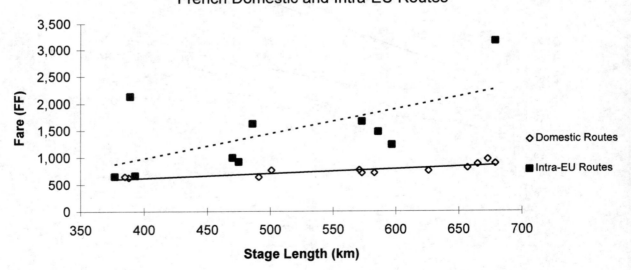

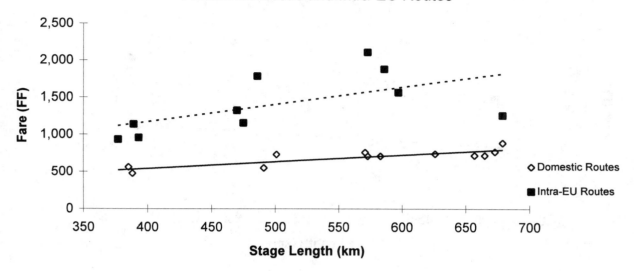

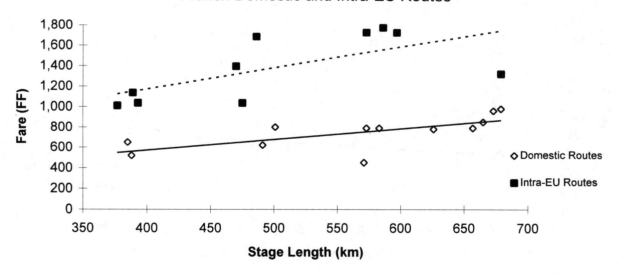

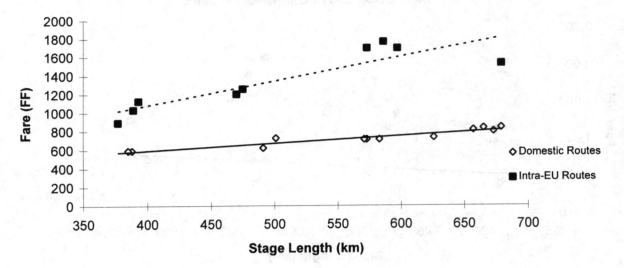

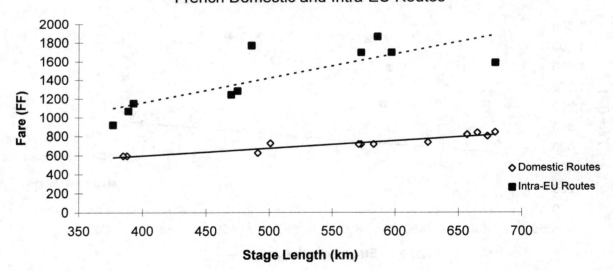

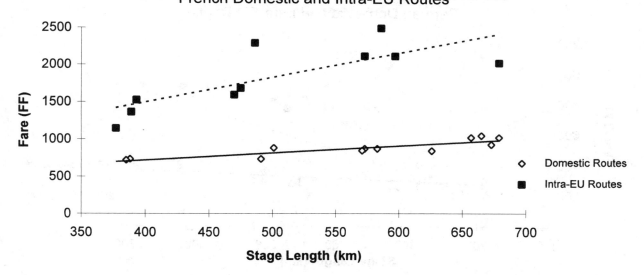

1992 One Way Fully Flexible Economy Fare vs Stage Length
French Domestic and Intra-EU Routes

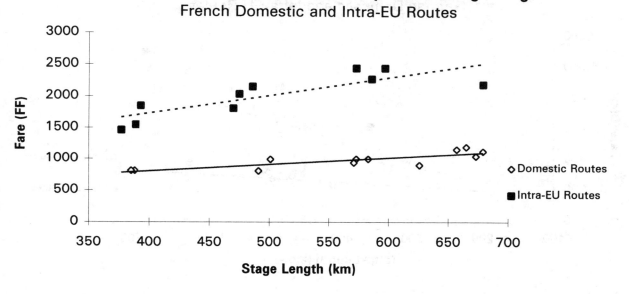

1995 One Way Fully Flexible Economy Fare vs Stage Length
French Domestic and Intra-EU Routes

D.6. Comparison of German domestic and intra-EU air fares

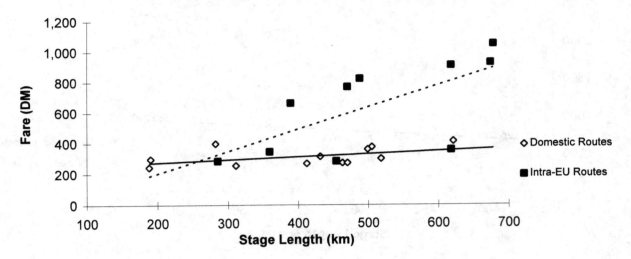

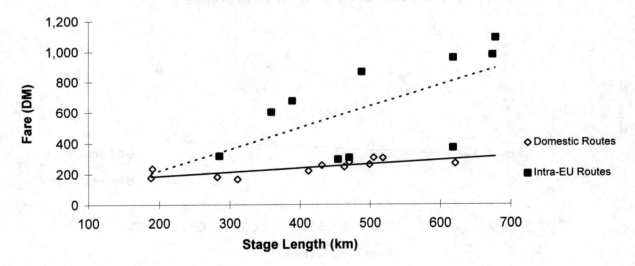

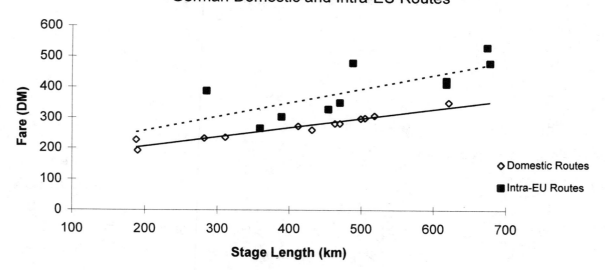

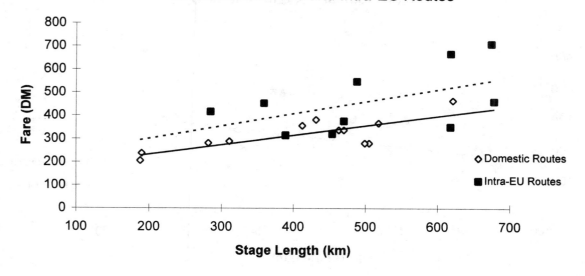

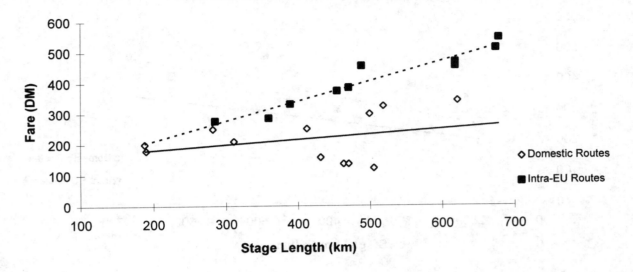

1986 One-Way Fully Flexible Economy Fare vs Stage Length
German Domestic and Intra-EU Routes

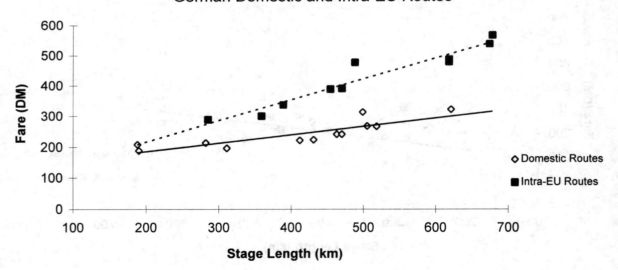

1989 One-Way Fully Flexible Economy Fare vs Stage Length
German Domestic and Intra-EU Routes

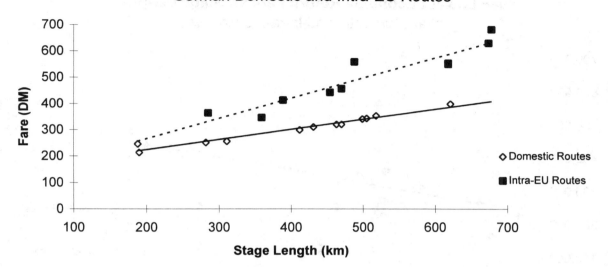

1992 One-Way Fully Flexible Economy Fare vs Stage Length
German Domestic and Intra-EU Routes

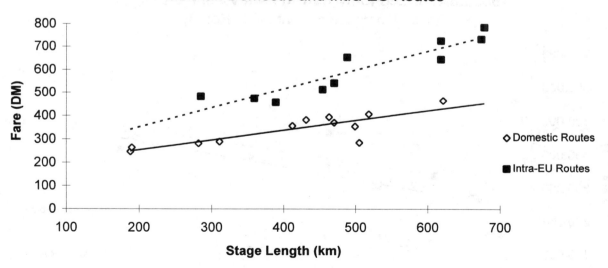

1995 One-Way Fully Flexible Economy Fare vs Stage Length
German Domestic and Intra-EU Routes

D.7. Comparison of Italian domestic and intra-EU air fares

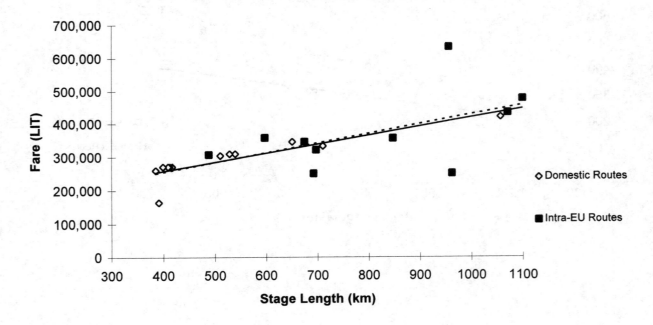

1986 Lowest Economy Return Fare vs Stage Length
Italian Domestic and Intra-EU Routes

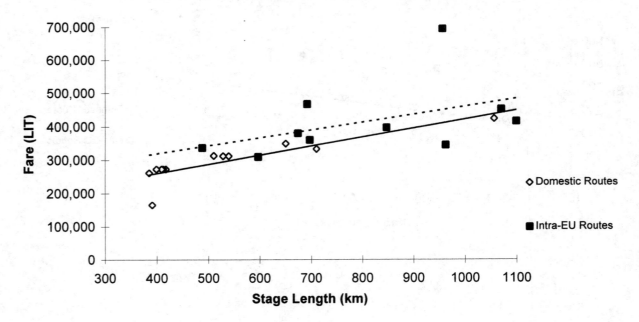

1989 Lowest Economy Return Fare vs Stage Length
Italian Domestic and Intra-EU Routes

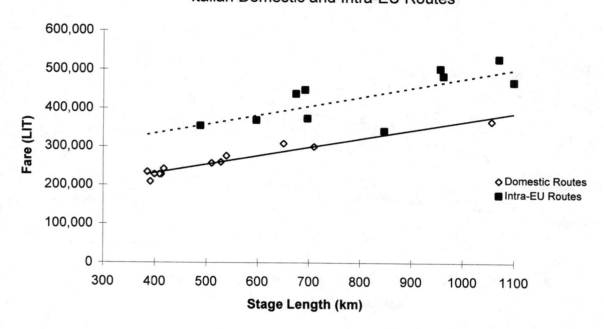

1992 Lowest Economy Return Fare vs Stage Length
Italian Domestic and Intra-EU Routes

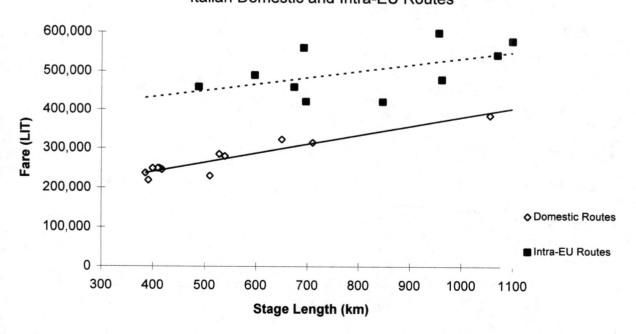

1995 Lowest Economy Return Fare vs Stage Length
Italian Domestic and Intra-EU Routes

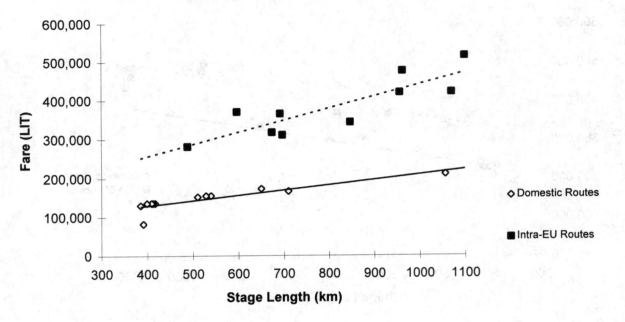

1986 One-Way Fully Flexible Economy Fare vs Stage Length
Italian Domestic and Intra-EU Routes

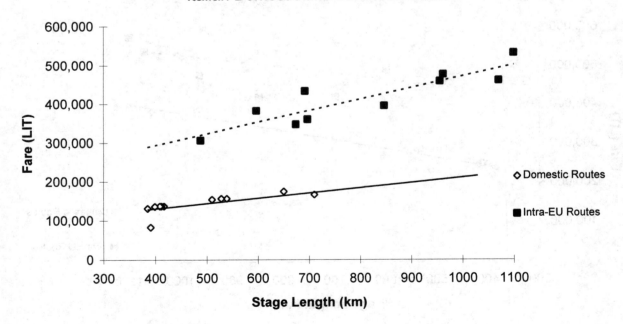

1989 One-Way Fully Flexible Economy Fare vs Stage Length
Italian Domestic and Intra-EU Routes

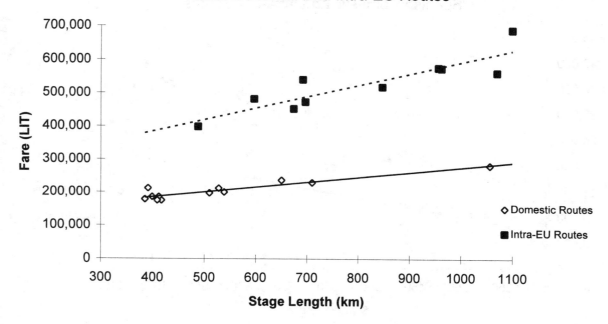

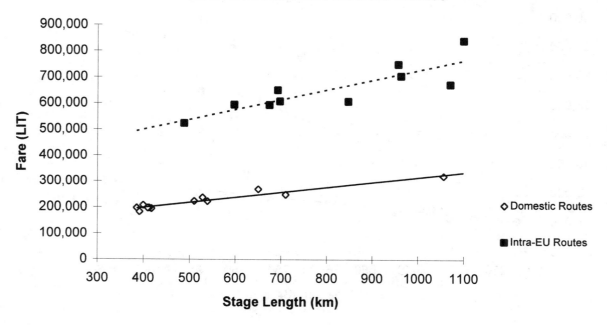

D.8. Comparison of Spanish domestic and intra-EU air fares

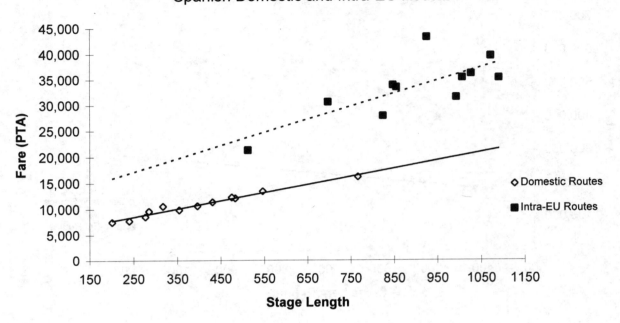

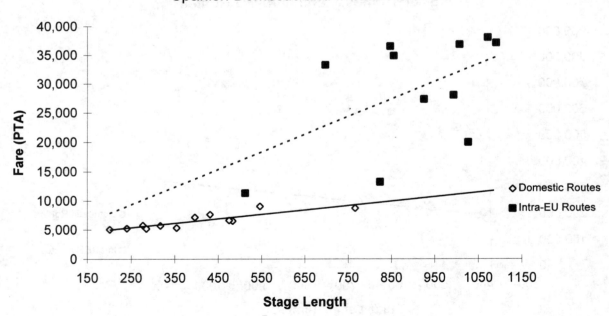

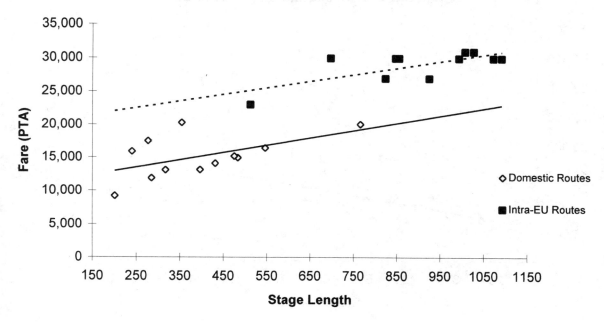

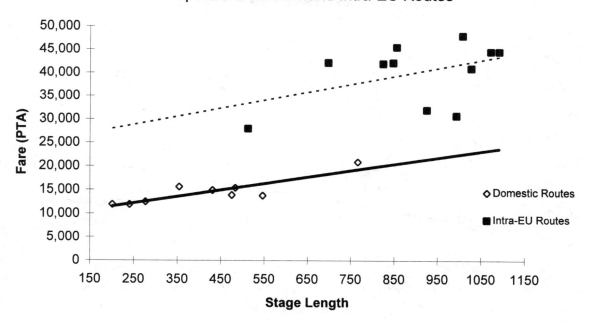

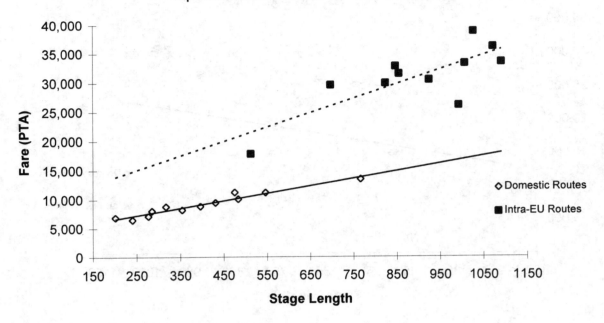

1986 One-Way Fully Flexible Economy Fare vs Stage Length
Spanish Domestic and Intra-EU Routes

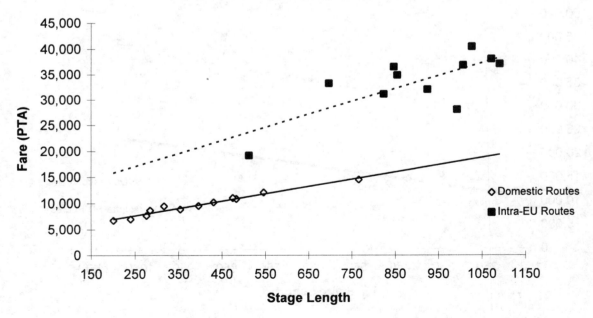

1989 One-Way Fully Flexible Economy Fare vs Stage Length
Spanish Domestic and Intra-EU Routes

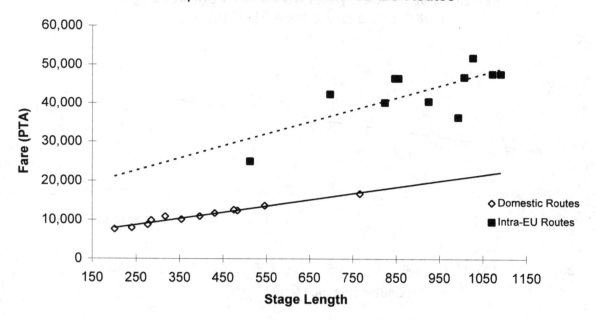

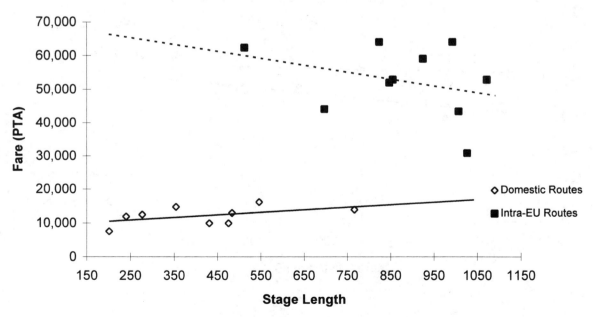

D.9. Comparison of UK domestic and intra-EU air fares

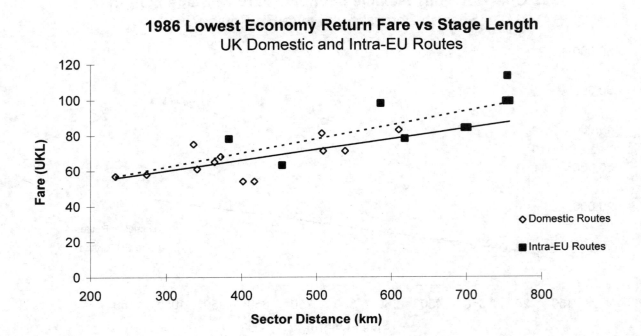

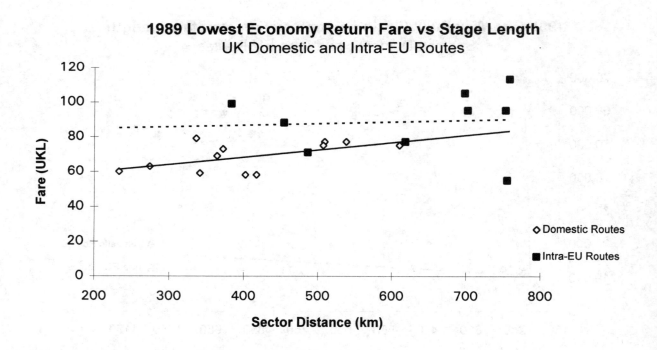

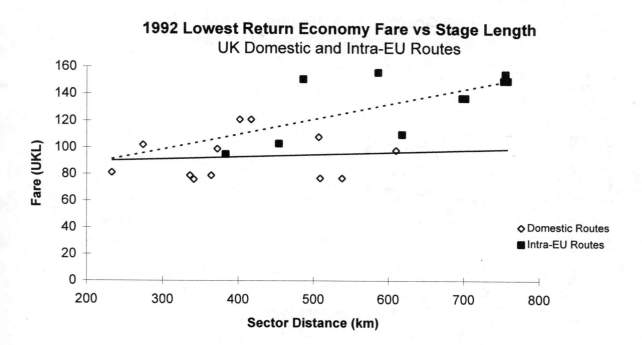

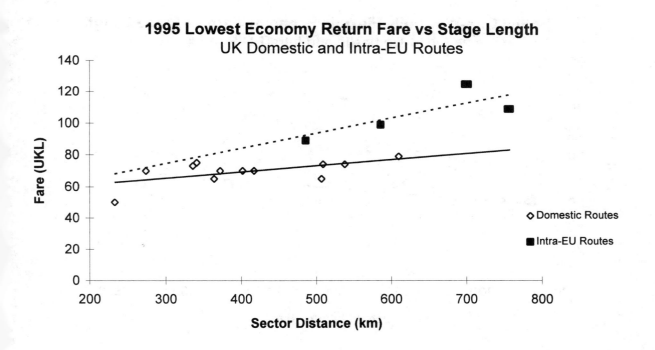

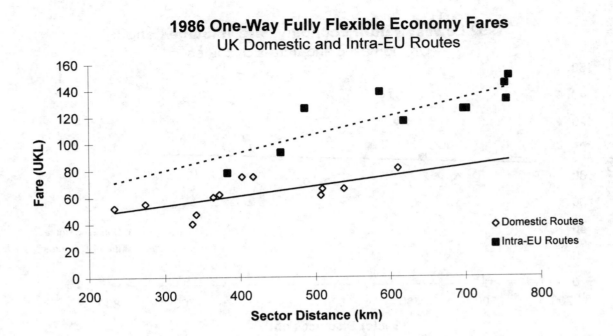

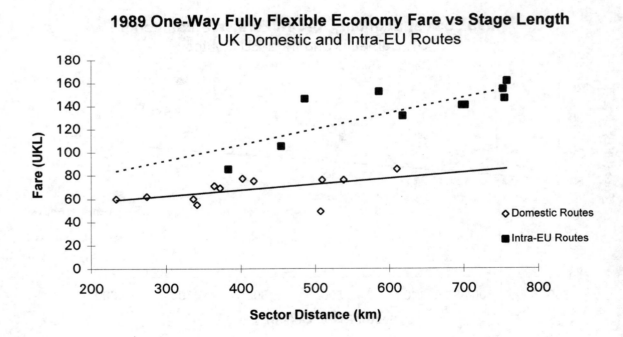

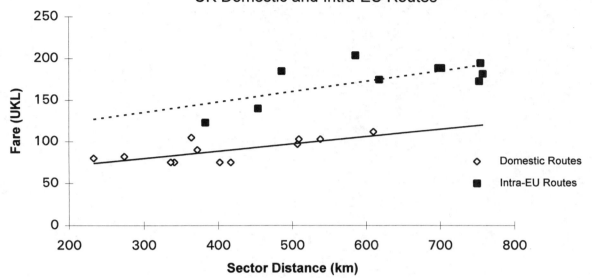

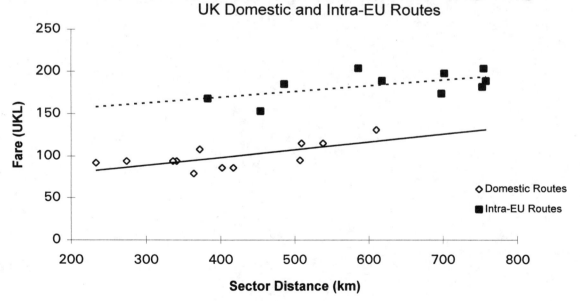

EU airline labour costs

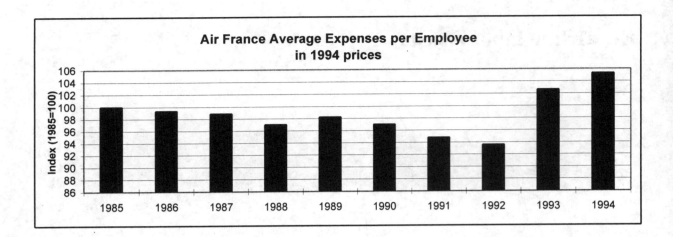

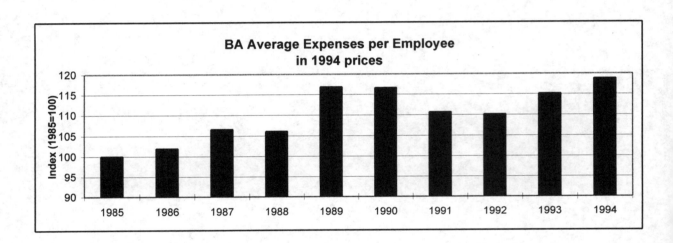

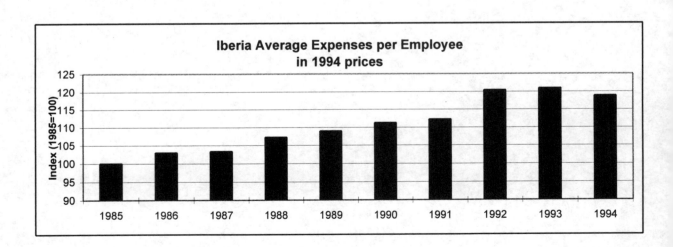

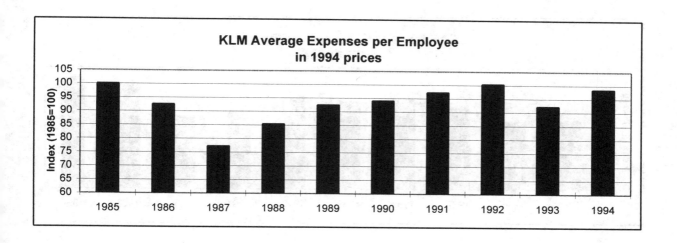

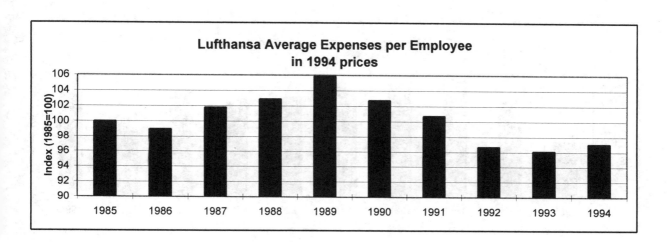

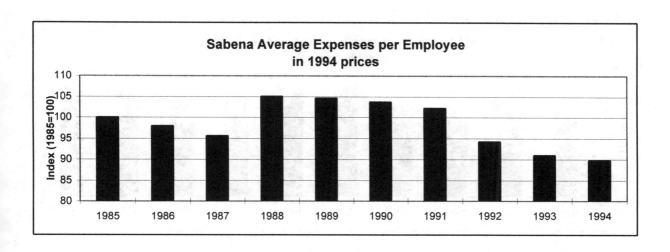

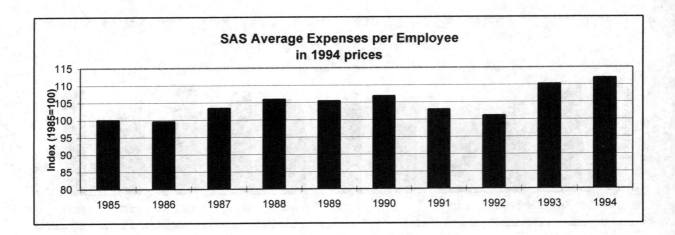

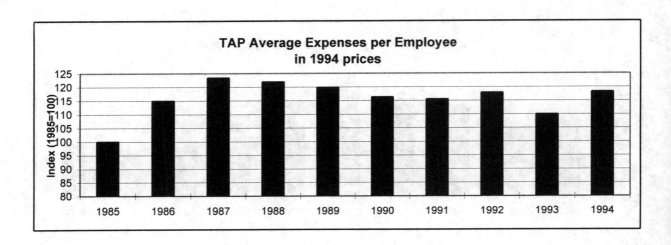

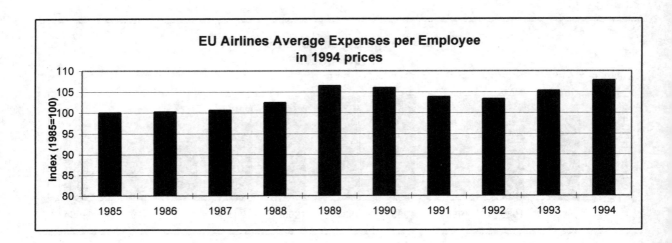

APPENDIX F

Airline case studies

F.1. Air France

F.1.1. Strategic responses

Throughout the 1990s Air France has faced the most profound difficulty in attempting to make the transition from highly protected carrier into one which has to face the full rigours of a competitive marketplace. Successive rounds of ever more stringent cost-cutting measures have yet to restore profitability. The broad consensus that existed in the late 1980s that Western Europe's airline industry would undergo rapid consolidation prior to the creation of the single European market had a strong influence in determining Air France's strategic policy for the 1990s. The company's perception that only large airlines with extensive route networks would survive in the global marketplace resulted in its decision to seek rapid expansion. To ensure its place in future events the company began rapidly to increase its fleet size, having some 52 aircraft on order in December 1989. In addition to organic expansion, the company embarked on a programme of developing alliances with other carriers.

The flag carrier's take-over of UTA in January 1990 marked the beginning of this period of rapid build-up in capacity as the airline prepared itself for the competitive onslaught to come. The elimination of UTA, a move that mirrored British Airways' acquisition of British Caledonian, was beneficial in two key areas for Air France. Whilst UTA had competed directly with the state airline on a small number of international routes, its real threat lay in its potential to develop a European route network. The second benefit derived by Air France was the control it gained of Air Inter. In the process of acquiring UTA, however, the company was required by the Commission to relinquish its shareholding in TAT.

In 1989 Air France had widened the alliance it had previously developed with Lufthansa (Amadeus, Atlas – a joint aircraft maintenance consortium, Euroberlin) to include staff training, aircraft purchasing and catering. The same year the company had acquired a 1.5% shareholding in Austrian Airlines. Despite worsening finances, the carrier continued with its acquisition policy in the early 1990s by taking a 19.9% stake in CSA and a 37.5% holding in Sabena.   The latter purchase, which received Commission approval in October 1992, followed an abortive attempt by British Airways and KLM to take over the Belgian flag carrier. Whilst the motivation for the Sabena purchase was clearly defensive, the marketing alliances established in 1992 with Aerovias de Mexico and Air Canada were viewed as a means of improving access to the US market. By comparison with British Airways, Air France's share of transatlantic traffic has been low, partly as the result of a less favourable bilateral agreement.

The long and deep economic recession of the early 1990s, exacerbated by the adverse impact of the Gulf War, produced a substantial decline in traffic, resulting in a dramatic decline in yields. Unfortunately for Air France this large downturn coincided with a period of high capital spending for the company. The outcome was one of mounting losses, which the carrier first sought to counter in September 1990. The Austerity Plan aimed to improve the carrier's financial plight, by freezing recruitment, lowering capital spending and reducing paid non-work periods. These measures, however, were clearly inadequate to deal with the fundamental problems faced by Air France. A second attempt to stem the company's losses was introduced by the Chairman, Bernard Attali, in September 1993. Under CAP 93, a three-point restructuring plan, 3,000 jobs were to be trimmed, representing some 5% of the carrier's workforce. In addition, a further FF 5 billion of capital was to be raised in order to fund the company's expansion and fleet renewal programme. The company's strategy remained clear: to reduce costs, absorb UTA, take a stake in Sabena and consolidate Air Inter.

Unfortunately, the strategy was flawed. A moribund economic climate in France and increasing competition from leaner airlines led to a rapid deterioration in the company's finances. Attempting to turn around and integrate Sabena, merge the activities of UTA, find some means by which to marry Air Inter's domestic operations focused at Orly with Air France's international network hubbing at Charles de Gaulle, develop Eastern European activities through its part acquisition of CSA and extract the benefits from the various marketing alliances it had established with carriers around the world, set against a background of declining yields and high operating costs, was an impossible task. Calls by Bernard Attali for even more draconian measures in September 1993, the carrier's fourth cost-cutting plan in three years, were not supported by the workforce. The inevitable strike action precipitated his departure from the airline in October of that year.

The cuts proposed by Mr Attali would have had the effect of reducing Air France's unit costs in 1995 by 19%. Another 4,000 jobs were to have gone by the end of 1994 and the number of routes served by the carrier would have fallen by 40% since 1990. Even given the scale of the cost-cutting, assuming its successful implementation, a further injection of capital would have been required from the state. In the event the French Transport Minister, Bernard Bosson, cancelled the company's restructuring plan.

The appointment of Christian Blanc as Chairman in October 1993 heralded the abandonment of the expansionist global strategy pursued by his predecessor. It was readily apparent that if Mr Blanc's plan was to succeed he would need the support of the workforce. The corporate plan announced in March 1994 called for a three-year wages freeze and further staff reductions. Unsurprisingly, it did not receive overwhelming trade union support. A direct approach to the company's employees, however, proved successful, with 81% of employees giving their consent to the new restructuring measures.

F.1.2. Routes, air services and capacity

The airline's ability to take advantage of a more liberalized air transport market in Europe has been severely limited as a result of its deteriorating financial position. Much of the route expansion embarked upon by the company at the end of the 1980s has had to be abandoned. During the early 1990s the company was forced to close some 50 loss-making routes linking French regional points with major European cities. Some lower yield destinations served by Air France from Paris, such as those in Spain and North Africa, were transferred to Air Inter.

Decentralization formed a key part of the company's 1994 corporate plan. The policy involved the establishment of 11 profit centres. Six of the profit centres are traffic based and the remainder concerned with logistical aspects of the carrier's operations, a horizontal organizational structure contrasting with the vertical arrangement that had existed previously. Long haul operations account for four of the six traffic profit centres (Americas, Africa and

Middle East, Asia-Pacific, Antilles-French Guyana-Indian Ocean), with European routes and cargo services forming the other two. A total of 20 destinations are served by the Americas profit centre (ten in the US, nine in South America, and Tahiti), using a mixed fleet of 747-400, A340, 767 and Concorde aircraft. The company's South American network was rationalized in 1994/95, with loss-making routes pruned. To serve the 37 locations in Africa and 11 in the Middle East, a fleet of ten A310 and eight 747-200 combi aircraft are employed. The company had reduced the number of destinations served in these two regions from 51 in 1993 to 40 in late 1994, but has since reinstated many of these routes.

The company's fleet of largest aircraft, the 747-400, is used mainly to operate to the 14 destinations served in the Asia-Pacific region. Operations to Malaysia, New Zealand, Pakistan and Sri Lanka were withdrawn during 1994 and those to Australia in 1995. The carrier's older fleet of 747 aircraft are used to operate routes to the French Overseas Departments and Territories, on which it faces stiff competition from both Air Liberté and AOM. Within Europe, Air France employs a mixed fleet of aircraft ranging from the 105 seat 737-200 and its more modern equivalent the 737-500, the 150 seat A320 and the considerably larger A300.

The company has a particularly large cargo division, operating a fleet of eleven 747 freighters. Substantial growth in traffic has been achieved over the past two years, resulting in a near 70% load factor.

At the regional level the carrier has a long history of contracting small, independent French airlines to operate services on its behalf on routes warranting the use of aircraft seating fewer than 100 passengers. Its use of the turbo-prop and small jet aircraft operated by Air Littoral, Brit Air and TAT (until its acquisition by British Airways) served the dual purpose of tying in potential competitors, whilst simultaneously enabling the company to operate lightly trafficked routes in a cost-effective way. The operation of a growing fleet of 50 seat Canadair Regional jets by both Air Littoral and Brit Air under the guise of Air France – Air Inter Express represents the most recent manifestation of this policy. The independent German regional carrier, Eurowings, also operates services on behalf of the company.

F.1.3. Marketing, traffic and market share

Within Europe, Air France has fared badly in terms of market share, when compared with the majority of its competitors. This situation has arisen for a number of reasons. The lack of an effective domestic feed for its international services at Charles de Gaulle and its record of industrial unrest have been two key factors. Whilst British Airways and Lufthansa have fully integrated route networks operating under a single brand name, the policy of maintaining Air France and Air Inter as two distinct airlines has been a major disadvantage in attracting traffic.

To help improve its image and catch up with the enhanced in-flight service provided by other carriers, Air France introduced its L'Espace and Tempo brands in 1995. The fact that Air Inter Europe continues to market a different in-flight service brand may well prove confusing to consumers.

F.1.4. Productivity and operating costs

The aim of the current restructuring plan is to restore the company to profitability by the beginning of 1997. In order to achieve this target, productivity has to be increased by 30% over 1993 levels. A continuing improvement in productivity was one of the conditions laid down by the Commission to enable payment of the second and final tranches of state aid. To achieve the 30% target, the number of staff employed by Air France is to be reduced to 35,000 by January 1997, down from 39,950 in January 1994. By the end of the 1994/95 financial year, half of the required reduction in staffing levels had been achieved.

Despite the severe cost reducing measures, Air France's unit operating costs continue to lag behind those of Lufthansa. The French carrier's direct operating costs were 7.5% higher than those of Lufthansa in the first half of 1995. This situation represents an improvement over the situation in 1993 when the differential was 10.6%. For long haul routes, the differential remains at the 1993 level. Overall, it is clear that Air France has some way to go to match the operating cost and productivity levels of British Airways and Lufthansa.

Apart from cuts in the labour force, productivity improvements are being sought through better utilization of aircraft, fleet rationalization, which has involved some downsizing, and longer flying hours from both flight deck and cabin crew. It remains to be seen whether these improvements can be achieved by early 1997. At present, the signs are not particularly strong that they will be realized. For example, in terms of aircraft utilization the carrier has yet to match the levels it achieved in 1989. Where its fleet is concerned, it would appear that the number of aircraft types employed has actually increased. During the 1990s, apart from replacing some older generation aircraft with more fuel efficient equipment, the number of different types and variants of aircraft operated has gone up from 11 in 1990 to 18 in 1995. Whilst providing the carrier with a greater degree of flexibility in terms of matching demand and supply across its route network, there is an undoubted disadvantage in terms of scale economies.

F.1.5. Pricing and yields

Yields have fallen throughout the 1990s. In the financial year 1994/95 the airline's average yield was some 9.9% lower than in 1993 (the 1993 yield was down by 7% on the 1992 figure). Whilst the company has been effective in achieving high load factors, 72% in 1994/95, it has an inappropriate mix of fares. The airline has acknowledged its poor yield management as being a major weakness. It is anticipated that this situation will improve during the spring of this year with the introduction of a new yield management system acquired from Sabre Decision Technologies. The Airmax Origin and Destination software performs forecasting and optimization across the carrier's entire route network, a feature lacking in the internally developed OPERA system.

F.1.6. Profitability and sources of finance

The extent of the company's difficulties is apparent from the scale of the financial aid required to set the airline on a sound footing. In July 1994 the Commission approved a restructuring plan which was dependent on FF 20 billion of state funding. A key element of the new strategy involved the creation of a new holding company, Groupe Air France SA. In addition to this new organization acquiring a 79% stake in Air France for a symbolic franc, it also took over the flag carrier's 72% shareholding in Air Inter. The plan aimed to tackle a major shortcoming of the previous strategy, namely the lack of co-ordination between these two carriers. The low level of interlining between the two airlines at Charles de Gaulle represented a substantial lost opportunity for the group. To overcome this difficulty a new company is to be set up which will combine the European services of Air France and all of Air Inter's activities. This could not be implemented before 1997, however, as a consequence of conditions imposed by the Commission.

The disposal of shareholdings acquired during the early 1990s in other carriers accompanied the new restructuring programme. Sabena's dissatisfaction with its shareholder partner led to an announcement by Air France in 1994 that it was disposing of its stake in the airline. In 1995 the carrier also sold its holding in CSA. Further sales have included the company's interests in the Meridien Hotel chain, a further condition of the state aid package.

A number of the aircraft ordered and held on option by the airline from Airbus and Boeing have been cancelled, whilst others have had their delivery dates deferred. A further requirement imposed by the Commission was that the fleet should be reduced in size by some 20 aircraft. However, this has had little impact, as the company already had 21 of its aircraft either on lease to other airlines or out of service.

Another major objective of Mr Blanc's corporate plan involved the modification of Air France's structure and status to enable employees of the airline to become shareholders. A law enabling joint stock companies with labour holdings to become ordinary limited companies was enacted in August 1994. Holders of labour shares were to receive shares in the new holding company, Groupe Air France, by way of compensation. The change in status enabled the airline to convert its salaried employees into shareholders, with a collective ability to hold up to 20% of the company's capital. At the end of 1994 some 12,000 of the carrier's staff became shareholders (owning 5% of the equity) in exchange for a reduction in their salaries.

Given the carrier's financial problems, it would seem unlikely that privatization of the company will be achieved during the 1990s.

F.1.7. Impact of EU measures and conclusions

As is evident, Air France has not been in a strong position to take much advantage of the opportunities presented by the third package. According to the company only three new services were started between June 1989 and June 1992 (Amsterdam-Copenhagen, Lisbon-Madrid, London-Strasbourg) and three in the following three years (Berlin-Strasbourg, Hamburg-Strasbourg, Munich-Strasbourg) as a consequence of EU legislation. The falling yields experienced by the carrier, however, bear witness to the high degree of competition evident in many of its markets. The pricing freedom given to carriers operating within Europe since 1993 has not been used to good effect by the company. Its weakness at managing yield has placed it at a great disadvantage to carriers such as British Airways and Lufthansa, who have placed considerable emphasis in this area.

It is readily apparent that Air France has still a considerable way to go before it can match the levels of profitability achieved by British Airways. A number of obstacles remain in its path. Given the confusion engendered by the continued separation of Air France and Air Inter (albeit now in the guise of Air Inter Europe), prolonging the distinction would appear to serve no useful purpose. Until the operations of the two companies are fully integrated under the well-known Air France brand name and effective hubbing occurs at both Paris airports, it will be difficult to match the marketing achievements of British Airways.

Whether Air France can achieve the targets set out as a condition of its FF 20 billion state aid package remains doubtful. It continues to experience fundamental difficulty in persuading its workforce of the necessity to change the company's culture from one of protected state monopoly to competitive enterprise. The strong bond between state and airline has acted to prolong this perception. For as long as the French government is willing to shield its flag carrier from the rigours of the free market this corporate culture will persist.

The real problem for Air France has been, and continues to be, that the goalposts are continually being moved. Whether the political will and sheer stamina required to maintain a sufficient degree of profitability over the longer term exist remains a matter of conjecture.

AIR FRANCE
TRAFFIC AND FINANCIAL STATISTICS 1985-94

PASSENGER TRAFFIC (thousand)

Year	Domestic	Europe	Int'nl	Total
1985	2,351	5,345	10,132	12,483
1986	2,424	5,425	9,602	12,025
1987	2,843	6,174	10,518	13,361
1988	3,144	7,029	11,625	14,769
1989	3,359	7,738	12,721	16,080
1990	3,276	7,759	12,412	15,688
1991	2,097	7,105	11,106	13,203
1992	1,940	7,393	11,813	13,754
1993	1,726	7,251	12,621	14,347
1994	1,830	7,968	13,762	15,592

RPK (million)

Year	Domestic	Europe	Int'nl	Total
1985	5,286	3,999	23,297	28,583
1986	5,593	4,009	21,978	27,571
1987	6,959	4,642	24,481	31,440
1988	7,793	5,356	26,540	34,333
1989	8,010	5,975	28,724	36,734
1990	7,630	6,081	29,023	36,653
1991	6,921	5,449	26,790	33,711
1992	7,289	5,826	29,746	37,034
1993	7,149	5,726	36,385	43,535
1994	7,969	6,333	42,151	50,119

ASK (million)

Year	Domestic	Europe	Int'nl	Total
1985	7,376	6,586	34,719	42,095
1986	7,657	6,786	34,609	42,266
1987	9,172	7,561	36,034	45,207
1988	10,448	8,805	36,491	46,939
1989	10,834	9,731	41,259	52,093
1990	10,535	10,224	42,402	52,938
1991	9,572	10,297	40,901	50,473
1992	9,932	10,725	44,821	54,752
1993	9,957	10,330	54,264	64,220
1994	9,957	10,263	57,957	67,914

ATK (million)

Year	Domestic	Europe	Int'nl	Total
1985	2,351	5,345	10,132	12,483
1986	2,424	5,425	9,602	12,025
1987	2,843	6,174	10,518	13,361
1988	3,144	7,029	11,625	14,769
1989	3,359	7,738	12,721	16,080
1990	3,276	7,759	12,412	15,688
1991	2,097	7,105	11,106	13,203
1992	1,940	7,393	11,813	13,754
1993	1,726	7,251	12,621	14,347
1994	1,830	7,968	13,762	15,592

RTK (million)

Year	Domestic	Europe	Int'nl	Total
1985	1,582	2,838	6,606	8,188
1986	1,612	2,837	6,001	7,613
1987	1,899	3,248	6,868	8,768
1988	2,000	3,760	7,475	9,474
1989	1,989	4,155	8,065	10,054
1990	1,976	3,996	7,807	9,783
1991	1,273	3,311	6,442	7,714
1992	1,149	3,512	7,005	8,154
1993	1,157	3,756	8,178	9,335
1994	1,405	4,836	10,335	11,740

WEIGHT LOAD FACTOR (%)

Year	Domestic	Europe	Int'nl	Total
1985	67.30%	53%	65%	66%
1986	66.50%	52%	63%	63%
1987	66.80%	53%	65%	66%
1988	63.60%	54%	64%	64%
1989	59.20%	54%	63%	63%
1990	60.30%	52%	63%	62%
1991	60.70%	47%	58%	58%
1992	59.20%	48%	59%	59%
1993	67.00%	52%	65%	65%
1994	76.80%	61%	75%	75%

PASSENGER LOAD FACTOR (%)

Year	Domestic	Europe	Int'nl	Total
1985	72%	61%	67%	68%
1986	73%	59%	64%	65%
1987	76%	61%	68%	70%
1988	75%	61%	73%	73%
1989	74%	61%	70%	71%
1990	72%	59%	68%	69%
1991	72%	53%	65%	67%
1992	73%	54%	66%	68%
1993	72%	55%	67%	68%
1994	80%	62%	73%	74%

PASSENGER REVENUE PER RPK (US cents 1985 prices)

Year	Domestic	Europe	Intern'l	Total
1985	5.19	15.06	8.37	7.78
1986	6.30	19.42	10.07	9.30
1987	6.48	21.21	10.42	9.55
1988	6.17	20.83	10.38	9.43
1989	5.56	18.88	9.70	8.79
1990	6.61	21.33	10.53	9.72
1991	5.83	21.92	10.53	9.56
1992	5.66	21.77	10.25	9.35
1993	N/A	N/A	N/A	N/A
1994	N/A	N/A	N/A	N/A

FREIGHT AND MAIL TONNE KM (million)

Year	Domestic	Europe	Int'nl	Total
1985	61	47	1,173	1,234
1986	61	52	1,226	1,287
1987	69	54	1,342	1,411
1988	73	57	1,390	1,463
1989	81	54	1,353	1,434
1990	90	60	1,479	1,568
1991	83	56	1,478	1,561
1992	63	56	1,371	1,435
1993	55	44	1,655	1,710
1994	54	48	1,788	1,842

AIR FRANCE
TRAFFIC AND FINANCIAL STATISTICS 1985-94

AVERAGE PASSENGER HAUL (km)

Year	Domestic	Europe	Int'nl	Total
1985	2,248	748	2,299	2,290
1986	2,307	739	2,289	2,293
1987	2,448	752	2,328	2,353
1988	2,479	762	2,283	2,325
1989	2,385	772	2,258	2,284
1990	2,329	784	2,338	2,336
1991	3,301	767	2,412	2,553
1992	3,756	788	2,518	2,693
1993	4,142	790	2,883	3,034
1994	4,355	795	3,063	3,214

TOTAL AIRCRAFT KM FLOWN (million)

Year	Domestic	Europe	Int'nl	Total
1985	21	47	146	166
1986	21	52	153	175
1987	25	61	167	193
1988	30	71	184	213
1989	33	79	198	231
1990	32	83	206	239
1991	27	80	199	226
1992	38	88	221	259
1993	36	89	255	291
1994	35	90	272	307

EMPLOYEES (units)

Year	Average
1985	35,325
1986	35,350
1987	35,580
1988	36,507
1989	38,117
1990	39,461
1991	39,640
1992	41,113
1993	42,425
1994	40,954

FLEET SIZE (units)

Year	Europe	Int'nl
1985	41	93
1986	44	98
1987	43	98
1988	50	97
1989	51	103
1990	56	112
1991	58	135
1992	67	139
1993	68	140
1994	61	126

TOTAL HOURS FLOWN (hours)

Year	Domestic	Europe	Int'nl	Total
1985	32,600	93,800	258,737	291,337
1986	34,000	102,900	271,020	305,020
1987	40,300	126,100	302,903	343,203
1988	47,800	153,100	344,635	392,435
1989	53,800	170,100	373,712	427,512
1990	53,500	180,300	387,261	440,761
1991	39,200	173,200	380,720	419,920
1992	37,500	189,400	413,339	450,839
1993	35,500	194,000	416,000	451,500
1994	34,800	196,900	439,500	474,300

AIR FRANCE FINANCIAL PERFORMANCE (current prices - million ECU)

Year	Op'ing Revenue	Op'ing Costs	Op'ing Profit	Net Profit
1985	3,966	3,658	307	109
1986	3,499	3,217	282	99
1987	3,533	3,221	312	103
1988	3,793	3,514	279	170
1989	4,329	4,212	117	99
1990	4,219	4,443	-224	-127
1991	5,060	5,135	-75	-87
1992	8,891	9,117	-227	-491
1993	5,876	6,531	-655	-1,187
1993	N/A	N/A	N/A	N/A

AIR FRANCE FINANCIAL PERFORMANCE (1990 prices - million ECU)

Year	Op'ing Revenue	Op'ing Cost	Op'ing Profit	Net Profit
1985	5,065	4,672	393	140
1986	4,234	3,893	341	119
1987	4,096	3,734	362	119
1988	4,212	3,902	310	189
1989	4,553	4,430	123	104
1990	4,219	4,443	-224	-127
1991	4,864	4,936	-72	-84
1992	8,301	8,513	-212	-458
1993	5,369	5,967	-599	-1,084
1994	N/A	N/A	N/A	N/A

FREIGHT AND MAIL YIELD (US cents 1990 prices)

Year	Domestic	Europe	Int'nl	Total
1985	23	56	24	24
1986	29	66	26	26
1987	32	72	26	26
1988	31	67	25	25
1989	28	61	23	23
1990	28	59	23	23
1991	29	60	24	24
1992	28	54	23	23
1993	N/A	N/A	N/A	N/A
1994	N/A	N/A	N/A	N/A

AVERAGE AIRCRAFT SIZE (seats)

Year	Domestic	Europe	Int'nl	Total
1985	360	140	239	254
1986	358	132	226	242
1987	361	124	216	235
1988	352	124	199	220
1989	332	123	208	226
1990	326	123	206	222
1991	361	128	205	224
1992	265	122	203	212
1993	280	116	213	221
1994	286	114	213	221

ATK PER EMPLOYEE (units)

Year	Average
1985	214,023
1986	224,942
1987	243,151
1988	263,381
1989	266,612
1990	265,260
1991	273,439
1992	273,476
1993	300,315
1994	315,161

DAILY AIRCRAFT UTILIZATION (hours)

Year	Europe	Int'l
1985	6.3	7.6
1986	6.4	7.6
1987	8.0	8.5
1988	8.4	9.7
1989	9.1	9.9
1990	8.8	9.5
1991	8.2	7.7
1992	7.7	8.1
1993	7.8	8.1
1994	8.8	9.6

F.2. British Airways

F.2.1. Strategic responses

British Airways (BA) is a classic case of a major EU airline which sees itself as a global carrier competing in a global marketplace; while operations within the EU are vital to its success, its overall strategy is driven by wider issues. For example, it identifies the three dominant regional air transport markets to be Europe, North America and Asia-Pacific and the three dominant intercontinental markets to be those linking these three. Its strategy is to be a major participant in all six markets, either directly or via long-term relationships. Its partnerships with USAir, Qantas, TAT and Deutsche BA (DBA) need to be seen in this light. Its interest in regulatory reform in North America (i.e. ownership rules), and Asia-Pacific (i.e. arrangements between Australia and New Zealand) are of similar importance to the EU single market process.

One of the most important events which acted as a catalyst to its strategic responses to a more competitive environment was the announcement by the British government in 1979 that the airline was to be privatized. This was nearly ten years before the adoption of the first package, but resulted in many actions to restructure the airline which other EU carriers did not begin to adopt until the final stages of the EU liberalization process. For them, British Airways provided something of a case study.

Because of this, British Airways indicates that the three packages have had no effect on product development, distribution strategy, the rate of marketing innovation or route rationalization. They have had only modest effect on alliances, pricing, cost-cutting and staff numbers.

The British Airways 1981–82 accounts recorded a UK£ 544 million deficit including special provisions for an extensive 'survival plan' which was also designed to prepare for privatization. It is interesting to note that this included staff cuts, suspension of unprofitable routes, disposal of surplus assets, the acquisition of a new fleet not constrained by political interference, and a major rebranding exercise. Many of these have parallels with current strategies being implemented with varying degrees of success by Aer Lingus, TAP, Sabena, Olympic, Air France and Iberia – and those being decided upon within Alitalia.

Unlike many other airlines in the EU, British Airways had to contend with a series of new-style bilaterals from the mid-1980s, which were precursors of the first two packages of liberalization measures. It also faced competition in specific markets from an efficient, largely deregulated charter sector. The momentum of the restructuring exercise was maintained and the airline was successfully privatized in February 1987 via a public flotation which was 11 times oversubscribed.

Over the last decade, British Airways has made a classic response to a more competitive market with a search for size and a set of new marketing strategies.

The former began with the acquisition of its main UK scheduled competitor, British Caledonian, in July 1987. The timing of this move was obviously not directly influenced by the EU packages of reform, but was a recognition that a reform process was under way. BA's move to secure interests in operators in the two next largest EU markets after the UK via Deutsche BA and TAT in 1992 (see Section 3.2) preceded the third package and the introduction of the concepts of Community ownership and common licensing. In any case, BA appears to have wished that these moves to ensure representation in one of the world's big regional markets did not result in adverse political and local consumer reaction to a 'British' brand. It was also concerned not to create difficulties with bilaterals with non-EU states for existing and future DBA and TAT operations.

In 1992 it took over the assets of the Gatwick-based carrier Dan Air and also began the process of securing a 24.6% stake in USAir. A further step in its strategy of global linkages was put in place with its agreement in 1993 to take a 25% stake in the Australian carrier Qantas.

The stake in USAir was in fact the culmination of a long search for a North American partner, which began with a marketing relationship signed with United in 1987. In 1989 it attempted to cement this arrangement with a 15% investment, but this had to be withdrawn when its other partners in the proposed buyout failed to raise the necessary funds, and United decided to start its own transatlantic services. A further unsuccessful partnership proposal, this time with KLM to acquire Sabena as part of a joint venture which opened the possibility of linking with Northwest, foundered in late 1990. The airline also held talks with KLM in early 1991 regarding a merger, again without any concrete results.

Partly as a result of its desire to secure its home market, and partly because it recognized that its own cost structure was not suited to low-density operations, BA pioneered the concept in 1993 of franchise operations. These arrangements can also be seen as part of its wider marketing response to liberalization. However, the UK industry, with its relatively large number of independent airlines, is uniquely open for non-UK airlines to gain a presence via acquisition. The setting up of an airline of significant size in the UK is made more difficult because of slot constraints. Recognizing that KLM and SAS had already made such moves via Air UK and BMA, a further motivation for BA to enter strong franchise arrangements was to provide a practical barrier to market entry by non-UK carriers at little investment cost to itself. It was also aware that these relationships would be difficult for the competition authorities to oppose.

F.2.2. Routes, air services and capacity

Much of BA's expansion within the EU has been via the growth of its franchisees and partners on relatively low density routes. These appear as BA code shares, and the traffic carried is not shown in the tables at the end of this section. Research carried out for this report using *ABC World Airways Guide* data reveals 10 new services opened between June 1989 and June 1992 and 40 routes opened between June 1992 and June 1995. According to BA (see questionnaire) only three of these (Paris-Rome, Brussels-Rome and Thessaloniki-Turin, all opened between 1992 and 1995) were not franchisees or partners.

F.2.3. Marketing, traffic and market share

British Airways increased its overall level of scheduled activity excluding franchise operations, as measured by revenue passenger-kilometres, by a factor of just over two (2.07) between 1985 and 1994. This was partly a result of organic growth, and partly because of mergers and acquisitions. Surprisingly, the airline's UK domestic traffic grew faster than this average, but this was explained largely by its acquisition of British Caledonian. On intra-European international routes (i.e. geographical Europe, not intra-EU) the traffic carried by

BA has grown at the same rate as its non-European international traffic, at first sight suggesting little effect of the single market process.

Over the same time period, the traffic of the AEA airlines grew slightly more slowly, by a factor of 2.01. Although it is difficult to make direct comparisons, because of changes in AEA membership and variations in definitions, it would appear that British Airways has at least maintained its market share at around 15% of AEA intra-European international revenue passenger-kilometres. In terms of total (world) international RPKs, it has advanced its share of AEA activity from around 20% to around 23%.

British Airways believes that the lack of airport slots within the EU is the most important barrier to market entry on cross-border routes. In 1990 it took the initiative to set up the Infrastructure Action Group, operating under the aegis of IATA, to lobby for better provision. In the charter sector it sees vertical integration with tour operators and travel agents as an important barrier. It does not see override commissions, frequent flyer programmes or airline alliances as particular barriers to entry. It has to be noted, however, that these are factors which are of considerable benefit to British Airways and its response needs to be interpreted accordingly.

F.2.4. Productivity and operating costs

In order to maintain productivity and control costs, BA has periodically been through a series of staff reduction, cost reduction and 'gap closing' exercises. It has admitted that its cost levels in several areas are still above those of some of the smaller UK airlines, but its brand position, its powerful marketing strategy and its domination of high yield business travel, particularly out of Heathrow, have helped it to maintain its profit record.

The biggest changes to the airline's staff productivity occurred prior to privatization in the first half of the 1980s. However, it has proven itself willing to react quickly to adverse economic conditions and reduce its headcount when necessary. For example, at the onset of the recession in the UK and in the aftermath of the Gulf War the airline reduced its workforce from a high of 52,252 in 1990, to 50,398 in 1991 and 47,103 in 1992. When reviewing these actions, the airline cites the need to remain competitive with US and Asian carriers as significantly more important than the three packages and the need to be competitive with EU airlines.

Amongst EU airlines, British Airways has taken the lead in outsourcing non-core activities and in creating internal profit centres to focus management attention on costs and efficiency. Its cargo operations and its engineering operations were the first departments to be made into profit centres, and the latter has recently been transformed into a separate, wholly-owned company.

It has pioneered amongst EU majors the concept of profit sharing (not an easy option for many EU carriers), performance related pay, flexible working and the location of labour-intensive tasks away from London with its high costs.

F.2.5. Pricing and yields

One of British Airways' strengths relative to its domestic, EU and global competitors is its yield management system. The airline has been able to combine a policy of gradually increasing its premium fares while participating fully but in a controlled way in the low fares market. Research presented elsewhere in this report shows that cross-border fares out of London are amongst the lowest in the Community. This is partly because of competition, but also because of successive depreciation of the UK pound. The airline has made use of its yield management system to direct intercontinental traffic from elsewhere in the EU over London to gain maximum benefit from network effects.

Its yields are typically below the AEA average, but its passenger seat factors are typically somewhat higher. It would see itself as innovative in terms of pricing and has recently taken steps to implement a system of remaindering excess capacity under the brand name of 'World Offers'.

F.2.6. Profitability and sources of finance

Although British Airways and its predecessor companies had a mixed profit performance prior to privatization, and changes in its accounting practices make year to year comparisons difficult, since privatization its record has been exceptionally good relative to industry and EU airline averages.

As part of its strategy of seeking additional funds, in 1992 it sought credit ratings from Moody's Investor Services and from Standard and Poor's. Both assigned it an 'A' grade or equivalent. In May 1993 it raised UK£ 442 million, net of expenses, by way of a rights issue. Some of this was used to pay for its stake in USAir, which many suggest was ill-advised. Unlike other EU carriers which are not disciplined by the financial markets, however, it has demonstrated a willingness to write off the investment in time, effort and money associated with what have turned out to be poor investments, for example in Air Russia.

It has to be recognized that the airline's global ambitions have not had an entirely positive effect on its financial performance. In addition to its losses on Air Russia, its investment in USAir has had to be written down in value – although British Airways claims that the principal benefits have been gained through increased feed through co-ordinated schedules, code sharing and joint operations. Neither TAT nor Deutsche BA are profitable, and this has provided a cautionary lesson about the difficulties of linking operations based in separate EU states.

Even when activities have been profitable, but have not been considered essential to the core business, it has been willing to dispose of them in order to focus management time and investment resources on airline operations (i.e. the sale of its engine overhaul business to General Electric, the sale of its charter operation Caledonian Airways to Inspirations). This process has moved ahead in parallel with the move towards greater out-sourcing and the creation of profit centres mentioned in Section B.2.4 above.

Since privatization, BA's shares have moved from trading between a high of 183 and a low of 158 pence in 1987, to trading between 436 and 398 in the first quarter of 1996. At flotation some 17% of shares were owned by foreign nationals. In March 1995, this proportion stood at 35%, with a large proportion held in the United States.

Like most private sector airlines, British Airways has acquired a proportion of its fleet under operating leases, with the majority of these off balance sheet. Of the March 1995 total fleet of 243 aircraft, excluding Deutsche BA and TAT, just under one-fifth (53 aircraft) were on off balance sheet operating leases. Although rather a simplistic view, the use of operating leases provides additional fleet planning flexibility, but in the case of British Airways this has not been brought about by the increased uncertainty associated with the creation of a single EU market in air transport. It is a reflection of wider planning uncertainties (i.e. tighter noise and emission rules) in a competitive global environment.

Although it is difficult to cite detailed evidence, British Airways has a reputation for being particularly aggressive with aerospace manufacturers when negotiating the acquisition of aircraft and engines. This covers not only price, but also guarantees, warranties and support. This is a skill which has reduced investment requirements and which other EU airlines, whose fleet planning has often been seen as part of their home state's industrial policy, may learn to apply.

In terms of factors affecting its financial performance, the airline sees the economic climate as most important. As with the spur for efficiency, it ranks the challenge from Asian and US carriers as more important than EU airlines or the three packages, which are seen as having little effect.

F.2.7. Impact of EU measures and conclusions

British Airways' motivation to become one of the world's leading airlines has not been stimulated by the EU's single market measures. Its drive to achieve the economies and other benefits of scale and scope are not driven primarily by rivalry with other EU airlines for the internal market.

EU traffic is important to BA, both because of its volume and because of feed to and network effects with the rest of its route structure. But success within the EU and being large in EU terms is not a sufficient condition to be competitive on a global scale.

British Airways sees the removal of restrictions on EU domestic services in April 1997 as being the final step in the liberalization process. It suggests that its investments in TAT and Deutsche BA provide vehicles for expansion within the EU – although the third package and cabotage rights make such investments unnecessary.

It believes that

'one of the biggest problems facing European airlines is the issue of fair competition. State ownership in Europe has resulted in subsidy and the legal battles currently being conducted by Europe's private airlines over the French government's latest state aid of FF 20 billion to Air France are witness to a competitive distortion that still exists within the Union. It is only when all airlines are subject to forces of a truly competitive market that real competition can flourish.' *(Source: British Airways Fact Book 1995)*

As the UK market and later the EU market were liberalized, British Airways has been one of the first EU airlines to find itself subject to general competition law rather than specific air transport regulation. For example, its takeover of British Caledonian, its proposed joint venture with KLM to acquire Sabena and its takeover of Dan Air have all been subject to scrutiny by authorities concerned with competition. It has found itself the subject of court action as a result of the so-called 'dirty tricks' campaign against Virgin Atlantic, and it has taken a leading role in challenging in the European Court of Justice the Commission's approval of a package of state aid to Air France.

A large measure of BA's success is due to its dominant position at London Heathrow, which is the largest hub in the EU. Although congestion puts a constraint on the airline's growth there, except by using larger aircraft, the lack of slots provides an effective barrier to additional competition. BA is unenthusiastic about the possibility of the Community negotiating Air Services Agreements with third countries. Part of the reason for this is the fear that greater access to Heathrow for the airlines of a non-EU state might be traded for some additional rights required by another EU Member State and airline.

BRITISH AIRWAYS
TRAFFIC AND FINANCIAL STATISTICS 1985-94

PASSENGER TRAFFIC (thousand)

Year	Domestic	Europe	Int'nl	Total
1985	4,144	8,203	12,824	16,968
1986	4,269	8,271	12,729	16,998
1987	4,618	9,336	14,482	19,100
1988	5,594	10,650	16,922	22,516
1989	5,216	11,296	17,965	23,181
1990	5,488	12,420	19,684	25,172
1991	4,942	11,029	17,927	22,869
1992	5,130	12,314	20,247	25,378
1993	5,766	13,751	22,377	28,143
1994	6,269	14,615	23,933	30,202

RPK (million)

Year	Domestic	Europe	Int'nl	Total
1985	1,920	6,533	39,182	41,103
1986	2,025	6,551	38,405	40,430
1987	2,215	7,439	44,085	46,299
1988	2,979	8,639	53,960	56,939
1989	3,195	9,248	57,563	60,757
1990	3,961	10,218	62,835	66,795
1991	3,581	9,500	59,254	62,835
1992	4,621	11,054	67,870	72,491
1993	5,042	12,654	75,044	80,086
1994	5,179	13,738	81,053	86,232

ASK (million)

Year	Domestic	Europe	Int'nl	Total
1985	2,970	9,786	56,909	59,879
1986	3,261	10,324	57,874	61,135
1987	3,392	10,859	61,065	64,457
1988	4,501	13,000	78,410	82,911
1989	4,810	14,013	80,652	85,462
1990	5,769	15,066	87,424	93,192
1991	5,612	14,867	85,379	90,991
1992	6,837	16,956	95,186	102,023
1993	7,322	19,768	107,176	114,497
1994	7,437	20,501	113,778	121,215

ATK (million)

Year	Domestic	Europe	Int'nl	Total
1985	305	1,032	7,447	7,752
1986	350	1,096	7,651	8,000
1987	368	1,162	8,081	8,449
1988	493	1,435	10,713	11,206
1989	531	1,553	10,981	11,512
1990	661	1,695	12,099	12,760
1991	659	1,769	12,042	12,701
1992	818	2,025	13,368	14,186
1993	875	2,349	14,765	15,639
1994	883	2,471	15,666	16,548

RTK (million)

Year	Domestic	Europe	Int'nl	Total
1985	178	639	4,803	4,981
1986	187	644	4,835	5,022
1987	205	723	5,487	5,692
1988	280	901	6,963	7,244
1989	302	964	7,335	7,637
1990	396	963	7,901	8,297
1991	368	915	7,587	7,954
1992	482	1,073	8,556	9,037
1993	522	1,233	9,420	9,942
1994	538	1,341	10,214	10,752

WEIGHT LOAD FACTOR (%)

Year	Domestic	Europe	Int'nl	Total
1985	58%	62%	64%	64%
1986	54%	59%	63%	63%
1987	56%	62%	67%	67%
1988	57%	63%	65%	65%
1989	57%	62%	66%	66%
1990	60%	57%	65%	65%
1991	56%	52%	63%	63%
1992	59%	53%	64%	64%
1993	60%	53%	64%	64%
1994	61%	54%	65%	65%

PASSENGER LOAD FACTOR (%)

Year	Domestic	Europe	Int'nl	Total
1985	65%	67%	69%	69%
1986	62%	63%	66%	66%
1987	65%	69%	72%	72%
1988	66%	66%	69%	69%
1989	66%	66%	71%	71%
1990	69%	68%	72%	72%
1991	64%	64%	69%	69%
1992	68%	65%	71%	71%
1993	69%	64%	70%	70%
1994	70%	67%	71%	71%

PASSENGER YIELD (US cents (1985 prices))

Year	Domestic	Europe	Int'nl	Total
1985	14.77	13.46	7.25	7.60
1986	17.41	15.82	7.97	8.44
1987	18.73	16.48	8.49	8.99
1988	17.87	17.60	8.93	9.41
1989	16.28	16.09	8.44	8.85
1990	15.99	17.76	8.88	9.30
1991	16.78	17.18	8.49	8.94
1992	14.61	16.75	7.88	8.31
1993	N/A	N/A	N/A	N/A
1994	N/A	N/A	N/A	N/A

FREIGHT AND MAIL TONNE KM (million)

Year	Domestic	Europe	Int'nl	Total
1985	5	51	1,275	1,280
1986	5	55	1,375	1,380
1987	5	55	1,520	1,525
1988	12	65	2,104	2,116
1989	14	70	2,158	2,172
1990	40	74	2,244	2,284
1991	45	64	2,252	2,297
1992	66	65	2,446	2,511
1993	60	79	2,538	2,598
1994	63	89	2,785	2,848

BRITISH AIRWAYS
TRAFFIC AND FINANCIAL STATISTICS 1985-94

FREIGHT AND MAIL YIELD
(US cents (1985 prices))

Year	Domestic	Europe	Int'nl
1985	102.07	60.99	23.19
1986	125.23	72.85	23.35
1987	141.26	83.10	22.31
1988	59.95	74.81	21.45
1989	65.71	65.06	20.47
1990	30.03	67.03	20.80
1991	28.37	62.96	20.01
1992	24.95	55.41	18.45
1993	N/A	N/A	N/A
1994	N/A	N/A	N/A

AVERAGE PASSENGER TRIP LENGTH
(km)

Year	Domestic	Europe	Int'nl	Total
1985	234	796	3,055	2,422
1986	245	792	3,017	2,379
1987	237	797	3,044	2,424
1988	280	811	3,189	2,529
1989	283	819	3,204	2,621
1990	319	823	3,192	2,654
1991	325	861	3,305	2,748
1992	375	898	3,352	2,856
1993	367	920	3,354	2,846
1994	354	940	3,387	2,855

TOTAL AIRCRAFT KM FLOWN
(million)

Year	Domestic	Europe	Int'nl	Total
1985	24	74	219	243
1986	25	78	288	313
1987	26	83	273	299
1988	32	101	310	342
1989	32	106	318	350
1990	31	117	346	378
1991	30	113	333	363
1992	32	121	363	395
1993	40	134	400	440
1994	43	138	426	469

AVERAGE AIRCRAFT SIZE
(seats)

Year	Domestic	Europe	Int'nl	Total
1985	123	133	260	246
1986	129	132	201	195
1987	132	132	223	216
1988	140	128	253	242
1989	151	132	253	244
1990	184	129	252	247
1991	188	132	257	251
1992	212	140	262	258
1993	183	148	268	260
1994	173	149	267	259

FLEET SIZE
(units)

Year	Europe	Int'nl	Total
1985	80	129	
1986	86	138	
1987	88	141	
1988	114	186	
1989	115	195	
1990	115	211	
1991	119	207	
1992	117	211	
1993	119	212	
1994	118	231	

DAILY AIRCRAFT UTILISATION
(hours)

Year	Europe	Int'l	Total
1985	4.9	7.0	8.3
1986	4.9	6.8	8.1
1987	5.0	7.0	8.3
1988	4.9	7.0	8.2
1989	5.1	7.0	8.1
1990	5.6	7.0	8.0
1991	5.2	6.7	7.8
1992	5.6	7.2	8.2
1993	6.0	7.9	9.1
1994	6.2	7.5	8.8

TOTAL HOURS FLOWN
(hours)

Year	Domestic	Europe	Intern'l	Total
1985	60,000	144,200	329,202	389,202
1986	62,100	152,900	344,616	406,716
1987	63,100	160,900	362,072	425,172
1988	80,800	203,600	474,809	555,609
1989	79,500	215,600	495,563	575,063
1990	79,400	236,500	539,547	618,947
1991	76,100	224,400	509,804	585,904
1992	79,100	237,300	551,833	630,933
1993	94,600	261,200	607,992	702,592
1994	104,800	267,000	634,900	739,700

ATK PER EMPLOYEE
(units)

Year	Average
1985	210,585
1986	212,790
1987	220,006
1988	257,127
1989	236,802
1990	248,957
1991	255,276
1992	305,150
1993	334,469
1994	350,751

EMPLOYEES
(units)

Year	Average
1985	36,967
1986	37,789
1987	38,688
1988	44,025
1989	49,623
1990	52,252
1991	50,398
1992	47,103
1993	47,334
1994	48,233

BRITISH AIRWAYS FINANCIAL PERFORMANCE
(1990 prices - million ECU)

Year	Op'ing Revenue	Op'ing Cost	Op'ing Profit	Net Profit
1985	5,521	4,887	634	348
1986	5,499	5,096	403	356
1987	4,513	4,220	292	236
1988	5,110	4,695	416	241
1989	6,318	5,767	551	284
1990	5,972	5,430	542	330
1991	6,165	5,939	225	129
1992	6,243	5,794	449	332
1993	5,817	5,462	355	204
1994	6,589	6,024	565	326

BRITISH AIRWAYS FINANCIAL PERFORMANCE
(current prices - million ECU)

Year	Op'ing Revenue	Op'ing Cost	Op'ing Profit	Net Profit
1985	4,323	3,826	497	272
1986	4,545	4,211	333	294
1987	3,893	3,640	252	204
1988	4,603	4,228	374	217
1989	6,008	5,484	524	270
1990	5,972	5,430	542	330
1991	6,412	6,178	235	134
1992	6,686	6,206	480	356
1993	6,367	5,978	388	223
1994	7,346	6,716	630	363

F.3. TAP Air Portugal

Portugal is a small country on the edge of Europe. Its population of around ten million enjoys a per capita GDP among the lowest in the EU. National territory extends to two Atlantic island groups, the Madeira archipelago and the Azores, respectively one-hour's and 2½ hours' flying time from Lisbon. Portugal inherited strong social, economic and political links with Africa and South America from its days as a colonial power: the nation's later economic decline created communities of emigrants and their descendants in the United States, Canada and South America. Continental Portugal and Madeira are the focus of strong, seasonal tourist movements from northern Europe. Until the recent past this environment has been the driving force behind the network development of TAP Air Portugal, and has defined the airline's commercial strategy.

F.3.1. Strategic responses

TAP began life as an offshoot of the Portuguese transport ministry in 1945, before being privatized in 1953. In the economic and political turmoil resulting from the end of the country's years of dictatorship in 1974 and immediate withdrawal from its colonial role, the airline was nationalized. Until then TAP had made heavy profits from its African network, serving as the only operator between metropolitan Portugal and the colonial territories of Angola, Cape Verde, Guinea-Bissau, Mozambique, São Tomé and Principe. In the years of independence war that preceded the 1974 revolution, the national carrier was awarded lucrative military transport contracts on these routes. These revenues allowed the carrier to subsidize its European and North American networks. The freshly nationalized carrier thus inherited a capacity, in terms of fleet, workforce and engineering facilities, suited to a major intercontinental operator but with a much reduced market. Since then, as Portugal moved into mainstream Europe after years of isolation, TAP began to focus on the integration of a European network with its intercontinental services. Building on its South American and African networks, the airline attempted to establish a mini-hub at Lisbon by adjusting schedules, and marketing connections, particularly in the United Kingdom. Heavy demand for these services from Lisbon and from the destination countries, at both premium and leisure fares, together with a growth of direct services from Europe to Johannesburg and Brazilian cities, gave the venture only limited success. Currently, TAP's intercontinental connections are marketed outside Portugal mainly through consolidators.

Since the late 1980s the airline has begun to face economic reality: its domestic market is low yield; its African market is characterized by political instability and difficulty in repatriating revenues; the airline faces strong competition from charter carriers for leisure traffic on European routes; Portugal's North American market is thin, low yield and highly seasonal. The airline had been slow to adapt to changes and opportunities in the European environment; its fleet mix was inefficient in terms of type and capacity; labour efficiency was low at all levels while union power maintained high levels of restrictive practices. The company had pursued high load factors on its European routes at the expense of yield and operating results: a high proportion of its seats were sold to tour operators and through consolidators.

In 1985 the carrier recognized that although the capacity it offered on routes to its principal leisure market, the United Kingdom, was roughly equal to that of UK scheduled carriers, its market share of total traffic between the UK and Portugal was probably less than 20%: the bulk of the market being carried by highly efficient charter operators based at London's

Gatwick and Luton airports. TAP responded by forming a charter subsidiary: Air Atlantis was successful in capturing some 30% of the charter market by operating for tour operators interested in developing the market from the UK's provincial airports, but the cost base of an ultimately state-owned airline was no match for year-round operators such as Britannia Airways, and the company ceased operations in 1992.

In the period 1986–89 TAP embarked on a programme of network expansion to North America and within Europe. The spreading of fixed costs was certainly one motivation for the move, and it was facilitated in Europe by the first package (Article 8) which gave Portugal and Ireland, as peripheral states, the right to introduce Fifth Freedom services within the Community ahead of general implementation of regulatory relaxation. Having to fly long, thin routes to Europe's major population centres, TAP was accustomed to developing routes by initially operating from Lisbon via Porto to, say, Manchester. The operation of Fifth Freedom services linking Lisbon to cities where demand was not sufficiently high to warrant a dedicated service operated by aircraft of a size available to TAP was therefore a concept which appealed to the airline. Between 1987 and 1988 it began operations from Lisbon to Dublin via Manchester, Vienna via Munich, Hamburg via Amsterdam, Stuttgart via Nice and Athens via Rome. Success of the strategy was mixed: at present Munich and Vienna are still linked by a Fifth Freedom service as are Athens and Rome; Manchester has not survived as a TAP destination; Dublin is operated once a week from Lisbon through Faro; Stuttgart is a code-share destination operated by Portugalia; while Nice is served as a consecutive cabotage through Lyon. Hamburg appears to be the only TAP Fifth Freedom destination to have successfully grown into a dedicated operation, although one of its weekly services goes on to Berlin.

Prestige routes to North America were intended to tap the ethnic markets of New England, Toronto and California. Thus the airline resumed its Boston service in 1986, began a Toronto service in 1987 and offered Los Angeles as a destination in 1989. Travel on these routes was likely to be predominantly leisure-based, targeting mainly population groups in the US and Canada with relatively low levels of disposable income visiting family in Portugal. Given that low-cost North American charter companies were geared up to providing the mainly seasonal service as they had been doing for years, the reasons behind the decision of a scheduled carrier to enter the market with a weekly year-round service are unclear. One justification for the route expansion was the dilution of unit costs across the TAP network. The period of expansion coincided with an improvement in the carrier's cash flow through a sale and lease back operation on its long-haul Lockheed Tristar fleet.

F.3.2. Routes, air services and capacity

The Portuguese domestic market consists of three types of air service: those in continental Portugal, dominated by the Lisbon-Porto route; public service obligation routes to the Azores and Madeira from the mainland and between the two island regions, and services within the Azores. TAP faces competition on continental routes from Portugalia, Portugal's private scheduled carrier. On services linking the continent with the Azores and Madeira, TAP operates under public service obligation rules defined in the third package, while services within the Azores are provided by SATA, owned by the regional government of the Azores and operating under the temporary exclusion of the Azores from application of Regulation (EEC) No 2408/92 of the third package.

Network growth within the EU has been achieved through:

(a)   development of Fifth Freedom services;
(b)   consecutive cabotage services in France and Germany;
(c)   operating direct services from Faro, Funchal and Porto through Lisbon;
(d)   capacity sharing and code sharing arrangements.

Only the first two of the above tactics have been facilitated directly by EU legislation.

TAP's greatest difficulties in initiating and developing successfully routes between Portugal and destinations outside the major European centres lie in the distance between Lisbon and potential markets and the capacity of aircraft available in the TAP fleet. The unit capacity of the airline's medium-range fleet is between 118 and 156 seats. This results in low frequency operations on non-trunk routes, for example to Nice three times weekly, which fail to stimulate the market to the extent that might be achieved by a daily operation. The airline attempts to overcome this by operating through Porto, amalgamating the traffic to and from the northern capital to Lisbon's traffic, and by increasing its code share operations with Portugal's second international scheduled operator, the privately owned Portugalia.

Between June 1989 and June 1992 Air Portugal initiated 15 new non-stop intra-European routes, between:

Lisbon and:	Berlin	Porto and:	Barcelona
	Bilbao		Bologna
	Bordeaux		*Bordeaux*
	Seville		*Lyon*
	Malaga		*Santiago de*
	Marseilles		*Compostela*
			Seville
Faro and:	*Brussels*	Funchal and:	London
			Frankfurt

Of these routes those in *italics* are no longer served by TAP. The Porto-Bologna and Porto-Barcelona services originate in Lisbon. Marseilles continues to be served from Lisbon, but on a stopping service operated by Air Toulouse. Porto-Bordeaux is now a route of Regional Air, a French carrier. Funchal is served from Frankfurt non-stop by Condor and LTU, but the TAP service has fallen to a one-stop through Lisbon.

Between June 1992 and June 1995 new non-stop intra-European routes were started between:

Lisbon and:	Munich	Funchal and:	*Paris*
Faro and:	Dublin	Porto and:	*Hamburg*
	Paris		*Luxembourg*

The Lisbon-Munich non-stop service survives, as do the weekly non-stops between Faro and Dublin, a service originating in Lisbon, and Faro-Paris, originating in Funchal and replacing the Funchal-Paris non-stop service. Hamburg is now served from Porto by Hamburg Airlines, Luxembourg no longer has a direct service from Porto.

It is worth noting that carriers which have taken over routes abandoned by TAP (the French carrier Regional Air and Hamburg Airlines) operate respectively 36-seat Saab 340 and 97-seat BAe-146 equipment. This compares with TAP's smallest aircraft, the Boeing 737, which can carry 118 passengers. Portugalia employs Fokker 100 jet aircraft, with seats for 101 passengers.

The TAP fleet at the end of 1994 included two newly purchased Airbus A340 aircraft, in partial replacement of the long-haul fleet of Lockheed Tristar-500. The purchase of these aircraft ended the airline's policy of acquisition through operating leases. In the same year the leases on two Boeing 737-300 aircraft terminated and they were not replaced. The airline has found it difficult to dispose of its Tristar fleet: one of the seven aircraft is leased to Angolan Airlines, another to BWIA. Since 1994 TAP has acquired two further A340 aircraft. The composition of the present fleet is set out in Table F.1:

Table F.1.   TAP fleet 1994

Units	Aircraft	No. of seats	Utilization (hours/day)	
			1994	*Increase from 1992 (%)*
8	Boeing 737-200	118	8.43	0
8	Boeing 737-300	132	8.93	4
6	Airbus A320-200	156	8.89	10
5	Airbus A310-300	215	8.42	4
5	Lockheed 1011-500	250	8.24	(-4)
4	Airbus A340-300	280	N/A	

Source: World Air Transport Statistics, IATA.

TAP enjoys certain advantages in aircraft utilization. High capacity aircraft can be used on the denser European routes during the day and on African and South American flights at night, benefiting from Lisbon airport's curfew-free night operations. Lower capacity aircraft can be employed outside the more attractive hours for European operations on TAP's public service routes to Madeira and the Azores.

F.3.3. Marketing, traffic and market share

Comparing TAP's capacity share in Europe with that of all AEA airlines, measured in ASK, TAP has increased production between 1992 and 1994 by around 4% over the two years while AEA members have reduced their total production by 7%. Thus TAP's share of AEA production has risen from 3.1% of AEA total of available seat-kilometres in 1992 to 3.6% in 1994.

In terms of marketing in Europe TAP has started a number of code sharing arrangements with Portugalia which have added new destinations to its network. An alliance with British Midland was established in 1995 which gives the airline access to six provincial UK destinations via London Heathrow from Faro, Funchal, Lisbon and Porto. Outside the European market, alliances have been signed with Air Afrique between Lisbon and Abidjan, and with Delta Airlines for code shares between Lisbon and New York's Kennedy airport (Delta service) and Newark (TAP service).

The airline has introduced a frequent flyer programme to encourage passenger loyalty, but faces the difficulties met by other smaller carriers in creating a product which is attractive to frequent flyers resident outside Portugal. The eventual solution for TAP will be to join the programme of a carrier with a global network.

TAP offers a premium product on all European services: Navigator Class. The carrier has invested in dedicated lounge facilities at all Portuguese airports, and buys space in similar facilities where possible at airports served outside Portugal.

It is difficult to assess the airline's market share on individual European routes. However, TAP's overall 1994 passenger load factor in European operations was 63% compared with the AEA average of 60%. But here it is important to stress the importance of the interplay between load factor and average passenger yield: there is little point in pursuing high load factors if this is achieved by loading the aircraft with low yield passengers. The market share of passengers paying premium, business class fares is crucial to commercial success. In Europe TAP produced 3.1% of all AEA members airlines' revenue passenger-kilometres in 1994. This was a fall from the 1993 figure of 3.8%, reflecting the carrier's rationalization of its European network.

Deservedly or not, TAP Air Portugal developed a generally poor reputation for reliability. Management has addressed the airline's image and punctuality, measured in percentage of departures leaving within 15 minutes of schedule, which rose each year from 1990 (74%) to 1994 (88%).

F.3.4. Productivity and operating costs

Between 1985 and 1994 TAP increased its activity on European routes, measured in terms of seat-kilometres produced, by around 160%, from 1,717 million ASK to 4,429 million ASK. The RPK, those seat-kilometres sold to passengers, rose by a smaller amount, reflected in the fall in average load factor on the carrier's European routes over the same period from 70% to 63%.

Growth on TAP's international services outside Europe has been much slower, with production measured in ASK increasing by 47% over the same period. This is a result of the airline's withdrawal from most North Atlantic routes: international, non-EU, ASK have fallen each year between 1992 and 1994.

Total 1994 current costs (before extraordinary items) showed an improvement of 7.7% over the previous year. Financial costs reduced to 9% of total, due largely to the Portuguese state's capital injection. Personnel costs, representing 29% of total costs, showed an improvement of over 4% on 1993.

In terms of personnel the airline is working towards the objectives set in its restructuring plan, reaching year end in 1994 with 614 fewer on the payroll than 12 months before. The highest drop (11%) came from reductions in staff overseas, as the network of sales offices and representatives was rationalized. Absenteeism, tackled in the restructuring programme, fell from the pre-restructuring levels of 9% to 5.5% in 1994.

F.3.5. Pricing and yields

Measured in terms of US cents per revenue passenger-kilometre, TAP's average yield on European services grew by around 33% between 1985 and 1992, while on services outside Europe it fell in real terms.

On many of its European routes TAP is in competition with major world carriers serving strong markets and international traffic fed into their European network through home-base hubs. These major carriers also enjoy the potential for wide-ranging capacity and code sharing arrangements with other majors. In this situation the Portuguese carrier is seldom a leader in pricing its products. An exception to this has been in the innovative marketing of its premium fare product, Navigator Class: this has been sold at discounts directly and through consolidators. Here the airline treads the difficult path between dilution of business class revenue and increasing the overall yield by creating a more flexible fare structure. Promotions to increase occupancy of the Navigator cabin include partner fares, complimentary or low cost overnight hotel packages and special fares to leisure destinations such as Funchal.

Part of TAP's restructuring programme is a commitment to increase average yields. This is to be achieved by reducing capacity available and improving the efficiency of its resale through the application of an increasingly sophisticated yield management system.

F.3.6. Profitability and sources of financing

The airline has failed to return a profit since nationalization. In 1994 TAP's financial performance reflected the company's efforts to reduce costs: the operating loss was reduced from ESC 14.1 billion to 2.6 billion, but the 1994 net result was a loss of almost ESC 30 billion (USD 190 million). The accumulated debt and narrow capital base has meant that the airline has been technically bankrupt for some years. At end 1992 the carrier's total assets represented 88.7% of its total outside liabilities. At end 1993 TAP's equity was over ESC 50 billion in the red (negative by around USD 350 million). State aid, directly or indirectly, has plugged some gaps while the financial guarantees of the state gave creditors a measure of confidence in the company. In 1988 the government transferred to the airline the land and buildings from which it operates at Lisbon airport. Annual state subsidies helped compensate for the high costs and the low, government imposed, fare structure of operations to the autonomous regions of Madeira and the Azores, while other subsidies offset losses associated with operating inherently unprofitable services to the ex-colony of São Tomé. Subsidies for services operated by TAP under public service obligation rules added ESC 4.7 billion (around USD 30 million) to its revenue in 1994. TAP's exemption from taxes is set to continue until 1997, when the current restructuring programme is complete and the final injection of state cash has been received (see below).

In 1994 the Portuguese authorities informed the Commission that they intended to increase the capital of the national carrier. This was to be accompanied by the adoption of a four-year restructuring programme aiming to restore the airline's economic and financial structure, with formal state guarantees for the company's credit operations.

Restructuring had begun earlier, when the Portuguese government realized that TAP's erratic decline would eventually lead to the total collapse of the national carrier:

(a)   the labour bill was attacked with a wage freeze and a programme of early retirement inducements, agreed redundancy and natural wastage to reduce the size of the workforce;

(b)   a number of activities were identified which could be run successfully as individual profit centres: among them was ground handling;

(c)   the operations of the charter subsidiary Air Atlantis were terminated.

The intention was to pay into the company in four annual instalments beginning in 1994, a total of ESC 180 billion (around USD 1.2 billion). The restructuring programme aims to return an operating profit in 1996, and an overall profit by the end of the programme, in 1997. The productivity target to be achieved was set at 242,000 ATK per employee, 780 hours per cockpit staff and 13,450 ASK per member of cabin staff. In broad terms this was to be achieved by:

(a)   elimination of chronically unprofitable routes within Europe (in 1992 one in ten European routes returned in revenue less than half the associated cost);

(b)   discontinuing all North American routes except Lisbon-New York;

(c)   reducing the size of the fleet to 32 units (from 38);

(d)   improving financial management, marketing analysis and yield management.

The Portuguese government contended initially that the capital was a necessary move which would be pursued by a rational private investor. The Commission ruled that unlikely and preferred to regard the money as state aid, which it would allow to continue subject to TAP implementing a restructuring plan it proposed and achieving performance objectives. A number of undertakings were also required, among them:

(a)   the capital would be used for restructuring the airline: there would be no purchase in whole or in part of any European carrier during the restructuring period;

(b)   the airline would at the end of the restructuring period begin a process which would eventually lead to its privatization;

(c)   tax exemptions would not continue after the restructuring programme was completed;

(d)   TAP should not increase its production (ASK) above an agreed proportion of total EEA supply.

Complete outsourcing of the maintenance and security of the company's buildings was achieved in 1994. Duty free shops at Portuguese airports have been a TAP concession but will become a joint-stock company with TAP's participation at 51%. Handling, maintenance and medical services will eventually become autonomous operations.

F.3.7. Impact of EU measures and conclusions

The reaction of TAP Air Portugal to European liberalization was slow to develop. The airline took advantage of early Fifth Freedom opportunities, but only recently has it considered capacity share with other airlines as an alternative to creating a more flexible fleet of its own to serve non-trunk routes between Portugal and the rest of the European Union. This has been paralleled by the carrier's reluctance to enter into strategic alliances with major world carriers and regional carriers, although these are now developing.

It appears that the greatest direct effects of Community legislation on the operating and management strategy of TAP have been:

(a)   operation of Fifth Freedom services within the Community (first package);

(b)   operation of consecutive cabotage services (third package);

(c)   increased flexibility of fares (second and third packages);

(d)   public service obligation rules (third package);

(e)   the formal requirement, imposed by the Commission as a condition of state aid, and reinforcing the airline's own judgement, of the adoption of an austerity plan and a series of measures aimed at restoring the carrier to financial equilibrium (Article 93 (2)).

Indirectly, an increasingly competitive air transport environment within the Community has induced the carrier to consider forming alliances with regional carriers within the Community, as well as major carriers on intercontinental services.

Following the recognition of the need for capital and operational restructuring of the airline, and the requirement to obtain EU agreement for state aid, TAP's management and technical resources have been focused sharply on the European market. The airline is making progress towards achieving the goals set out in its agreement with the Commission (and the third tranche of state aid was recently approved by the Commission). Figure F.1 sets out the relevant statistics describing TAP's labour efficiency of production in relation to the 1997 target, and shows achievement to date.

Figure F.1. TAP's productivity and the targets of its restructuring plan

	1992	1993	1994	1995 target
ATK per employee	137,000	157,000	165,000	242,000
ASK per cabin staff	7,966	9,435	9,568	13,450
Rev hours per cockpit crew (est.)	466	465	488	780

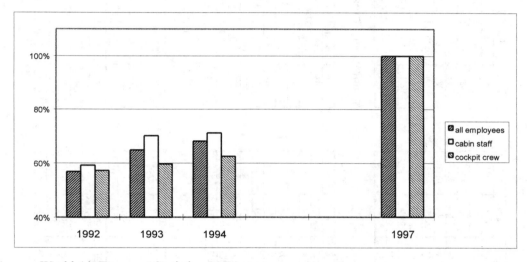

Source: World Air Transport Statistics, IATA.

TAP AIR PORTUGAL
TRAFFIC AND FINANCIAL DATA 1985-94

PASSENGER TRAFFIC *(thousand)*

Year	Domestic	Europe	Int'nl	Total
1985	719	867	1,306	2,026
1986	732	934	1,401	2,133
1987	841	1,104	1,598	2,439
1988	818	1,269	1,817	2,635
1989	730	1,465	2,060	2,791
1990	796	1,656	2,304	3,100
1991	829	1,728	2,359	3,188
1992	879	1,890	2,600	3,479
1993	940	1,978	2,677	3,617
1994	1,003	1,863	2,498	3,501

RPK *(million)*

Year	Domestic	Europe	Int'nl	Total
1985	603	1,196	3,637	4,240
1986	626	1,294	3,850	4,475
1987	717	1,560	4,261	4,978
1988	761	1,853	4,879	5,640
1989	733	2,151	5,498	6,231
1990	768	2,446	6,067	6,836
1991	825	2,608	6,200	7,025
1992	879	2,838	6,793	7,671
1993	897	2,992	6,971	7,868
1994	970	2,812	6,616	7,586

ASK *(million)*

Year	Domestic	Europe	Int'nl	Total
1985	854	1,717	5,308	6,162
1986	881	1,896	5,814	6,695
1987	984	2,190	6,037	7,021
1988	1,088	2,811	7,083	8,171
1989	1,031	3,359	8,150	9,181
1990	1,020	3,785	8,698	9,718
1991	1,121	4,084	9,169	10,290
1992	1,152	4,620	9,992	11,144
1993	1,198	4,656	10,011	11,209
1994	1,352	4,429	9,695	11,047

ATK *(million)*

Year	Domestic	Europe	Int'nl	Total
1985	95	197	707	802
1986	98	217	769	867
1987	112	251	807	919
1988	126	330	958	1,084
1989	122	406	1,102	1,224
1990	125	460	1,166	1,291
1991	136	508	1,236	1,372
1992	138	550	1,333	1,471
1993	142	545	1,317	1,459
1994	162	533	1,280	1,442

RTK *(million)*

Year	Domestic	Europe	Int'nl	Total
1985	61	125	427	488
1986	63	136	454	517
1987	73	162	495	569
1988	79	192	565	644
1989	79	230	651	730
1990	85	260	709	794
1991	89	273	716	805
1992	94	294	775	869
1993	96	305	794	890
1994	104	293	771	875

WEIGHT LOAD FACTOR *(%)*

Year	Domestic	Europe	Int'nl	Total
1985	65%	63%	60%	61%
1986	65%	63%	59%	60%
1987	66%	65%	61%	62%
1988	63%	58%	59%	59%
1989	64%	57%	59%	59%
1990	68%	57%	61%	60%
1991	66%	54%	61%	61%
1992	68%	54%	58%	59%
1993	68%	56%	58%	59%
1994	64%	55%	60%	61%

PASSENGER LOAD FACTOR *(%)*

Year	Domestic	Europe	Int'nl	Total
1985	71%	70%	69%	69%
1986	71%	68%	66%	67%
1987	73%	71%	71%	71%
1988	70%	66%	69%	69%
1989	71%	64%	67%	68%
1990	75%	65%	70%	70%
1991	74%	64%	68%	68%
1992	76%	61%	68%	69%
1993	75%	64%	70%	70%
1994	72%	63%	68%	69%

PASSENGER YIELD *(US cents - 1985 prices)*

Year	Domestic	Europe	Int'nl	Total
1985	4.89	8.61	7.21	6.88
1986	6.10	10.27	7.42	7.24
1987	6.48	11.34	8.02	7.79
1988	6.70	11.33	8.23	8.02
1989	6.24	10.62	7.86	7.67
1990	7.10	11.54	8.55	8.39
1991	7.32	11.37	8.96	8.77
1992	8.54	11.47	8.58	8.58
1993	N/A	N/A	N/A	N/A
1994	N/A	N/A	N/A	N/A

FREIGHT AND MAIL TON KM *(million)*

Year	Domestic	Europe	Int'nl	Total
1985	7	17	95	102
1986	7	20	108	114
1987	9	22	112	121
1988	10	25	126	137
1989	13	36	156	169
1990	16	40	163	179
1991	15	38	158	173
1992	15	38	164	179
1993	12	32	157	169
1994	14	36	226	239

TAP AIR PORTUGAL
TRAFFIC AND FINANCIAL DATA 1985-94

FREIGHT AND MAIL YIELD
(US cents - 1985 prices)

Year	Domestic	Europe	Int'nl	Total
1985	36	54	33	33
1986	49	75	42	42
1987	43	73	41	41
1988	39	66	38	38
1989	33	53	33	33
1990	24	44	29	28
1991	42	58	36	36
1992	52	59	35	36
1993				
1994				

AVERAGE PASSENGER TRIP LENGTH
(km)

Year	Domestic	Europe	Int'nl	Total
1985	839	1,380	2,784	2,093
1986	854	1,386	2,748	2,098
1987	853	1,414	2,666	2,041
1988	930	1,460	2,685	2,140
1989	1,003	1,468	2,669	2,233
1990	965	1,477	2,633	2,205
1991	996	1,509	2,628	2,204
1992	999	1,501	2,613	2,205
1993	954	1,512	2,604	2,175
1994	967	1,510	2,648	2,167

TOTAL AIRCRAFT KM FLOWN
(million)

Year	Domestic	Europe	Int'nl	Total
1985	7	12	28	34
1986	7	13	30	37
1987	8	15	32	40
1988	8	20	38	46
1989	8	23	43	51
1990	8	26	47	55
1991	9	28	50	58
1992	9	33	56	65
1993	9	34	57	66
1994	10	34	56	67

AVERAGE AIRCRAFT SIZE
(seats)

Year	Domestic	Europe	Int'nl	Total
1985	129	146	192	180
1986	128	144	192	180
1987	130	144	189	178
1988	130	142	187	176
1989	136	147	190	182
1990	126	144	185	177
1991	132	145	184	177
1992	131	140	178	172
1993	136	139	176	171
1994	133	132	172	166

FLEET SIZE
(units)

Year	Europe	Int'nl
1985	14	28
1986	13	26
1987	13	25
1988	15	25
1989	16	26
1990	16	27
1991	17	27
1992	20	32
1993	23	38
1994	22	38

TOTAL HOURS FLOWN
(units)

Year	Europe	Int'nl
1985	19,200	40,336
1986	21,600	42,956
1987	25,100	45,560
1988	32,800	54,321
1989	38,300	61,548
1990	44,000	67,164
1991	46,700	72,042
1992	54,500	81,574
1993	55,000	82,664
1994	54,800	84,500

EMPLOYEES
(units)

Year	Average
1985	9,786
1986	9,685
1987	9,580
1988	9,580
1989	9,662
1990	10,102
1991	10,681
1992	10,829
1993	10,123
1994	9,108

ATK PER EMPLOYEE
(units)

Year	Average
1985	88,900
1986	93,324
1987	99,055
1988	116,895
1989	127,423
1990	128,450
1991	128,767
1992	136,085
1993	144,500
1994	158,630

DAILY AIRCRAFT UTILISATION
(hours)

Year	Europe	Int'l
1985	3.76	3.95
1986	4.55	4.53
1987	5.29	4.99
1988	5.99	5.95
1989	6.56	6.49
1990	7.53	6.82
1991	7.53	7.31
1992	7.47	6.98
1993	6.55	5.96
1994	6.82	6.09

TAP FINANCIAL PERFORMANCE
(1990 prices - million ECU)

Year	Op'ing Revenue	Op'ing Cost	Op'ing Profit	Net Profit
1985	680	694	-15	-40
1986	564	613	-49	-32
1987	N/A	N/A	N/A	N/A
1988	681	712	-31	-21
1989	N/A	N/A	N/A	N/A
1990	787	821	-35	-12
1991	841	861	-20	-29
1992	803	969	-166	-140
1993	748	943	-196	-169
1994	N/A	N/A	N/A	N/A

TAP FINANCIAL PERFORMANCE
(current prices - million ECU)

Year	Op'ing Revenue	Op'ing Cost	Op'ing Profit	Net Profit
1985	532	544	-11	-31
1986	466	506	-41	-27
1987	N/A	N/A	N/A	N/A
1988	613	642	-28	-19
1989	N/A	N/A	N/A	N/A
1990	787	821	-35	-12
1991	875	896	-21	-30
1992	860	1,037	-178	-149
1993	818	1,032	-214	-185
1994	N/A	N/A	N/A	N/A

F.4. Maersk Air

Maersk Air was formed in 1969 as a wholly-owned subsidiary of the A P Moller (Maersk Line) Group. Developed primarily as a charter airline, Maersk Air has developed an extensive Danish domestic network and, in 1984, launched international scheduled flights from Billund to London Southend. This route was subsequently replaced by a service from Billund to London Gatwick. Scheduled services are now operated from Copenhagen to London Gatwick, the Faroe Islands and Kristiansand and from Billund to Amsterdam, Brussels, the Faroe Islands, Frankfurt, Paris and Stockholm. In 1993 Birmingham European Airways was bought by Maersk Air and the former now operates as Maersk Air UK.

F.4.1. Strategic responses

The A P Moller Group has interests in shipping, oil exploration, shipbuilding and retailing. Maersk Air is a self-supporting subsidiary of the Group. Initially, the airline operated scheduled services between Copenhagen and Odense, Skrystrup and Stanning although the core business gradually developed into charter and inclusive-tour operations and further significant development of scheduled services did not occur until the mid-1980s.

Initially, the growth of Maersk was constrained by the regulatory regime of Denmark. This was because of limits imposed on the number of charter operations and package-tour duration. During the 1970s and the early 1980s, the Scandinavian governments (Norway, Denmark and Sweden) set up and imposed a joint aviation policy whereby 50% of the domestic route licences were awarded to SAS and the remaining 50% to private operators. This was to protect national government investment in SAS.

As an example, when a new non-flag-carrier entrant applied to operate a scheduled service on an unserved route, SAS was given first refusal. Also, SAS held a monopoly between major city pairs within Scandinavia. Therefore, for many years, airline competition on scheduled routes has been constrained by the regulatory authorities.

The 1983 EC Regional Directive gave Maersk the opportunity to establish a scheduled service between Billund and London (Southend). This operated from 1984–90 and, during this period, was the only scheduled international service operated by Maersk. Shortly after operations commenced, allegedly because of pressure from competing airlines flying from Copenhagen to London (Heathrow), London (Southend) was changed to Southend in the ABC airline guide.

The joint aviation policy continued until 1988 when, as the result of pressure from the other non-flag-carriers, the Scandinavian authorities allowed the non-flag-carriers to operate intra-Scandinavian services, except between seven major cities, and also from Category 1 to Category 2 airports in the EC. In the case of the latter routes, this was provided that SAS was not interested in operating these routes and that there was no existing service to the same Category 2 airport from other airports in Scandinavia. This partial liberalization was unattractive as small carriers could operate and develop thin routes to feed SAS hubs but with the possibility of having these routes taken over by SAS if traffic grew.

In 1988 Maersk also purchased a 40% stake in Plymouth (UK) based Brymon Airways which in turn bought loss-making Birmingham Executive Airways (which shortly afterwards was renamed Birmingham European Airways). This financial investment was seen at the time as an initial stepping-stone towards the transfer of flights from Southend to Gatwick and initial preparation for the single European market. In August 1993, Birmingham European Airways became wholly owned by Maersk and was renamed Maersk Air UK. The airline now operates under a franchise agreement with British Airways. At the same time, Brymon became a wholly-owned subsidiary of British Airways.

These partial measures towards full liberalization permitted smaller independent airlines to serve trans-Scandinavian routes without harming SAS, which the governments were determined to protect. However, the Danish government did not want to see any erosion of Copenhagen's importance as an international gateway which might happen if there were a sudden proliferation of services from provincial airports to Stockholm and Oslo. Back in 1986 Air Business unsuccessfully applied for licences from Billund and Esbjerg through Aarhus to Stockholm, Oslo and Gothenburg. Cimber and Maersk were equally unsuccessful with similar applications. Ten years later, the only one of these routes that is being operated is by Maersk between Billund and Stockholm.

The 1990 second package allowed new entrants to serve routes between national Category 2 airports and other Category 1 airports and between national Category 1 and other Category 2 airports within the EU. In addition, multiple designations by a state were allowed for major routes. For example, the Copenhagen-London (Gatwick) route was fully liberalized although each country was allowed to do what they wanted with their designation policy, for example, to ensure the protection of state-owned airlines. Therefore, in 1990 there was the prospect of BA and Air Europe being in competition with SAS and Maersk, although it was up to the Danish Minister of Transport to decide if a second Danish carrier be allowed.

As it turned out, the second package enabled Maersk to take a major step forward as an international scheduled carrier. Firstly, SAS pulled out of the Copenhagen-London (Gatwick) route (to be followed by Air Europe some time later) leaving the way clear for Maersk and, secondly, Maersk was able to introduce services from Billund to Amsterdam, Brussels, Frankfurt, London (Gatwick) and Stockholm.

The third package, effective 1 January 1993, introduced the principle of free pricing, route designation of airlines no longer applied and capacity was unrestricted. So far, the third package has provided little benefit to the route development strategy of Maersk and other problems, discussed later, have exercised some constraints on the subsequent development of the airline. One example of this is that under the third package the potential commercial benefits depend on the catchment and services that are already operating. Therefore, Maersk as a new entrant had reduced potential for developing Copenhagen traffic (SAS being the incumbent airline) and had therefore chosen to concentrate their activities on Jutland.

F.4.2. Routes, air services and capacity

Between 1989 and March 1996 Maersk have gradually expanded their portfolio of scheduled services. These are shown in Table F.2 together with weekday service frequencies in each direction.

Table F.2.   Maersk scheduled, services 1989–96

Route	1989	1990	1991	1992	1993	1994	1995	1996
From Copenhagen								
Billund	10	10	10	10	10	10	9	9
Bornholm					6	6	7	7
Esbjerg	8	7	7	7	7	8	7	7
Faroe Islands	1	1	1	1	1	1	1	1
Kristiansand						3	3	3
London - Gatwick				2	2	2	2	2
Odense	8	8	9	9	9	8	8	8
Vojens			5	6	6	6	6	6
Total routes	*4*	*4*	*5*	*6*	*7*	*8*	*8*	*8*
From Billund								
Amsterdam			1	1	1	1	2	3
Brussels			1	2	2	2	3	3
Copenhagen	10	10	10	10	10	10	9	9
Esbjerg	1	1						
Faroe Islands				<1	<1	<1	<1	<1
Frankfurt					1	2	2	2
London - Gatwick			1	2	2	2	3	3
Odense								2
Paris - CdG								1
Southend	2	2						
Stavanger		1						
Stockholm			1	1	2	1	1	2
Total routes	*3*	*4*	*5*	*6*	*7*	*7*	*7*	*9*

While Table F.2 is of interest, there are specific factors which have influenced the development of these routes. Between 1986 and 1996 domestic scheduled services in Denmark have been provided on a continuous basis by SAS, Maersk, and Cimber Air. The domestic routes were split up in the late 1980s between the three airlines and run under the auspices of the Dan Air organization (no relation of Dan Air which was absorbed by British Airways) which set the fares. The ownership of Dan Air was split 38% (Maersk), 57% (SAS) and 5% (Cimber). With the onset of full liberalization Dan Air was wound up in late October 1995 and each of the airlines can now fly where they want. Because of the restricted domestic market, in autumn 1995 Maersk claimed that they would not be introducing an extensive range of new domestic scheduled services, although a new service to Odense from Billund is shown in the March 1996 OAG timetable.

Apart from the Billund to London (Southend)/London (Gatwick) service, Maersk's development of international scheduled services has been a policy of staged development. Billund has been developed as a hub in view of the SAS dominance of Copenhagen. In fact, Copenhagen-London is the only city pair in which Maersk is in competition with SAS (who operate to Heathrow). From the start (1991) the Billund-Brussels service was operated as code share between Maersk and Sabena. It is understood the Billund-Amsterdam service has gone the same way, following a code share agreement between Maersk and KLM.

Outside Western Europe, the range of destinations served by scheduled services from Denmark are dominated by the SAS monopoly. Even the development by Maersk of new routes to Eastern Europe would, subject to demand, be possible only should there be a lack of interest by SAS. Maersk indicated that 'it could never be visualized that Maersk would be in a position to commence scheduled operations to New York'.

Although other Danish operators (Muk Air, Newair) have operated cabotage routes, Maersk have never done so, nor are there any plans to do so in the future.

In 1992 it had been predicted that Maersk would take advantage of the third package and launch routes from Copenhagen to Oslo, Stockholm and Gothenburg. This has yet to happen, although Maersk now operate from Billund to Stockholm and the other two cities are considered to be long-term options for future services from Billund. In addition, a more recent document, 'CAP 654 - The Single European Aviation Market - Progress So Far' (UK Civil Aviation Authority) suggested a number of routes from Copenhagen with potential for new entrants. Apart from Oslo and Stockholm, the additional routes identified were Frankfurt, Amsterdam and Helsinki.

Maersk have identified route viability to be dependent on prospects for interlining, costs and travel times to the destination city centre. As an example, Milan (Linate) is considered to be a non-starter because of its designation as a domestic airport while Milan (Malpensa), designated for international services, is unattractive because of the airport distance from the centre of Milan.

The recent introduction of a scheduled service from Billund to Paris (Charles de Gaulle) was an example of where the lack of slots can constrain the development of new services. In the case of Maersk, initial operations had three different evening departure times during the week with, in one case, only a 20 minute turnaround time.

Maersk have also commented that en-route and airport charges have, on average, increased above the rate of inflation and, therefore, while in theory there are no problems for new entrants into new routes, in practice there still appears to be a number of constraints which prevent the operation of a truly free market.

The other barrier is the number of flights that would have to be operated by a new entrant to achieve a proportionate market share. Copenhagen-Oslo is effectively an SAS monopoly with a current daily frequency (March 1996) of 16 flights in each direction. According to CAP 654, a new entrant would require to have an entry frequency of at least 4 flights in each direction in order to achieve a reasonable market share. Similarly, Copenhagen-Stockholm would require a new entrant frequency of at least three flights in each direction. This, of course, assumes that the slots are available.

The thinner routes from Copenhagen to Frankfurt, Amsterdam and Helsinki are even less attractive. On the Amsterdam route Maersk would be in competition with SAS and KLM and on the Helsinki route the competition is SAS and Finnair. On the Copenhagen to Frankfurt route, services were operated by SAS and Lufthansa. With the recent code sharing agreement between these two airlines, this route is now a monopoly and offers some opportunities for new entrants particularly as the European Commission has stipulated specific conditions (slots, interlining) which would be of benefit to a new entrant.

For all three routes, adopting a rule of thumb that a new entrant should ideally have the same frequency as the smallest incumbent, then all three routes would require an entry frequency of three flights per day in order to achieve a proportional market share.

The Maersk aircraft fleet has consisted for some years of a mixture of Fokker 50 turbo-props and variants of the B737 family. The policy of Maersk is to keep the average age of the fleet low. There appears to be an ongoing policy of both leasing in and leasing out aircraft. Table F.3 shows a summary of the aircraft types and numbers that are known to have been used for Maersk's scheduled and charter operations; actual levels of ownership are higher than those shown in the table.

Table F.3.   Aircraft types used by Maersk Air

	1988	1989	1990	1991	1992	1993	1994	1995
BAe 125								1
S-360				1	1	1	1	
DHC.7	5	2						
F50		6	6	6	7	7	8	9
B737-200	2	2	2					
B737-300	3	2	2	3	2	3	3	4
B737-400							1	
B737-500				4	5	3	4	3
Total	**10**	**12**	**10**	**14**	**15**	**14**	**17**	**17**

F.4.3. Traffic and market share

Between 1985 and 1994 Maersk increased the level of scheduled activity and, with the continuing modest introduction of new routes and increased frequencies, this trend is continuing. What is interesting is the lack of growth in the domestic scheduled market; in fact traffic levels have declined from a peak reached in 1988/89. At the same time, there have been wild fluctuations in the number of charter passengers with traffic levels only now exceeding those experienced in the mid-1980s (just under 500,000 passengers a year). Other operating statistics have moved in line with the fluctuation in passenger numbers. There is no readily available information on traffic levels for individual routes.

F.4.4. Productivity and operating costs

In 1994 Maersk produced 440 million seat-kilometres on its domestic network and sold 263 million of them to give a passenger load factor of 59.7%, little changed over the previous year. International services, however, showed an increase of 19% in ASK in 1994, to give a total of 533 million. The airline was less successful in selling its production on international routes, averaging a passenger load factor of just 37.1%, a modest increase from the 36.1% achieved in 1993. When combined, the international and domestic networks produced 973.5 million ASK, and achieved a load factor of 49.3%.

The airline's increasing involvement in the charter market is reflected in the growth of the proportion of total ASK attributable to charter operations: 45% in 1993 grew to 59% in 1994.

Unit operating costs measured in US cents per available tonne-kilometre of production were USD 1.16 in 1994. These figures include charter operations.

Between end-1993 and end-1994, the number of people employed by Maersk rose by 22.3% to 1,310.

F.4.5. Pricing and yields

Pricing strategies of Maersk have to be seen in context with a number of factors. Firstly, on the majority of Maersk routes there are no competitors. For example, from Billund, code-sharing deals have been reached with Sabena and KLM; the remaining routes are operated by Maersk alone. Likewise, from Copenhagen, with the exception of flights to the Faroe Islands, the only city-pair route on which there is competition is Copenhagen-London.

Secondly, although against the spirit of the third package, Maersk gave the impression that, under certain circumstances, incumbent carriers could object to fares set between a specific city-pair but via an alternative routing. For example, consider the development of Billund by Maersk as a rival hub to Copenhagen. Major carriers have an interest in protecting their own hubs so SAS would not welcome Billund as an alternative hub to Copenhagen, in particular, if cheaper through-fares are offered through the former.

Probably the most competitive pricing strategies are in operation on the Copenhagen-London route which, as previously mentioned, is the scene of competition between Maersk, BA, SAS and Air UK. On this route Maersk has offered a lower C2 fare (business, maximum stay 1 year, no stopovers) for some time. In November 1994 this was 20% (from London) and 24% (from Copenhagen) lower than the Heathrow carriers (BA, SAS). Maersk also offers a Y2 (as C2 but economy) fare, which in November 1994 was 29% (from London) and 33% (from Copenhagen) below the BA and SAS fare. This was available in 1992 but the penalty for reservation changes no longer applies. Note, also, that Air UK fares between Copenhagen and London are extremely competitive. However, for both Maersk and Air UK it could be argued that the lower fares are a bid to attract traffic, away from Heathrow, to the less attractive airports of Gatwick and Stansted.

Other pricing strategies by Maersk include volume discounts for corporate accounts and Maersk's long-term strategy includes proposals to 'attack' the trunk route market on price by the introduction of new fares that might offer savings of up to 60% on pre-liberalization levels. Other possibilities mooted in late 1995 included a cut-price air pass for multi-destination travel by international visitors; in March 1996 it was announced that Finnair, Maersk, Braathens and Transwede had banded together to launch an air pass scheme with individual sectors costing as little as £48.

F.4.6. Profitability and sources of finance

There is limited information available on the financial status of Maersk. What information there is indicates that, overall, the last 15 years of operations have proved to be profitable. Highlights include the announcement of a £10 million profit for 1986 and that the reported loss in 1991 was the first for a decade. In 1994, the airline made a net profit of USD 20.8

million, up 4.2% from the previous year on total revenues of USD 266.7 million (up 17.7% from the previous year). This indicates a very healthy operating ratio.

Much of the success can be attributed to being a subsidiary of the A P Moller shipping company. Although running a consistent operating profit in its own right, the financial backing of the parent company has enabled Maersk to have the confidence to purchase new aircraft on a regular basis (and the phasing out of old aircraft) and diversification into other air transport activities. Apart from monopoly domestic and international (almost) scheduled traffic, other activities include charter flights, long-term aircraft leasing, a North Sea helicopter company, a travel agency chain and a stake in the handling company Copenhagen Air Services.

F.4.7. Impact of EU measures and conclusions

From this case study it can be seen that the EU measures influenced the development of Maersk Air in three main ways.

(1)   The measures forced a relaxation in the domestic regulatory environment under which Maersk (and other Danish non-flag carriers) operated.

(2)   The second package encouraged the development of new international services fromBillund.

(3)   Lastly, the third package gave Maersk the right to operate on routes outside of Denmark and the right to acquire or set up carriers in other EC countries. As part of AP Moller's shipping strategy has been to set up subsidiaries in the United Kingdom, Spain, the United States and Asia, it would be natural to do the same for company aviation activities. The creation of Maersk Air UK and the development of Copenhagen Air Services activities outside of Denmark are initial steps in this process.

However, there are a number of factors which are seen as constraints on the future development of Maersk. The most important are:

(a)   high salaries, social legislation and taxes that have to be paid by Danish operators;
(b)   market domination of major carriers (including alliances and frequent flyer programmes);
(c)   state aids to flag carriers;
(d)   slot constraints and environmental measures at major airports;
(e)   air traffic control and airport charges increasing faster than the rate of inflation.

MAERSK AIR
TRAFFIC AND FINANCIAL STATISTICS 1985-94

PASSENGER TRAFFIC *(units)*

Year	Intern'l Scheduled	Domestic Scheduled	Total Scheduled	Total Charter
1985		720,000	720,000	409,000
1986	14,305	818,495	832,800	435,000
1987		881,000	881,000	412,000
1988	39,565	876,435	916,000	369,000
1989	42,206	873,964	916,170	309,333
1990				
1991	118,945	715,180	834,125	245,932
1992				
1993	162,342	732,032	894,374	298,552
1994	232,850	743,910	976,760	488,696

RPK *(thousand)*

Year	Intern'l Scheduled	Domestic Scheduled	Total Scheduled	Total Charter
1985		259	259	1,055
1986	11	283	294	1,197
1987		326	326	1,243
1988	30	283	313	1,095
1989	35	278	313	804
1990				
1991	114	249	363	630
1992				
1993	161	263	424	716
1994	200	263	463	1,284

ASK *(thousand)*

Year	Intern'l Scheduled	Domestic Scheduled	Total Scheduled	Total Charter
1985		417	417	1,275
1986	27	434	461	1,341
1987			519	1,438
1988	60	505	565	1,304
1989	78	483	561	874
1990				
1991	321	463	784	783
1992				
1993	447	448	895	741
1994	533	440	973	1,414

ATK *(million)*

Year	Intern'l Scheduled	Domestic Scheduled	Total Scheduled	Total Charter
1985		45	45	131
1986	3	44	47	138
1987			54	133
1988	7	52	59	126
1989	9	49	58	91
1990				
1991	40	64	104	87
1992				
1993				
1994	47	39	86	141

RTK *(million)*

Year	Intern'l Scheduled	Domestic Scheduled	Total Scheduled	Total Charter
1985		26	26	99
1986	1	32	33	108
1987			29	112
1988	2	26	28	99
1989	3	25	28	70
1990				
1991	10	24	34	57
1992				
1993				
1994				

WEIGHT LOAD FACTOR *(%)*

Year	Intern'l Scheduled	Domestic Scheduled	Total Scheduled	Total Charter
1985		58%	58%	76%
1986	36%	73%	70%	78%
1987			54%	84%
1988	33%	49%	47%	79%
1989	35%	51%	48%	77%
1990				
1991	26%	37%	33%	66%
1992				
1993				
1994				

TOTAL AIRCRAFT KM FLOWN *(thousand)*

Year	Intern'l Scheduled	Domestic Scheduled	Total Scheduled	Total Charter
1985	0	6,689	6,689	10,347
1986	648	6,523	7,171	10,615
1987		8,217	8,217	11,085
1988	1,335	7,053	8,388	9,334
1989	1,723	6,645	8,368	6,989
1990				
1991	3,673	6,077	9,750	5,863
1992				
1993	4,973	5,943	10,916	6,890
1994	6,426	5,834	12,260	9,904

PASSENGER LOAD FACTOR *(%)*

Year	Intern'l Scheduled	Domestic Scheduled	Total Scheduled	Total Charter
1985		62%	62%	83%
1986	41%	65%	64%	89%
1987			63%	86%
1988	50%	56%	55%	84%
1989	45%	58%	56%	92%
1990				
1991	36%	54%	46%	80%
1992				
1993	36%	59%	47%	97%
1994	38%	60%	48%	91%

FREIGHT AND MAIL TON KM *(thousand)*

Year	Intern'l Scheduled	Domestic Scheduled	Total Scheduled	Total Charter
1985		2,241	2,241	35
1986	31	7,085	7,116	
1987		7	7	
1988	1	7	8	
1989	55	206	261	6,000
1990				
1991				
1992				
1993				
1994	589	683	1,272	

MAERSK AIR
TRAFFIC AND FINANCIAL STATISTICS 1985-94

AVERAGE PASSENGER HAUL (km)

Year	Intern'l Scheduled	Domestic Scheduled	Total Scheduled	Total Charter
1985		360	360	2579
1986	769	346	353	2752
1987			370	3017
1988	758	323	342	2967
1989	829	318	342	2599
1990				
1991	958	348	435	2562
1992				
1993	992	359	474	2398
1994	859	354	474	2627

DAILY AIRCRAFT UTIL'N (hours)

Year	Total
1985	5.45
1986	5.21
1987	5.49
1988	4.28
1989	3.71
1990	3.08
1991	
1992	
1993	2.65
1994	4.71

ATK PER EMPLOYEE (units)

Year	Total
1985	208284
1986	
1987	
1988	195664
1989	164278
1990	
1991	
1992	
1993	
1994	190676

AVERAGE AIRCRAFT SIZE (seats)

Year	Intern'l Scheduled	Domestic Scheduled	Total Scheduled	Total Charter
1985		62	62	123
1986	42	67	64	126
1987			63	130
1988	45	72	67	140
1989	45	73	67	125
1990				
1991	87	76	80	134
1992				
1993	90	75	82	108
1994	83	75	79	143

MAERSK LTD FINANCIAL PERFORMANCE (current prices - million ECU)

Year	Operating Revenue	Operating Cost	Operating Profit	Net Profit
1985	118	110	8	14
1986	125	116	9	15
1987	132	122	10	10
1988	131	113	18	9
1989	142	129	13	5
1990				
1991				
1992				
1993				
1994				

MAERSK LTD FINANCIAL PERFORMANCE (1990 prices - million ECU)

Year	Operating Revenue	Operating Cost	Operating Profit	Net Profit
1985	151	141	10	18
1986	152	140	11	18
1987	153	141	12	12
1988	145	126	19	10
1989	149	136	13	5
1990				
1991				
1992				
1993				
1994				

HOURS FLOWN (units)

Year	Total Scheduled	Total Charter	Total
1985	18,598	15,230	33,828
1986	18,243	15,970	34,213
1987	21,566	16,526	38,092
1988	18,701	15,650	34,351
1989	17,071	12,735	29,806
1990			28,075
1991	16,952	7,963	24,915
1992			
1993	19,010	9,017	28,027
1994	21,477	12,877	34,354

EMPLOYESS (average)

Year	Total
1985	845
1986	
1987	
1988	946
1989	907
1990	967
1991	
1992	
1993	1,187
1994	1,191

FLEET SIZE (units)

Year	Total
1985	17
1986	18
1987	19
1988	22
1989	22
1990	25
1991	
1992	15
1993	29
1994	20

F.5. Eurowings

Eurowings was formed in 1992 as the result of a merger between NFD Luftvekehr and RFG Regionalflug, which was completed at the beginning of 1994. Talks had been held in November 1991 on the possibility of RFG taking a 30% stake in NFD, following the collapse of Air Europe which originally owned 49% of NFD. Prior to the merger, the two carriers had co-operated on joint aircraft purchase, spares pooling and pilot training. The merger was the result of RFG's need for additional capacity for expansion, and NFD's financial situation following over-expansion and the burden of having to buy back the Air Europe stake. The industrialist, Albrecht Knecht, holds 93.66% of the shares in the new company, the remainder owned by the chief executive and other employees.

F.5.1. Strategic responses

NFD started scheduled operations in 1975, and by 1987 were carrying around 80,000 passengers with a fleet of 2 ATR-42, 6 Metro III and 3 Cessna aircraft. At that time some services were flown for Lufthansa, with aircraft painted in Lufthansa colours, and closer co-operation was envisaged in the future. It carried 184,300 passengers in 1987, and operated a fleet of 2 ATR42s, 8 Metro IIIs and 1 Dornier 228. Close co-operation was also started at that time with Air France and KLM. The airline operated some services on behalf of Lufthansa, the remainder focused on scheduled services from their Nuremberg base. A second hub was started at Hanover, which they saw as having considerable longer term potential. However, one of their Hanover routes (Manchester-Hanover) was later withdrawn. The negative reaction to their Metro III was given as the main reason for the losses on this route. NFD started operating jet aircraft in 1988 with BAe 146-200 charters for the express cargo company, TNT.

RFG started scheduled operations in 1979 with the Dortmund-Munich route, followed by Nuremberg-Paris in 1980, and by 1985 were carrying around 33,000 passengers. Scheduled services were operated between Dortmund and Paderborn and Munich, and Paderborn/London Gatwick was served as part of British Caledonian Commuter Services.

The two airlines started co-operating in 1985, both realizing that they lacked the necessary economies of scale to survive alone. A joint purchasing agreement was signed, and both airlines ordered ATR-42 aircraft under this agreement, which they saw as ideal for their relatively short sectors. Further orders for ATR-42s and the larger ATR-72 followed in 1987.

The two airlines were finally integrated in 1994, and initially focused on internal German routes. In 1995, however, the airline shifted its focus onto developing cross-border, rather than domestic German routes, due to competition from high speed trains and the high cost of operations. It signed a 10 year co-operation agreement with Air France, and further cemented the relationship with KLM, taking over the latter's Amsterdam to Nuremberg and Hanover services. Discussions took place with Lufthansa in 1994 on a closer partnership with Lufthansa, but these broke down because of what Eurowings described as 'internal resistance within Lufthansa'. Subsequent talks with Delta Air Lines and British Airways on linking Eurowings' services with those carriers networks also ended without agreement.

It also operated charter flights with an Airbus A310-300 on behalf of Hapag Lloyd Flug, principally to Mediterranean destinations. However, this is to be discontinued because of union objections. Eurowings' strategy is now based on three types of business: its own scheduled services, increasingly on cross-border routes, and in niche markets of 20,000 to 100,000 passengers a year; charter services with its own aircraft; and some third party work for Lufthansa, TNT and other carriers.

F.5.2. Routes, air services and capacity

Prior to the merger, RFG had a number of scheduled services out of Dortmund, and NFD out of Nuremberg. NFD was the second designated carrier between Germany and France, with international routes operated between Stuttgart and Lyon, and Nuremberg/Paris. In 1987, NFD added Hanover/Manchester to its network, and strengthened its sales and reservations effectiveness by appointing Lufthansa as its world-wide GSA.

Between 1992 and 1995, a number of new routes were initiated, for example between Düsseldorf and Newcastle, and Dresden and Paris. They also started a number of summer only routes to Guernsey, Jersey, Olbia, Nice and Bastia. In 1994, several routes between Amsterdam and Germany were transferred from KLM to Eurowings under code sharing arrangements. The majority of these new routes could have been operated without the benefit of the freedom of entry allowed under the three packages. The airline's Poland network was also expanded in 1995, with Krakov being added to existing routes from Berlin to Warsaw and Frankfurt to Wroclaw. They plan also to operate between Dresden and Poxnan.

International passenger services are now operated to the following cities on a year-round basis:

Paris:	from Munich, Dortmund, Hanover, Nuremberg, Leipzig, Dresden, Münster
Lyon:	from Munich/Dortmund
Amsterdam:	from Dresden, Leipzig, Düsseldorf, Hanover, Stuttgart, Nuremberg (and from Summer 1996, Paderborn and Dortmund)
Brussels:	rom Hanover and Nuremberg
London:	from Paderborn
Newcastle:	from Düsseldorf.

Hubs are operated at Dortmund, Berlin (Templehof), Dresden, Münster, Nuremberg and Paderborn, with smaller hubs at Munich, Leipzig, Hanover and Düsseldorf.

Jet aircraft operate the Nuremberg-Paris and Amsterdam-Stuttgart routes.

The Air France agreement includes 50% block seat arrangements on:

(a)   Nuremberg-Paris;
(b)   Munich-Lyons;
(c)   Hanover-Paris;
(d)   Dresden-Leipzig-Paris.

Eurowings moved up to jet passenger operations in 1994, with the acquisition of two BAe 146s, in addition to the two BAe 146 freighters that they operated for TNT. A third passenger BAe 146 aircraft (-300 series) was acquired from Crossair, and will be used for charter flights in Summer 1996, operating to Mediterranean destinations from smaller German regional airports, such as Hof, Erfurt and Kassel, which could not support larger jets. They expect to operate a total of ten jet aircraft in the future, mainly on international routes, and do not rule out moving up to larger jet aircraft.

Dortmund is a key hub for Eurowings, but it has a relatively short runway of 1,050 metres. Proposals for extending the runway to 2,000 metres, which would allow scheduled operations with larger B737 or A320 jets and charters, were recently blocked by the Green Party, who are part of the ruling coalition in North Rhine Westfalia. Even though an extension would allow direct competition from Lufthansa, Eurowings are in favour of upgrading this airport which has a very large catchment area in the Ruhr region, and considerable potential, given runway constraints at Düsseldorf.

F.5.3. Marketing, traffic and market share

Eurowings operates at a serious disadvantage in terms of size and economies of scale and scope. Even before the merger it had tried to overcome this problem by linking with a larger carrier (NFD with Lufthansa and later Air Europe, and RFG with British Caledonian). It also focuses on niche markets in which it will not have direct competition with the larger carriers. These markets are unlikely to be operated by larger airlines like Lufthansa on an economic basis, because of their higher cost base. On the other hand, Eurowings needs the help of larger carriers on the marketing side, which could take the form of interline agreements, or better still the code sharing agreements that the airline has concluded with both KLM/Northwest and Air France. The carrier also operates the Münster-Osnabruck route under a joint code with Lufthansa, as well as the wet lease Frankfurt to Münster and Nuremberg routes for Lufthansa, although they also compete strongly with Lufthansa's Cityline subsidiary on one or two domestic routes. Services are offered in single class configuration, but they have been seriously considering adding a business class.

The airline does not have a frequent flyer programme, and has complained to the German competition authorities that Lufthansa's programme is anti-competitive. With around 80% of passengers travelling on business, the airline negotiates rebates directly with corporate customers, with money returned if pre-determined targets are reached. Overrides are not offered to travel agents, but business agents can make use of the corporate rebate scheme.

Eurowings is interested in ticketless travel, and has a pilot scheme operating with the large company, Siemens, where only boarding passes are needed and these are issued at the airport.

Eurowings did not operates on any of the ten most dense domestic German routes in 1993, and competes with other German carriers to a very limited extent (for example, they competed with Lufthansa on eight routes in 1994, with DBA and other small regional carriers usually only on one or two routes). Eurowings entered three routes in competition with Lufthansa in 1993 (Frankfurt/Münster, Frankfurt/Hanover and Düsseldorf/Leipzig). Its average frequency share when competing with Lufthansa was 38%. On the Nuremberg-Berlin route, Eurowings competes with Lufthansa and claims a 50–60% market share. This may be helped by the fact that it serves the more convenient Templehof Airport, whereas Lufthansa flies to Tegel.

International traffic increased steadily from 1987 to 1994 in terms of passengers carried, and rose sharply in 1995 to reach just over half a million passengers. Domestic traffic increased rapidly between 1988 and 1992, with a small drop in 1993. In both 1994 and 1995, however, domestic passengers have grown substantially to reach just under 1 million in 1995.

The passenger load factor has generally been in the range of 40–50% for domestic services, with international services somewhat lower. Such levels are low even for this type of regional operation, which carry mainly business traffic at relatively high yields.

F.5.4. Productivity and operation costs

Labour productivity in terms of ATKs per employee increased rapidly over the period 1988–1990, with staff numbers remaining stable and high traffic growth rates. Between 1990 and 1994, however, labour productivity has remained constant as a result of a rise in staff numbers, with a large increase in 1995.

Average aircraft utilization was just over five block hours per day per aircraft in 1994. This is relatively low compared to regional airlines such as the UK-based City Flyer Express, which operated its ATR-42s for 8.1 hours per day on average in 1994 (and ATR-72s 6.7 hours). On the other hand, City Flyer's Shorts 360s only achieved 4.9 hours a day, over an average sector of 290 km (as opposed to 380 km for the ATR-42s). Eurowings' average sector length for both international and domestic flights was 370 km in 1994.

F.5.5. Pricing and yields

In 1995 Eurowings introduced a scheme of discounts for large customers: those giving the airline DM 50,000 or more per year would get a discount starting at 6%, and increasing in steps. While the threshold is based on total revenues, including both leisure and business fares, the discount is only applied to the business revenues.

Its Wings fare structure was introduced in 1994, with four basic fare levels:

(i)   Full fare;
(ii)   Full fare less 20%;
(iii)   Full fare less 55%;
(iv)   Full fare less 70%.

Availability and flexibility are reduced in line with the increased discounts offered. The initial result of the new fare structure was an increase in passengers carried of around 25%.

The average yield was DM 262 per passenger in 1994, falling DM 222 in 1995, although the percentage of scheduled service traffic fell from 95% to 82% over the same period.

F.5.6. Profitability and sources of finance

Prior to the merger, NFD had generally produced small operating profits and net losses in some years. After merging with RFG, Eurowings made an operating loss of DM 2.85 million in 1993 and DM 5.8 million in 1994. These became net losses of DM 6.8 million and DM 7.7 million respectively. Their operating ratio was 99% in 1993 and 98% in 1994. Turnover increased marginally from DM 305 million in 1993 to DM 316 million in 1994, but jumped to DM 400 million in 1995, when the airline will to go into profit.

A subsidy is paid by the government of the Free State of Bavaria for the operation of the Hof-Bayreuth-Frankfurt services. However, this is small in relation to total turnover, and the limited equipment at the two Bavarian airports results in costly diversions and delays in Winter.

NFD/RFG and Eurowings have invested over DM 500 million between 1987 and 1994. All their BAe 146 aircraft are leased, as well as four of the ATR-42/72 fleet. The airline has an aircraft maintenance subsidiary, NAYAK GmbH, based at Cologne, and a tour operator, Eurowings Touristik GmbH.

F.5.7. Impact of EU measures and conclusions

EU liberalization has not been so important for Eurowings' route expansion, since the German domestic market was already deregulated at the beginning of the 1990s, and international routes were already available under bilaterals. However, the lifting of the restrictions on fare filing in the third package were seen as a significant advantage for the carrier. They also saw opportunities for services to Austria which, with that country's entry into the EU, would now have no restrictions.

Some of the features of the EU packages, on the other hand, have had a negative impact on Eurowings. Consecutive cabotage allows foreign carriers entry into German domestic markets, often on thin routes, and on routes which Eurowings were developing. Many of these routes which were originally initiated have now been discontinued (eg SAS), but British Airways' London-Hanover-Leipzig remains. While BA do not carry many cabotage passengers between Hanover and Leipzig, even ten passengers a day have a serious impact on Eurowings' traffic on that sector.

The airline's co-operation with Air France pre-dates the three packages, and the KLM/Northwest agreement was dictated more by transatlantic bilateral changes, rather than any EU measures.

Progress towards the single market has also led to the easing the restrictions on leasing in aircraft from other EU countries, as well as hiring staff from other EU countries. However, they face a problem of attracting and keeping skilled staff, such as pilots, who often move to jobs with better pay and prospects at Lufthansa. Future harmonization of pilot hours might actually have a negative effect on the airline's productivity, since their levels are higher than, for example Lufthansa or Air France.

The airline would like to see more stronger EU measures aimed at airports (slots) and air traffic control (delays and costs). They also consider that they are at a disadvatage when official travel or public contracts are awarded, since, in Germany, Lufthansa tends to be the automatic choice. Corporate and indirect taxation and social legislation heavily penalize air transport operations in Germany and by German based carriers, and further harmonization in these areas can only benefit the airline.

Table F.4. Eurowings data

Passengers	1994	1995
Scheduled domestic	843 107	963 141
Scheduled International	307 334	504 017
Operated for other airlines	9 152	48 757
Own charters	48 336	91 102
Hapag Lloyd charters	-	192 983
TOTAL	**1 207 929**	**1 800 000**

Fleet (1996)	Number	Seats
ATR-42	17	46/48
ATR-72-200	6	68
ATR-72-210	5	68
BAe 146-200 *(Scheduled passengers)*	2	84/92
BAe 146-300 *(Charter passengers)*	1	n/a
BAe 146-200QT *(Charter freight)*	2	
Total	**32**	

APPENDIX G

Community legislation, etc.

G.1.   Regulations

Council Regulation (EEC) No 3975/87 of 14 December 1987 laying down the procedure for the application of the rules on competition to undertakings in the air transport sector (OJ L 374, 31.12.1987, p. 1).
Council Regulation (EEC) No 3976/87 of 14 December 1987 on the application of Article 85(3) of the Treaty to certain categories of agreements and concerted practices in the air transport sector (OJ L 374, 31.12.1987, p. 9).
Council Regulation (EEC) No 2299/89 of 24 July 1989 on a code of conduct for computerized reservation systems (OJ L 220, 29.7.1989, p. 1).
Council Regulation (EEC) 4064/89 of 21 December 1989 on the control of concentrations between undertakings (OJ L 395, 30.12.1989, p. 1)
Council Regulation (EEC) No 2342/90 of 24 July 1990 on fares for scheduled air services (OJ L 217, 11.8.1990, p. 8).
Council Regulation (EEC) No 2343/90 of 24 July 1990 on access for air carriers to scheduled intra-Community air service routes and on the sharing of passenger capacity between air carriers on scheduled air services between Member States (OJ L 217, 11.8.1990, p. 8).
Council Regulation (EEC) No 2344/90 of 24 July 1990 amending Council Regulation (EEC) No 3976/87 on the application of Article 85(3) of the Treaty to certain categories of agreements and concerted practices in the air transport sector (OJ L 217, 11.8.1990, p. 15).
Commission Regulation (EEC) No 84/91 of 5 December 1990 on the application of Article 85(3) of the Treaty to certain categories of agreements, decisions and concerted practices concerning joint planning and coordination of capacity, consultations on passenger and cargo tariff rates on scheduled air services and slot allocation at airports (OJ L 10, 15.1.1991, p. 14).
Council Regulation (EEC) No 294/91 of 4 February 1991 on the operation of air cargo services between Member States (OJ L 36, 8.2.1991, p. 1).
Council Regulation (EEC) No 295/91 of 4 February 1991 establishing common rules for a demied-boarding compensation system in scheduled air transport (OJ L 36, 8.2.1991, p. 5).
Council Regulation (EEC) No 2407/92 of 23 July 1992 on licensing of air carriers (OJ L 240, 24.8.1992, p. 1).
Council Regulation (EEC) No 2408/92 of 23 July 1992 on access for Community air carriers to intra-Community air routes (OJ L 240, 24.8.1992, p. 8).
Council Regulation (EEC) No 2409/92 of 23 July 1992 on fares and rates for air services (OJ L 240, 24.8.1992, p. 15).
Council Regulation (EEC) No 95/93 of 18 January 1993 on common rules for the allocation of slots at Community airports (OJ L 14, 22.1.1993, p. 1).
Council Regulation (EEC) No 3089/93 of 29 October 1993 amending Regulation (EEC) No 2299/89 on a code of conduct for computerized reservation systems (OJ L 278, 11.11.1993, p. 1).

G.2.   Directives

83/416/EEC: Council Directive of 25 July 1983 concerning the authorization of scheduled inter-regional air services for the transport of passengers, mail and cargo between Member States (OJ L 237, 26.8.1983, p. 19).

87/601/EEC: Council Directive of 14 December 1987 on fares for scheduled air services between Member States (OJ L 374, 31.12.1987, p. 12).

87/602/EEC: Council Directive of 14 December 1987 on the sharing of passenger capacity between air carriers on scheduled air services between Member States and on access for air carriers to scheduled air-service routes between Member States (OJ L 374, 31.12.1987, p. 19).

90/314/EEC: Council Directive of 13 June 1990 on package travel, package holidays and package tours (OJ L 158, 23.6.1990, p. 59).

93/13/EEC: Council Directive of 5 April 1993 on unfair terms in consumer contracts (OJ L 95, 21.4.1993, p. 29).

96/67/EC: Council Directive of 15 October 1996 on access to the groundhandling market at Community airports (OJ L 272, 25.10.1996, p. 36).

G.3.   Case law

Case 167/73 *Commission* v *France* [1974] ECR 359.

Case 209/84 *French Republic (Public Prosecutor)* v *Asjes* [1986] ECR 1425.

Case 66/86 *Ahmed Saeed Flugreisen and others* v *Zentrale zur Bekämpfung unlauteren Wettbewerbs* [1989] ECR 103, [1990] 4 CMLR 102.

Case C-364/92 *SAT Fluggesellschaft* v *Eurocontrol* [1994] ECR I-43.

G.4.   Other

The contribution of the European Communities to the development of a Community air transport policy (COM(79) 311 final).

Civil Aviation Memorandum No 2: Progress towards the development of a Community air transport policy (COM(84) 72 final).

Report on the first year (1988) of implementation of the aviation policy approved in December 1987 (COM(89) 476 final, 2.10.1989).

Commission Recommendation 87/598/EEC of 8 December 1987 on a European Code of Conduct relating to electronic payment (OJ L 365, 24.12.1987, p. 72).

Amended proposal for a Council Directive on the protection of consumers in respect of contracts negotiated at a distance (COM(93) 396 final, 7.10.1993).

Proposal for a Council Regulation (EC) on air carrier liability in case of accidents (COM(95) 724 final, 20.12.1995).

APPENDIX H

Data sources and bibliography

1.   Legal and administrative measures

European Commission. *The Community Internal Market*, annual reports on the operation of the single market, 1993 and 1995; and *The Single Market in 1995*, COM(96) 51 final Luxembourg, Office for Official Publications of the EC.

European Commission. Series of six booklets on the *Internal Market*, latest update 1st July 1994, Vols 1–4, Luxembourg, Office for Official Publications of the EC.

European Commission. *23rd and 24th Annual Reports on Competition Policy*, 1993 and 1994, Luxembourg, Office for Official Publications of the EC.

Other reports and studies supplied by the Commission to the Coordinating Consultant, in particular cross-section studies on Customs and fiscal formalities at frontiers, Public procurement, Social and labour policy and Economies of scale.

(1)   Official reports and studies of the Commission and Member States. For instance, Commission Decisions concerning the granting of state aids as reported in the *Official Journal of the European Communities.*

European Commission. *Report on the first year (1988) of implementation of the aviation policy approved in December 1987,* COM(89) 476, Luxembourg, Office for Official Publications of the EC.

European Commission (DGIV). *Report on Frequent Flyer Programmes,* December 1992.

Avmark. *The Competitiveness of the European Community's Air Transport Industry,* Luxembourg, Office for Official Publications of the EC, 1992.

Coopers & Lybrand. *The Application and Possible Modification of Council Regulation 95/93 on Common Rules for the Allocation of Slots at Community Airports,* Final Report, 17th October 1995.

(2)   Articles written by Commission officials or other experts relating to the development and implementation of the three packages and the competition rules. Such articles are too numerous to list here in total. However, key articles or papers included the following:

Balfour, J. 'Competition rules – a seven year assessment', *Avmark Aviation Economist*, December 1994.

Balfour, J. 'The Control of State Aids in the Air Transport Sector', *Air and Space Law*, No 4/5, 1993.

Balfour, J. 'The EC Commission's Policy on State Aids for Airline Restructuring: Is the Bonfire Alight?', *Air and Space Law*, No 2, 1995.

Chataway, C. *The charter airline industry: a case history of successful deregulation*, Institute of Economic Affairs lectures on regulation, November 1994.

Civil Aviation Authority (UK). *Airline Competition in the Single European Market*, November 1993, CAP 623.

Civil Aviation Authority (UK). *Slot Allocation: A Proposal for Europe's Airports*, February 1995, CAP 644.

Civil Aviation Authority (UK). *The Single European Aviation Market – Progress So Far*, September 1995, CAP 654.

Crans, B. 'EC Aviation Scene', *Air and Space Law*, Vol. XVII, No 4/5, 1992.

Dutheil de la Rochière, J. 'European Community Policies on Airline Concentration', *Journal of Air Transport Management*, No 2, 1994.

Euroscope. *The Relevant Market in Air Transport*, Study commissioned by the Association of European Airlines, November 1989.

van Houtte, B. 'Community Competition Law in the Air Transport Sector', *Air and Space Law*, Nos 2 and 6, 1993.

IATA Regulatory Affairs Review.

International Civil Aviation Organization. *Digest of Bilateral Agreements* (Doc 9511), 1988.

International Civil Aviation Organization. *The World of Civil Aviation, 1993–96*, Circular 250-AT/102, Montreal, October 1994.

Katz, R. 'Liberalization of Air Transport in Europe', *Travel and Tourism Analyst*, March 1987.

OECD. *Deregulation and Airline Competition*, Paris, 1988.

Stasinopoulos, D. 'The Third Phase of Liberalization in Community Aviation and the Need for Supplementary Measures', *Journal of Transport Economics & Policy*, September 1993.

Villiers, J. 'For a European Air Transport Policy', *ITA Magazine*, No. 57, September/October 1989.

Wheatcroft, S and Lipman, G. *Air Transport in a Competitive European Market*, EIU Special Report No 1060, 1986.

Wheatcroft, S and Lipman, G. *European Liberalization and World Air Transport*, EIU Special Report No 2015, May 1990.

(3)   Interviews with key officials of airlines and civil aviation authorities in Member States (see Appendix B).

2.   Airline strategic responses

(1)   Data from the International Civil Aviation Organization (ICAO), the International Air Transport Association (IATA), the Association of European Airlines (AEA), Eurostat and the Organization for Economic Co-operation and Development (OECD).

(2)   Airline annual reports during the period 1985–94. These were complemented by reports in the aviation press, notably *Airline Business, Avmark Aviation Economist, Flight International, Aéroports Magazine, Luftfahrt, Commercial Aviation* and *Airfinance Journal.* Also conference papers and research journals.

(3)   Network changes were monitored through the *ABC Airways Guide*, the 1989, 1992, 1994 and 1995 scheduled timetables for all European services on a computerized database, and past copies of the *Guide*.

(4)   Reports from the *Comité des Sages* and the Commission response *(The Way Forward for Civil Aviation in Europe*, COM(94) 218 final).

(5)   The UK CAA Reports (see also (1) above) on EU airline competition and various research publications from finance houses and stockbrokers.

(6)   *The Globalization of the Civil Aviation Industry, and its Impact on Aviation Workers*, a report published by the International Transport Workers' Federation, February 1993, re-issued in November 1994.

(7)   Questionnaire responses and interviews with 18 airlines (both scheduled and charter).

(8)   Articles or papers such as:

Smith, P D. 'Airlines' Diversification and Investment Strategies', *EIU Travel & Tourism Analyst*, No 4, 1989.

3.   Impact of EU measures on EU airlines

The data sources used for this part of the study are largely the same as those listed for the analysis of airline strategies (above). Of particular value for this part of the work were:

(1)   the computerized ABC timetables for 1989, 1992, 1994 and 1995;

(2)   the detailed statistical reports of the Association of European Airlines (Brussels), and studies commissioned by the European Commission's Directorate-General for Transport (DG VII);

(3)   the interviews and questionnaires, mentioned in 2.(7) above, with key managers from a sample of about 18 European airlines (scheduled, new entrants and charters).

The following books, articles or papers are also relevant:

Alamdari, F. Doganis, R. and Lobbenberg, A. *Efficiency of the world's major airlines*, Department of Air Transport, Cranfield University, Research Report 4, March 1995.

Barrett, S. *Sky High: Airline price and European deregulation,* The Adam Smith Institute, 1985.

Bureau of Transport and Communications Economics. *Deregulation of domestic aviation in Australia, 1990–1995,* Information Sheet 6, 1995.

Comité des Sages. *Expanding Horizons,* A report for the European Commission, January 1994.

Edwards, A. 'Changes in real air fares and their impact on travel', *EIU Travel and Tourism Analyst,* No 2, 1990.

European Commission. *European Economy: The economics of 1992,* No 35, March 1988, Luxembourg, Office for Official Publications of the EC.

French, T. *Regional airlines in Europe: strategy for survival,* EIU Research Report R462, 1995.

GRA Inc. *A study of international airline code sharing,* A study for the US Department of Transportation, December 1994.

International Air Transport Association. *Airline Economic Results and Prospects,* 1991–1995.

International Civil Aviation Organization. *Survey of international air transport fares and rates,* Circular 198-AT/76, September 1985.

International Civil Aviation Organization. *Survey of international air transport fares and rates,* Circular 246-AT/100, September 1992.

International Civil Aviation Organization. *The world of civil aviation, 1994–1997,* Circular 258-AT/107, September 1995.

Jet Finance SA. *Analysis of the comparative ability of the European airline industry to finance investments,* Report for the European Commission, June 1995.

Marin, P. L. 'Competition in European Aviation: pricing policy and market structure', *Journal of Industrial Economics,* Vol. XLIII, No 2, June 1995.

McGowan, F. and Seabright, P. *Deregulating European airlines,* Economic Policy – A European Forum, October 1989.

Meyer, J. R. Oster, C. V., Morgan, I. P., Berman, B. and Strassmann, D. *Airline deregulation: the early experience,* Auburn House, 1981.

Pryke, R. *The competition among international airlines,* Trade Policy Research Centre, London, 1986.

Pryke, R. 'European air transport liberalization', *EIU Travel and Tourism Analyst,* No 1, 1989.

Smith, P. 'European Charter Airlines', *EIU Travel and Tourism Analyst,* No 2, 1991.

Youssef, W. and Hansen, M. 'Consequences of strategic alliances between international airlines: the case of Swissair and SAS', *Transportation Research*, Vol. 28A, No 5, 1994.